Your Guide to Understanding Investing

Kenneth M. Morris, Alan M. Siegel
and Virginia B. Morris

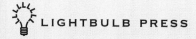

LIGHTBULB PRESS:

Creative Director Dean Scharf
Design Dave Wilder
Editor Jason Forsythe
Production Chris Hiebert, Thomas F. Trojan, Kwee Wang
Illustration Krista K. Glasser, Barnes Tilney
Film Quad Right, Inc.

SPECIAL THANKS TO:

Dow Jones & Co. Dan Austin, William Casey, Joan Wolf-Woolley

SECURITIES INDUSTRY ASSOCIATION:

Project Director James David Spellman
Project Editor Melissa Levy
Copy Editors Margaret Draper, Elizabeth Rives, Dianne Miller

SIA thanks the following committees for their thoughtful review and contributions: Investor Education, Public Trust and Confidence, and Self Regulation and Supervisory Practices. SIA also thanks: the Office of Investor Education and Assistance of the Securities and Exchange Commission; the Securities Investor Protection Corporation; the National Association of Securities Dealers; and the Corporate Communications, Legal and Compliance Departments of SIA member firms.

PICTURE CREDITS:

The Bettmann Archive, New York (page 136)
Chicago Board of Trade (page 119)
Comstock, New York (pages 52, 53, 152, 172, 173, 174)
FPG, New York (pages 148, 152, 174, 175)
The Image Bank, New York (pages 92, 154, 164, 165, 175)
Jeff Mermelstein (pages 106, 107)
New York Stock Exchange (pages 64, 65, 94)
Andy Shen (pages 58, 163)
UPI/Bettmann, New York (page 175)

CONTENTS

Your Guide to Understanding Investing

CONTENTS

BONDS

MUTUAL FUNDS

FUTURES AND OPTIONS

EMPLOYER RETIREMENT PLANS

INDIVIDUAL RETIREMENT PLANS

Taking the First Steps

Getting started is tough, but the earlier you start investing, the more it will pay off in the long run.

Americans today are investing in record numbers. About one out of every three American households now invests in mutual funds—up from just 6 percent in 1980. In March 1996, stock, bond and money market funds had combined assets of a staggering $3 trillion—that's over $10,000 for every man, woman and child in the country.

Americans are paying more attention to their financial future because they face more challenges to meeting their financial goals than ever before. Affording a comfortable retirement is perhaps the most daunting. Of course, building a nest egg for retirement has always been a key motivating factor behind investment. Unfortunately, the burden of planning for retirement in recent years has shifted from the employer to the individual. Average Americans can no longer depend on Social Security and their company pension funds to pay for the kind of retirement they want. And because Americans are living longer, there's a good chance that their retirement will last 20 years or more.

The rising cost of education is another factor. While the cost of tuition at both private and public institutions has increased beyond the rate of inflation in recent years, federal and state grants to students have been cut back, forcing parents to plan ahead more than ever. In 1996, a single year at a public university could cost $9,000, and it's realistic to assume those costs will continue to climb.

Take Responsibility

The first step toward financial security is to make yourself aware of the responsibilities that you face now, and those you are likely to face in the years ahead. Then you need to educate yourself about investing. The more you know about selecting investments and building a portfolio, the easier managing your finances and reaching your goals will be.

Set Goals

Investing usually involves creating a financial plan and sticking to it. It can be a formal document or simply a list of things you wish to do in the future. But it must include the financial steps you'll take to achieve them. Some will be short-term goals, like buying a new car, making a downpayment on a home or starting a new business. Others are mid-term goals, like financing your children's education, paying for extended travel, or purchasing a second home. Finally, there are long-term goals—most notably, planning for a comfortable retirement.

CAN I AFFORD TO INVEST?
Many non-investors think investing is only for rich people. This simply is not true. Some mutual funds allow you to invest as little as $25 at a time.

Still, starting an investment plan can be intimidating. If you are having trouble getting started, you might want to consider the slow and steady approach. If you are earning $40,000 a year, for example, putting aside 5% of your income means just $5.50 a day. By the end of the year, you'll have enough to invest in a $2000 Individual Retirement Account (IRA)—a sizable investment without much sacrifice. And remember—that $5.50 a day is money you are paying yourself.

Start Now

There is no perfect time to invest, but starting when you begin earning gives you a head start. Simply stated, it's not easy to get rich fast, and there will be many ups and downs along the way. The younger you are, the more earning potential you have in front of you, and the more financial risk you can, at least theoretically, afford to take. And if you invest for the long haul, you can ride out the down periods of the market and wait for the market to become profitable again.

STICK WITH IT

Historical data show that if you keep your money invested for long periods of time in stocks and bonds—five to ten years or longer—your money may grow faster than it would in a bank account. While there will be setbacks along the way, stock and bond investments will also, over the years, outpace earnings on cash investments in money market funds, CDs and even short-term Treasury bills.

Plan for Retirement

A good place to start planning for retirement is to look at what you need to live on now. The rule of thumb many people use is that you'll need to replace 80% of what you're earning when you retire. Investments can help provide that income.

TAKE ADVANTAGE OF RETIREMENT PLANS

If you're putting money into an employer-sponsored pension plan or an IRA, you're already investing for retirement in one of the most productive ways you can. That contribution may be most, or even all, of what you feel you can put away. Yet the truth is, being able to afford the kind of retirement you want will depend, in most cases, on the personal investments you make in addition to the money you put into these plans. If you don't start until retirement is within sight, it's tough to invest enough to produce the income you'll need.

THE POWER OF COMPOUNDING

| | STARTING EARLY | | STARTING LATER | |
Year	Contribution	Year-end value	Contribution	Year-end value
1	$2,000	$2,200		
2	2,000	4,620	$40,000	
3	2,000	7,282	invested	
4	2,000	10,212	over	
5	2,000	13,431	20 years	
6	2,000	16,974	↓	
7	2,000	20,871		
8	2,000	25,158		
9		27,674	$2,000	$2,200
10	↑	30,441	2,000	4,620
11		33,485	2,000	7,282
12	$16,000	36,834	2,000	10,210
13	invested	40,517	2,000	13,431
14	over	44,569	2,000	16,974
15	8 years	49,026	2,000	20,871
16		53,929	2,000	25,158
17		59,322	2,000	29,874
18		65,254	2,000	35,061
19		71,779	2,000	40,767
20		78,957	2,000	47,044
21		86,853	2,000	53,948
22		95,583	2,000	61,643
23		105,092	2,000	69,897
24		115,601	2,000	79,087
25		127,161	2,000	89,196
26		139,877	2,000	100,316
27		153,865	2,000	112,548
28		169,252	2,000	126,003

Earnings after 35 years	**$169,252**	Earnings after 25 Years	**$126,003**

Growth based on a hypothetical 10% rate of return, and does not represent the return of any particular investment.

Your Net Worth

Once you create a snapshot of what you've got, you'll know how much you need to put away.

Figuring your net worth is not only a critical first step in financial planning. It will also come in handy in many financial situations.

For example:

- **Banks and other lenders may require a statement of net worth for a mortgage application.**
- **College financial aid is based on net worth, so you'll have to report your assets and liabilities when your children apply.**
- **Certain high-risk investments may require that you have a minimum net worth—say $1 million or more.**

It's a good idea to update your personal balance sheet periodically just to see where you stand.

FINDING NET WORTH

Your balance sheet shows your net worth: your assets—the value of what you own or have invested—minus your liabilities—the money you owe. If your assets outweigh your liabilities, you are said to have a positive net worth. If your liabilities are larger, you have a negative net worth.

FINDING MONEY TO INVEST

You can include investment as a part of your household budget. If you don't do it already, you can find several ways to squeeze investment savings out of your existing budget.

Five Tips to Reach Your Goals

1 **Pay off your credit card balance. Then start putting an amount equal to the monthly interest you were paying into a new investment account.**

2 **Put as much money as you can into your retirement plan at work, or into an IRA.**

3 **Arrange to have a percentage of your income deducted from your paycheck and invested for you automatically. Or make sure to write an investment check when you pay your monthly bills.**

ASSETS

Current Estimated Value

Cash in Banks	
Money Market Accounts	
Amount Owed to Me	
Stocks/Bonds	
Other Investments	
Life Insurance (cash surrender value)	
IRA & Keogh Accounts	
Pension & Profit Sharing (vested interest)	
Real Estate: home	
other	
Business Interests	
Personal Property	

(Include furnishings, jewelry, collections, cars, security deposit on rent, etc.)

TOTAL ASSETS

– Total Liabilities

= TOTAL NET WORTH

LIABILITIES

Amount

Mortgages	
Bank Loans	
Car Loans	
Lines of Credit	
Charge Accounts	
Margin Loans	
Alimony	
Taxes Owed: income	
real estate	
other	
Other Liabilities	

TOTAL LIABILITIES

(Subtract liabilities from assets for net worth)

4 Try to invest any extra money from gifts, bonuses or freelance jobs that come your way unexpectedly.

5 Reinvest any money you make from investments instead of spending it.

REORGANIZING YOUR BUDGET

Many financial experts urge clients to invest 10 percent of their income. By reducing your spending in some of the more flexible expense categories, you can reorganize your budget to reach that goal. This is how one household making $75,000 a year might do it:

Expense Categories	Typical Expenditures	
	Without Investment	With 10% Investment
Housing	$31,500	$31,500
Food	13,425	11,925
Transportation	12,825	11,325
Health	4,650	4,650
Clothing	4,575	3,075
Entertainment	3,300	1,800
Other	4,725	3,225
Investment	0	7,500

Source: Bureau of Labor Statistics

The Retirement Marathon

Planning your financial future is planning for retirement— and having the money to enjoy it.

In 1900, retirement wasn't a hot topic. Employers didn't offer pensions, there was no Social Security, and the average life expectancy was 50.

But nearly a century later, everything has changed. More than a million people retire every year, at an average age of 63—and they expect to live to be nearly 85. Current estimates even suggest that a million or more people now in their 40s can expect to live to be 100 or more.

READY, SET, GO

The general wisdom is that planning your financial future starts with your first job. That's when you can begin putting money into a tax-deferred Individual Retirement Account (IRA). Even though you'll probably have lots of shorter-term reasons to invest, such as buying a car or a home, you should be thinking early on about long-term goals: your financial security and the security of those you care about. You'll quickly discover that there are lots of ways to invest for the future—including some that have tax advantages built in.

In Your 20s: Getting Started

You can get a head start on building your financial future if you start early. The two opportunities you don't want to pass up:

- Contributing to a **voluntary tax-deferred retirement plan.**

- Setting up one or more **investment accounts** with mutual funds, brokerages or banks.

While you may be paying off college debts or struggling to meet living expenses, the advantages of getting an early start on a long-term investment plan are too good to pass up.

Ideally, you should be investing up to 10% of your income, but half of that is better than nothing. If you're in an employer-sponsored plan that deducts your contribution from your salary, your taxable income will be reduced. That means tax savings—a reward for doing the right thing.

Though some of what you've put aside should be **liquid**, or easy to turn into cash, the best long-term investments are generally stocks or stock mutual funds. The growth they provide usually justifies the risk of possible setbacks in the short term.

In Your 30s & 40s: Hitting Your Stride

Even while you're juggling your income to pay for things that might seem more pressing, like buying a home, supporting a family, or anticipating your children's college expenses, you need to build a diversified portfolio of long-term investments.

One technique is to split the amount you invest between long- and short-term goals. Even if you put less into long-term plans than you'd like, at least these investments will grow, especially if you're building on a portfolio you started in your 20s. Most experts agree that long-term investments should be in stocks or stock mutual funds, but short-term investments should usually be in less volatile securities.

Keep in mind that investing for the long term is good for your current financial situation too:

- **You save on taxes by participating in a salary-reduction plan.**

- **You may qualify for a mortgage more easily if you have investment assets.**

- **You can borrow from some retirement investments without incurring taxes and penalties.**

WHAT THE FUTURE HOLDS

The truth is that retirement age is relative, not fixed. Many government workers retire after 20 years of service—sometimes as soon as their early 40s. Some people work productively through their 80s, thinking of retirement as something other people do. Many people retire the first day they're eligible. Still others leave work unwillingly, taking early retirement packages they can't refuse.

What you do about retirement may fit one of those patterns, or you may design your own approach. But whether retirement is a long way off, or sneaking up on you faster than you care to admit, planning for your financial future has three main ingredients:

- **Your financial security**
- **Adequate health care**
- **Benefits for your heirs**

In Your 40s & 50s: The Far Turn

You may be earning more than before, but you may be spending more, too. College expenses can wreak havoc on long-term investment goals. So can expensive hobbies, or moving to a bigger house.

On the other hand, if you've established good investing habits—like participating in a salary reduction plan and putting money into stocks and stock mutual funds—your long-term goals should be on track. You may also find that the demands on your current income eventually begin to decrease: the mortgage gets paid off, the children grow up, or you inherit assets from your parents.

That means you can begin to put more money into your long-term portfolio—through your employer's voluntary salary-reduction plans, mutual funds or brokerage accounts and some income-producing investments such as CDs and bonds.

AN EASY FORMULA

One rule of thumb for deciding what investments to make: add a percent sign to your age. You should have no more than that percentage of your money in fixed-income investments like bonds or CDs. The rest should be in stocks.

In Your 60s: The Home Stretch

When you start thinking seriously about retirement, you have to be sure you will have enough money to live comfortably. If you have a good pension and substantial investments, you'll have the flexibility to retire when you want.

Because you can expect to live 20 or 30 years after you retire, you'll want to continue to invest even as you begin collecting on your retirement plans. One approach is to reinvest earnings on certain investments into an account earmarked for making new ones. Another is to time the maturity dates of bonds or other fixed-income assets, like CDs, so that you have capital to reinvest if a good opportunity comes along.

Some of the other financial decisions you'll be facing may be dictated by government rules about when and what you must withdraw from your retirement accounts. Others may be driven by your concerns about health care or your desire to leave money to your heirs. At the least, you'll have to consider:

- **Shifting some investments to produce more income with fewer risks, in case of a sudden downturn in the stock market**

- **Rolling over retirement payouts to preserve their tax-deferred status**

- **Finding ways to reduce estate taxes and to pay for those that are unavoidable**

Planning for the Future

To live comfortably after you retire, you have to be realistic about how much you'll need to pay the bills.

Good health is wonderful. So is a nice place to live. But what you really need when you retire is money— money to pay your bills, with enough left over to do the things you want. The general rule of thumb is this: you'll need 70% to 80% of what you're spending before you retire, more if you have expensive hobbies or plan to travel extensively. For example,

CURRENT INCOME X 80% = PROJECTED NEED

if your gross income while you're working is $6,000 a month—that's $72,000 a year— you'll probably need $4,800 a month, or about $57,600 a year, after you retire.

UP OR DOWN?

You can be pretty sure some living expenses will shrink after you retire, but others are equally certain to go up. Planning your financial future includes anticipating those changes.

WHAT COSTS LESS

- By the time you retire, you'll have probably paid off your mortgage.

- Unless you were older than average when your children were born, you will have finished paying for their educations.

- If you commuted to work, you'll probably spend less on day-to-day travel and restaurant meals. You may need only one car, and will probably spend less on clothes and make fewer visits to the dry cleaner.

WHAT COSTS MORE

- Home maintenance costs and property taxes tend to go up, not down, over time, unless you move to a smaller place or to a state with lower taxes.

- If you're home all the time, your utility bills may increase.

- Home and car insurance are apt to increase.

- Medical expenses, including the cost of insurance, tend to skyrocket—500% or more over pre-retirement costs isn't unheard of. These costs will continue to rise as employers cut back on health care coverage in general, and for retirees in particular. For example, the average retired person spends $500 a year on prescription drugs, which aren't covered under most insurance plans.

LOOKING AHEAD

INFLATION'S BITE

Inflation is another factor you have to consider when planning your retirement budget. If you were retiring this June, for example, you'd need 80% of what you were spending in May. But next June you'll probably need more money to pay for the same goods and services.

That's because of **inflation**, the increase in the cost of living. Inflation has averaged 4% in the U.S. since 1926, and while it has been lower in the last few years, it has sometimes been substantially higher—hitting 14% in the early 1980s, for example.

That means if you're planning on a 20-year retirement, you'll need more than double the income in the 20th year than you do in the first, just to stay even. How can you manage that, especially if you're not working any more? The surest way is by earning money on your investments at a rate that tops the rate of inflation.

DOING THE MATH

While it might take a long time to estimate your retirement needs if you were doing the math yourself, you can use one of the software programs available through computer stores, mutual fund companies and brokerage houses to get a sense of where you stand. Often, the packages are free for the asking.

The software programs are generally easy to use. All you have to do is plug in the financial information they ask for, along with details about your plans for the future. The program will tell you how much more you'll need to invest to have enough money to retire on. Not surprisingly, you'll also get suggestions for ways to invest through the company that has developed the program.

If a financial planner or bank officer does the analysis for you, you may be charged a fee. But chances are they'll use programs similar to the ones you could use yourself for free.

ADDING IT ALL UP

If you start investing 35 years before you're ready to retire, and you save only 10% of what you earn each year, you'll have enough put aside to replace 70% of your salary.

STARTING AGE	PERCENT SAVED	SALARY REPLACED
30	10%	70%
40	21%	70%
50	48%	70%
55	84%	70%

For each year you delay, you'll have to save more of your yearly earnings to build up the same reserves. Most people would have trouble taking that much out of their salary, no matter how important they know it is to save.

SPECIAL CASES

You may have certain special advantages in planning your financial future. Veterans, for example, can apply for mortgages, health care coverage and disability benefits through the Veteran's Administration. They may also qualify for local tax breaks and get pension credit for their years on active service.

Union members and members of professional and other organizations may qualify for health and life insurance at lower rates than those available to the general population, or for other kinds of reduced-rate goods and services. Sometimes members of the clergy are offered discounts too.

In any case, you should check with any groups you're part of for the long-term financial advantages that may come with your membership. The larger ones may also keep you up-to-date on tax and other changes that affect your finances directly, through newsletters, journals or other publications.

Cost of a College Education

Going to college is the norm for many Americans. But paying for it can be an extraordinary expense.

Next to your home, one of the biggest expenses you may face is college tuition. If you send your children to private or prep school as well, the price tag for education can be very hefty indeed.

Since these costs keep going up—college and private school tuitions consistently exceed the rate of inflation and rise even in a down economy—planning ahead is essential.

How Much Will You Have to Save?

Four-year college costs, including tuition, room and board, books and transportation, and the monthly investments required to finance them. Table assumes 8% annual increase in college costs and 6% annual after-tax investment return, and no additional investments or earnings on balance invested once the child starts college.

YEARS UNTIL CHILD STARTS COLLEGE	PROJECTED COST OF 4-YEAR PROGRAM		MONTHLY INVESTMENT FOR 4-YEAR COST	
	PUBLIC	PRIVATE	PUBLIC	PRIVATE
1	$47,728	$99,724	$3,808	$7,957
3	53,627	112,050	1,314	2,746
5	60,255	125,900	815	1,702
7	67,703	141,461	600	1,253
9	76,071	158,946	480	1,003
15	107,908	225,467	310	647
20	144,406	301,726	244	509

Source: T. Rowe Price Associates, Inc., 1996.

THE GROWING COST OF EDUCATION

Tuition at private colleges and universities has increased anywhere from 5% to 13% every year since 1980. What cost $8,000 then costs nearly $30,000 now. If the current rate of increase continues, the cost could skyrocket to more than $50,000 in 2008, when today's first graders will start college. Tuition at public institutions has also increased, sometimes dramatically,

reflecting the crunch of tighter state budgets. Decreasing federal aid has made matters even more difficult for students.

The more prestigious the school, the higher the cost. The exception: top-flight state universities. Compare the 1995-1996 tuition plus room and board bill at Yale—$27,630—to $8,460 at the University of Virginia ($17,846 for an out-of-state student).

Average annual cost for
PUBLIC EDUCATION: $8,990*
(in state, 4 years)

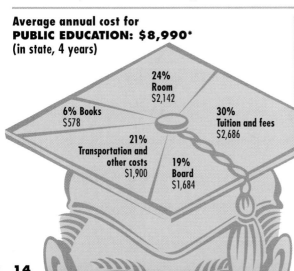

24% Room $2,142

6% Books $578

30% Tuition and fees $2,686

21% Transportation and other costs $1,900

19% Board $1,684

TUITION
The charge for instruction, including salaries, and the general operations of the institution. Public, tax-supported schools cost less than private ones.

ROOM
Housing in the dorms. Other housing options, like apartments, fraternities and sororities, aren't billed through the college, but such costs are comparable.

INVESTING FOR A COLLEGE EDUCATION

Putting away money for education calls for special investment strategies, such as:

- **Start early by establishing separate college savings accounts with the birth of each child.**
- **Plan on adding money every month to each account.**
- **Choose investments according to your children's ages.**
- **Invest in stocks and mutual funds when your children are young to maximize growth.**
- **Gradually shift to more conservative, income-producing investments as your children get older. These include equity income funds and mid-term Treasury bonds.**
- **As your child reaches college age, time your investments to mature when tuition bills come due.**

HOW DIFFERENT INVESTMENTS MAY HELP

Zero-coupon bonds
Bonds can be scheduled to come due on a staggered basis during the years you need the money, so you can calculate the amount you will have available. Some bonds are tax-free.

Mutual funds
Growth funds emphasize long-term gains. You can transfer profits from riskier funds into safer ones as your child gets closer to college age. Regular contributions are convenient, and may even be arranged as a payroll deduction.

CDs
Return on investment is guaranteed, so you'll know what's available, but yield may be low. Reinvestment rates change, so your long-term yield is unpredictable.

U.S. Savings Bonds
Interest is completely tax-free if you use the money to pay for education—provided your income is less than $60,000 a year (or $40,000 if you're a single parent).

SAVING IN YOUR CHILD'S NAME
You can save for college by opening a custodial account in your child's name. The advantage is that the earnings will probably be taxed at a lower rate once the child reaches age 14. (Before then, some of a child's earnings are taxed at your rate.)

But the tax savings can be marginal, and you lose control of the money when your child turns 18 or 21, depending on the state.

What's more, the strategy can backfire if your child applies for financial aid.

That's because most financial aid formulas require students to contribute 35% of their savings, while parents are required to supply only 5.6% of theirs.

Borrowing is another source of college funds. You can take out a home equity loan, or borrow from your profit-sharing or 401(k) plan. You can also borrow most of the cash value of your life insurance policy.

BOARD
Dining hall meals. Most schools offer several different plans at different costs. Students who don't live in college housing can opt for a meal plan or pay for food individually.

ACTIVITY FEES
Extra money for clubs, the yearbook, school newspaper and graduation. Everyone pays them.

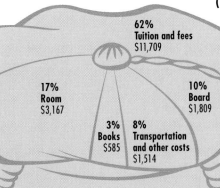

Average annual cost for
PRIVATE EDUCATION: $18,784*
(4 years)

62%
Tuition and fees
$11,709

17%
Room
$3,167

10%
Board
$1,809

3%
Books
$585

8%
Transportation and other costs
$1,514

*Source: The College Board, 1996.

Financial Planning

A financial plan should help you evaluate your current financial situation, estimate the cost of life-long goals, and establish strategies to meet them.

A financial plan is a blueprint that evaluates your current assets and debts, identifies the things you want or need and lays out a strategy to pay for them. Developing the plan is the first challenge. Sticking to it is the next.

In putting a plan together, you need to consider the present and the future so you can balance what's important to you now with what you can reasonably anticipate. But it's equally important to remember that you're not committing yourself irrevocably. You're likely to change your goals, and even more likely to change your approach to investing as you gain knowledge and experience.

Once you get a handle on how much you'll need, then it's easier to choose investments that are best suited to achieving your goals.

What a Successful Financial Plan Can Do

A professionally prepared financial plan is typically a computer-generated document that summarizes the information you've provided, explains appropriate financial planning strategies and recommends specific steps you should take to achieve your objectives.

Before you start a financial plan, you'll need to know your:

NET WORTH
Your total assets minus your total debt

CASH FLOW
The money you have coming in and the money you'll be spending

YOUR GOALS
The plans you have for the future

Without a financial plan in place, you run certain financial risks. For example, you may not have enough in reserve to meet large costs, such as college tuition or a downpayment on a home, or you may have to postpone retirement or continue to work part time.

If you decide to create a plan yourself, make sure to update it periodically, especially if there is a major change in your family or financial situation. Major changes in the economy, such as the rise and fall of interest rates, or new tax laws that affect you, should also trigger a review.

SIX OUT OF TEN
Americans rate a steady source of retirement income as their primary financial goal.

PROFESSIONAL FINANCIAL PLANNING

A professional financial plan usually begins with a *profile*—a questionnaire that a planner completes in an initial interview. You'll need to provide some basic documents—recent tax forms, insurance policies and retirement plans—and be prepared to discuss your financial goals.

Profiles vary in level of detail and sophistication. The more elaborate they are, the more customized information they provide. The cost is usually greater as well.

BEAT INFLATION

Helps your money earn more than the rate of inflation. (Money saved, rather than money invested, doesn't grow.)

MINIMIZE TAXES

Uses tax-free investments to avoid income taxes, and tax-deferred investments to postpone income taxes. Sets up trusts to reduce the taxes your heirs will owe later.

MANAGE THE UNEXPECTED

Provides a cash fund plus adequate health and life insurance as a hedge against unexpected expenses and illness.

PROVIDE MONEY FOR SPECIAL EXPENSES

Lets you afford things that are important to you, including college expenses, a vacation home, or travel and leisure activities.

ENRICH YOUR RETIREMENT

Encourages investments to supplement pensions and Social Security so you can maintain your lifestyle when you retire.

Tax Planning for Investments

Don't overlook the tax consequences when figuring the return on your investments.

Taxes are a vital part of any investment decision. But always remember that taxes are only a part of an overall investment strategy. Financial advisors recommend that you make investment choices not solely on tax avoidance—but on what you can expect to earn, the level of risk you're taking, and the diversity of your portfolio.

A capital gain is the profit produced by buying and selling stock or property.

CAPITAL GAINS
Capital gains taxes should be a primary concern of any investor. A **capital gain** is the profit that results from buying and selling stock or property. Capital assets include everything you own for investment and personal use—stocks and bonds, your home and furnishings, jewelry, cars and collectibles.

Gains from selling these assets are usually taxable. Losses are deductible only if you held the item for investment and not for personal use. So, you also need complete records for all of your transactions and expenses. See IRS Publication 550, "Investment Income and Expenses." You can get a copy by visiting the IRS Internet homepage at:
http://www.irs.ustreas.gov

LONG- AND SHORT-TERM GAINS
If you hold an asset for a year or less, any increase or **appreciation** in its value will result in a **short-term gain**. These gains are taxed at your highest ordinary income-tax rate. But an asset you hold for more than a year is a **long-term gain** and is taxed at no more than the maximum capital gains rate, 28 percent as of 1996.

That means a long-term gain is taxed like ordinary income for taxpayers in the 15- and 28-percent brackets. But the 28-percent maximum is a boon for people whose marginal tax rate is 31 percent, 36 percent or 39.6 percent.

DEDUCTING CAPITAL LOSSES
If you lose money on an investment, you may be able to deduct your losses. You combine short-term gains and losses to see if you have a net loss, and then do the same for long-term gains and losses. If you have an overall net loss, you may deduct it from ordinary income (your salary, for example) up to a maximum of $3,000 in one year ($1,500 if you're married, filing separately). If your loss is greater than what you are allowed to deduct, you carry over the excess and deduct it in later years.

Specific rules apply to figuring losses on investments you receive as a gift. You may want to consult your tax advisor to be sure you handle reporting them correctly.

FIGURING GAIN
You figure gain or loss by subtracting your **basis** from the proceeds of a sale. Basis is the price paid for the item, plus the expense of buying, holding and selling it. For example, the commissions and costs of an investment transaction are subtracted from the proceeds of a sale when you figure a gain or loss. If you received the item as a gift, your basis is the same as the giver's was. If you inherit an asset, your basis is the market value on the date of the giver's death. See IRS Publication 551, "Basis of Assets."

PROCEEDS The amount you get when you sell your asset

– BASIS The original cost of the asset, plus the cost of buying, holding and selling it

= GAIN OR LOSS

Here's how you would figure a capital gain:

	$ 22,000	Gross proceeds from the sale of stock
–	20,000	Amount you paid for the stock
–	385	Broker's commission and fees on sale
=	$ 1,615	Your capital gain

THE LONG AND THE SHORT OF IT

An investor in the 36% tax bracket sells stock resulting in a capital gain of $20,000. She saves $1,600 if she has a long-term gain.

SELL ON OR BEFORE ONE YEAR

$20,000 taxed at 36%

= **$7,200 TAX DUE**

SELL AFTER ONE YEAR

$20,000 taxed at 28%

= **$5,600 TAX DUE**

PASSIVE INCOME

Passive income, or **losses**, comes from businesses in which you aren't an active participant. These include limited partnerships, rental real estate and other rental activities that you don't help manage.

Most tax shelters are passive partnership ventures designed to let investors deduct or take tax credits for more dollars than they actually put up in cash. Shelters are designed for high-income taxpayers willing to take risks.

The 1986 tax act eliminated most of these tax shelters. Losses from passive investments may now be deducted only from income from similar ventures. The losses can no longer shelter other income. That is, they can't be deducted from active income, such as wages and salaries, or portfolio income, such as interest, dividends and capital gains. Losses not taken can only be deducted when the passive investment is sold or disposed of in a taxable transaction. A gift is not a taxable transaction.

HOLDING STOCKS DEFERS CAPITAL GAINS TAXES

Short-term gains are taxed at your highest income-tax rate.

Long-term gains are taxed at a maximum rate of 28%.

While you're holding an investment, you don't pay any tax on its increase in value. The market price of a stock you bought for $5 a share may climb to $50, but the tax on that capital gain is deferred until you sell the stock and collect the proceeds. If you've held the stock for more than a year, you owe the maximum capital gains rate when you sell.

For this reason, well-off investors often pick stocks for long-term growth prospects rather than for regular dividends. Dividends are taxed as they're paid and at high ordinary income rates.

TAX SHELTER

THE GAIN OF GIVING

If you donate appreciated property, such as stock or a house, that you've held for over a year, you may deduct the market value and avoid capital gains tax on the appreciation. If a stock's value has dropped, you can sell it, take the capital loss and donate the proceeds of the sale.

Once your child is over age 14, you can save taxes by giving the child stock that has appreciated in value while you owned it. The child sells the shares and pays capital gains tax at a lower rate than yours.

TAX-DEFERRED INVESTMENTS

You can take advantage of a variety of **tax-deferred investments** that allow you to accumulate earnings on which you owe no tax until you begin withdrawing money, usually after you retire. Then you pay at whatever your current rate is.

There are often, though not always, contribution limits on the amount you can invest each year in tax-deferred plans. But sometimes the amount you invest is also tax-deductible, saving you even more.

The 1993 tax act provides a 50 percent capital gains tax exclusion for investors in certain new small businesses.

GRAND OPENING

Finding an Investment Professional

Expert advice can make investing easier—
and more profitable.

When you're ready to choose an advisor, you should take care to find one who will take the time to understand your financial goals. Before you start looking, figure out what you want your investments to accomplish. Everyone wants to make money. Yet it's better to narrow down your objectives to definable goals—like financing your daughter's education or preparing for retirement.

QUALIFICATIONS TO LOOK FOR

Judge qualifications of financial advisors just as you would any professional you hire. Key qualifications to consider:

EXPERIENCE
Five years isn't too much to require. As a general rule of thumb, the less experience you have, the more experience you want in an advisor. Educational background is another factor to consider.

REPUTATION
Referrals from people you trust—especially professionals in the field—are most helpful. Ask for the names of an advisor's current clients who are similar to you and are willing to act as references. Then call them.

EXPERTISE
Financial advisors differ in the services they provide to clients. Some have expertise in particular industries or investment strategies. Others provide broader-based service.

COMPATIBILITY
Face-to-face meetings will tell you a lot about your advisor's skills. Ask many questions and expect clear and concise answers.

An advisor will be asking you whether you are investing to meet short- or long-term goals, and how much financial risk you are comfortable with. Other questions to consider: Do you need current income from your investments, or are you seeking capital appreciation? Do you have any special tax concerns that might affect your investing? The answers will help your advisor guide you in the right direction.

When you interview potential advisors, ask them to explain how the investments they would recommend will help you achieve your financial goals. Make sure you understand the answer. The better you grasp the strategy, the better you'll feel about following the advice you are paying for.

REVIEWING PROFESSIONAL RECORDS
Several organizations track regulatory violations by brokers or firms, as well as disciplinary actions that securities regulators have taken against them. One source is the NASDR (800-289-9999) which has a database of 500,000 brokers. It can tell you if any self-regulatory organization has disciplined the advisor or firm. They'll send you a free printout of their findings. Another source is your state securities office. It can tell you about complaints filed by customers against a broker or firm. Bear in mind that these claims may not have been substantiated or proven true.

CHOOSING A BROKER

Different firms offer different levels of service, and different fees. If you are planning to choose your own investments, then a **discount brokerage** may be best for you. Discount brokerages charge lower fees and commissions than full-service brokerages. The drawback is that they do not offer the same level of advice and research that higher fees buy for you. If personal attention is important to you, hiring an investment advisor from a **full-service brokerage** is a good idea.

TYPES OF INVESTMENT ADVISORS

Most financial institutions—including banks, brokerages, mutual funds and insurance companies—provide financial planning and investment advice. Typically, these institutions pay their advisors a salary, or a commission on the investments they sell, or both. It's helpful for you to know how advisors are paid, so you can better evaluate their recommendations, especially when the investments are offered by their own institutions.

STOCKBROKERS/ FINANCIAL CONSULTANTS (Registered Representative, Account Executive, Financial Advisor)

Stockbrokers work in brokerage firms and provide advice on specific investments. They buy and sell stocks, bonds and mutual funds for their clients on commission. They must pass an examination to sell securities to the public and participate in continuing education programs.

BANK INVESTMENT REPRESENTATIVES (Customer Service Representative)

Advisors who work for banks can help you with annuities, mutual funds, CDs and money market funds available through that particular bank. They can also help you with loans, money transfers and other banking-related transactions. You can find them at most banks and bank branches, and, more recently, over the phone and even by computer. In addition to their salaries, bank representatives may receive commissions on annuities and mutual funds they sell.

CERTIFIED PUBLIC ACCOUNTANTS (CPAs)

CPAs may work independently in private practice or as part of a large company. They provide financial planning advice, and, in certain cases, investment advice. Their expertise, however, is often in tax planning and preparation. They are paid a fee for their services, but no commissions.

FINANCIAL PLANNERS (Financial Consultant, Financial Advisor)

Like CPAs, financial planners can work independently or as part of larger companies. They specialize in creating financial plans and providing investment advice. Most sell investments, life insurance and annuities. Some are paid on commission, some by fee, and others a combination of both.

INSURANCE AGENTS (Financial Advisor, Financial Planner, Registered Representative)

Besides selling life insurance and annuities, insurance agents may also offer financial planning. Some sell investments as well. They are paid primarily on commission.

MONEY MANAGERS (Asset Manager, Personal Banker, Bank Trust Officer)

Typically found in banks and other financial institutions offering banking services, money managers manage assets of well-to-do clients, and handle loans and mortgages. They work by fee, often based on the size of the portfolio. Asset managers, typically, have more discretion over the money entrusted to them than the others.

More than 20 million Americans rely on investment professionals to help them manage their portfolios. They choose from a pool of about a half-million investment advisors.

Making the Most of Your Partnership

Building a partnership means taking an active role with an advisor you trust—and get along with.

After you have chosen your financial advisor, it's time to move ahead. To make your new relationship work, think of it as a partnership. As with any partnership, taking an active role yields the best results. Communicate effectively and be involved in the decisions. Be as candid as possible about your goals and your assets. Be as specific as you can.

Here are several steps you can take to ensure you get the service and long-term results you are paying for.

STAY IN SYNC

Review your investment objectives before you meet. Consider your willingness to take financial risks, and whether you can live without the money you are about to invest. Let your advisor know if you are planning a major purchase—like a house—and when you will be needing the money. Then together you can calculate your net worth, decide how much money you have to invest, and develop a financial plan.

Put a premium on clear communication. Make sure you understand the investment strategy your advisor is laying out for you. One way to ensure you understand each other is to ask your advisor to put it in writing. Ask for a letter summarizing what you've agreed about your goals, your risk tolerance and your overall financial situation. If the letter reflects your feelings, you are on the right track. Sign it, and keep a record of it.

Ask many questions. If there is something you don't understand, even something you feel embarrassed about not knowing, don't be afraid to ask. Remember: It's your money you are investing. It's up to you to let your advisor know if you need more information.

Understand the role of each investment in your portfolio. The investments in a diversified portfolio are designed to complement each other. One may offset the risk of another. Some will pay dividends, others will yield capital gains and still others accrue interest. You need to understand the differences and the tax consequences of each, and be aware of the role each one plays in your overall investment strategy.

Read your mail. You'll be receiving account statements, transaction confirmation orders, prospectuses, annual reports and written investment advice from your portfolio manager. The more attention you can give to these materials, the more you'll learn about your investments and the other options available to you.

DOs

✓ **Be candid and specific about your goals and your assets.**

✓ **Be serious and stick to your plan.**

✓ **Read the financial press and material from your advisor.**

✓ **Ask questions.**

✓ **Expect market fluctuations.**

DON'Ts

✓ **Don't be passive.**

✓ **Don't panic. Take a long-term view and give investments a chance to pay off.**

✓ **Don't have unreasonable expectations.**

✓ **Don't blindly follow advice. Check it out.**

Be aware of changes in the value of your account. Make sure you understand the risks of your portfolio, and what might cause the value of your portfolio to fluctuate. If you own bonds, for example, understand how changes in interest rates will affect the value of your holdings.

Keep good records. Keep a file of any letters you exchange, along with your transaction confirmation statements. They not only will help you monitor trends, but will be useful during tax season. You'll need to report to the IRS, for example, the profit or loss you make from the sale of an investment.

SECOND OPINIONS

Although many people prefer to work with a single financial advisor, working with two can give you access to greater expertise. One advisor, for example, can help you with your employee retirement plan. Your personal investment account could be managed by another professional. You may even choose to seek advice from a third advisor—an accountant or a tax attorney, for example—to help you make investment decisions that reduce the amount of tax you or your heirs will owe.

Naturally, using two advisors allows you to bounce ideas from one advisor off the other. But be careful: If you do have two advisors, it's up to you to be aware when both accounts invest heavily in stocks in the same industry. Investments concentrated in a single industry could increase your risk if stock prices in that industry tumble.

Most advisors are willing to work on specific assignments—like investing a lump sum payment you receive from a retirement plan. Once you have been able to evaluate the recommendations for a specific goal, then you can choose to make a longer-term commitment to work together.

Resolving Problems

There are many actions you can take if the partnership turns sour.

Any partnership—especially one based on money—can go awry. If you have a specific complaint, or believe your financial advisor mishandled your account, there is plenty you can do to resolve the problem. In many cases, it won't cost you anything to get results.

FIRST THINGS FIRST

Before you register your complaint, ask yourself the following questions:

- **Were you misled by the information given you by your advisor, or did you not understand it completely?**
- **Did your advisor ignore your wishes, or was the mistake an honest one?**

If part of the blame lies with you, then you'll just have to resolve to avoid the same problem next time around. If your advisor is clearly at fault, act quickly.

LAST THINGS LAST

If enough money is at stake, and you've exhausted all your other options, you can sometimes take your case to court. This option is the most expensive, and may not be available to you if you signed an arbitration clause when you opened your brokerage account.

There's also a time limit for you to initiate your claim. If you are considering a court case, make sure your lawyer is a specialist in securities law. You can call your local or state bar association for referrals.

THREE WAYS OF SETTLING COMPLAINTS

Talk To Your Advisor

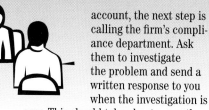

First, look over your account statements and transaction confirmation slips to clarify the problem. Then, call your advisor, and bring your complaint to his or her attention. In most cases, that alone should resolve the problem. Remember: Advisors need customers like you, and should act quickly to keep your business.

If this doesn't bring satisfaction, call the branch manager and arrange an appointment. Bring all your paperwork with you, along with a written account of your complaint, complete with dates of conversations. It's also a good idea to write a letter confirming your call.

If your complaint is the misappropriation of funds or the unauthorized trading of securities in your account, the next step is calling the firm's compliance department. Ask them to investigate the problem and send a written response to you when the investigation is over. This should take about a month.

If this doesn't work, send a detailed complaint, along with an account of your attempts to resolve the issue, to the chairman or president of the firm. Also be sure to let the authorities know about any violations or inappropriate sales. The Office of Investor Education and Assistance of the Securities and Exchange Commission (800-SEC-0330) will send you a free brochure about filing a complaint. If your advisor is a broker, you can go to your state's securities division. If your advisor is an insurance agent, you can appeal to your state's insurance commission.

Mediation

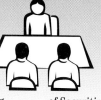

If you can't get the problem resolved, you might consider mediation. Mediation means using an impartial third party to help come to an agreement. But unlike binding arbitration, the mediator doesn't impose a decision. Mediation is less expensive than arbitration or traditional litigation. Call the Mediation Department (212-858-4400) of the National Association of Securities Dealers Regulation, Inc. (NASDR), for more information.

Arbitration

Arbitration may be your only remaining option if you signed an arbitration clause, as most brokerage customers do when opening an account.

You or your lawyer present your case before a panel assembled by the financial market you dealt with, or by the American Arbitration Association (212-484-4000), an independent arbitration forum. The decision is based on fairness rather than legal precedent.

In most cases, their decision is binding, which means there is no appeal and you cannot file suit in a court. If your dispute is $10,000 or less, a single arbitrator will review your claim.

Any firm that is a member of the NASD or the New York Stock Exchange (NYSE) is required to go to arbitration if a customer requests it. The fee for a hearing is modest, and is tied to the amount of your claim. Arbitration procedures can be obtained from the American Stock Exchange (212-306-1000), the NYSE (212-656-2772) and the NASDR (301-590-6500). They'll tell you how to file your claim with them, any regional exchange, or the American Arbitration Association.

Understanding Your Statement

Keeping tabs on your investment paper trail gives you a leg to stand on.

Paying close attention to your account statements will give you a valuable snapshot of your financial position. A brokerage statement gives you a record of all the trades you made during the most recent account period. You can track the value of your individual holdings from statement to statement. You will also find a summary of income produced by each security, including any dividends, interest and capital gains.

Statements also give you a chance to make sure your records are correct. Checking your brokerage account statement is just like balancing your checkbook.

PHONE INQUIRIES

Most brokerage houses have a phone inquiry system to allow you to get information about your balance and the daily performance of particular funds. You can usually do this by entering your account number and providing a password or personal identification number. Most firms also provide account information via computer modem. Or you can talk regularly with your financial advisor.

A typical monthly or quarterly statement includes two basic sections.

PORTFOLIO SUMMARY
The bottom line in a portfolio summary tells you the current market value of your cash and securities at the firm holding your account. Comparing the summary from month to month can give you an idea of exactly how volatile your holdings are. If there are wide fluctuations from month to month, it shouldn't be cause for panic. Month-to-month and even year-to-year fluctuations are to be expected. The important thing is keeping a long-term perspective. Ask your advisor to explain

CONFIRMATION STATEMENT

The confirmation statement you get from your broker after you buy or sell a security spells out the details of a trade. The type of transaction, the exchange where the trade was made and the terms and conditions are explained on the back. You should keep all transaction confirmations as part of your tax records.

Most brokerages are covered by the Securities Investor Protection Corporation (SIPC), which insures your account up to $500,000.

Securities Company, Inc.

MEMBER
SiPC
SECURITIES INVESTOR
PROTECTION CORPORATION

B - YOU BOUGHT S - YOU SOLD	DESCRIPTION	PRICE
B 200	SYNTEX CORPORATION E	45:0000

Most investors buy stocks in multiples of 100, or round lots. If they aren't round lots, they're called odd lots. With odd lots, the commission may be higher.

The price per share reports the price you paid. You can buy or sell either at the current market price, or you can authorize a trade when the price hits a certain amount.

The base amount of your purchase is figured by multiplying the number of shares by the market price.

Investments Corp.

Individual Retirement Account
August 29 - September 30, 1996

Account number 111-00011-19 415 SALLY SEP

IRA activity summary

Amounts added to your IRA

The IRS requires Shearson Lehman Hutton to report only the total amount contributed to your IRA during the calendar year. It is your responsibility to determine which contributions, if any, are deductible when you calculate your income tax. The designations shown below are based on information you provided to your financial consultant.

Employer's contributions

				Total
Description				$ 30.00
Contributions made in past prior calendar year				30.00
Contributions made in prior calendar year				30.00
Contributions made in current calendar year				

Employee's voluntary contributions

	Deductible portion	Non-deductible portion	Unspecified	Total
Description	$ 30.00	$ 30.00	$ 30.00	$ 90.00
Contributions for prior tax year made in prior year	30.00	30.00	30.00	90.00
Contributions for prior tax year made in current year	30.00	30.00	30.00	90.00
Contributions for current tax year				

Employee's elective deferral (salary reduction) contributions

		$ 30.00
Contributions made in prior year		30.00
Contributions made in current year		

Rollovers

	$ 30.00
Amounts rolled over from IRAs and other qualified plans	

Transfers in

	$ 30.00
Cash transferred directly into your Shearson Lehman Hutton IRA from other financial institutions (Not including value of securities)	

Amounts withdrawn from your IRA

Distributions

	$ 30.00
Amounts paid to you since Jan 1 of current year	30.00
Federal taxes withheld	

Transfers out

	$ 30.00
Cash transferred directly from your Shearson Lehman Hutton IRA to other financial institutions (Not including value of securities)	

the reasons behind price movements that concern you.

Typically, a portfolio statement breaks down your holdings by categories such as stocks, bonds and mutual funds. You may get a separate statement for your IRA.

ACCOUNT ACTIVITY

The account activity section shows all additions and subtractions from your accounts, including sales and purchases, cash deposits and withdrawals. It also includes information about reinvested dividends and income or capital gains distributions.

The Securities and Exchange Commission (SEC) imposes a fee on most transactions. Some brokerages impose a modest handling charge as well.

You pay brokers' commissions every time you buy or sell stock. The charges are added to the amount you pay when you buy, and deducted when you sell.

The net amount includes the cost of the security plus commissions and fees.

Confirmation

UPON THE TERMS AND CONDITIONS OF THE AGREEMENT PRINTED ON THE BACK HEREOF AND NONE OTHER.

Please retain for tax purposes.

AMOUNT	INTEREST OR STATE TAX	S.E.C. FEE AND/OR HANDLING	COMMISSION OR CHARGE	NET AMOUNT
900000		225	19024	919249

INV. OBJ.	ACCOUNT NUMBER	TYPE OF ACCT.	TYPE OF TRANS.	TRADE DATE	SETTLEMENT DATE
	AT1 234 567	1	25	10/30/96	11/02/96

These numbers, explained on the back, confirm whether you made a cash trade, bought on margin, sold short or any one of several other transactions.

The trade date is the day of the transaction—usually either the day you authorize a trade or the day the security reaches the price you specify to buy or sell it.

The settlement date is the deadline for paying your bill or getting your proceeds. Investors must settle their security transactions within three business days.

Winning Investment Strategies

You've got to develop a strategy to win at investing.

There is no single right way to invest. In fact, flexibility in choosing investments is essential. As economic trends and market conditions change, you have to modify your approach and move your money into different products.

Certificates of Deposit (CDs) are a good example. In the 1980s, CDs offered double-digit rates of return. But in the 1990s they frequently paid 5% or less. That meant CD investors earned less,

AVOID RANDOM BUYING

Random buying—a few stocks here, a bond there—is rarely a winning strategy. In fact, it's no strategy at all. Rather, you should plan your investments carefully, allocating some of your money to stocks or stock mutual funds, some to bonds and some to cash or cash equivalents.

THE MONEY YOU HAVE TO INVEST

IMPATIENT— OUT OF MARKET TOO SOON

RANDOM BUYING

NO MATTER HOW MUCH MONEY YOU HAVE TO INVEST, ALWAYS MAKE SURE YOU:

- **Make a plan**
- **Keep track of your investments**
- **Invest for the long term**

and made less progress toward meeting their goals.

Flexible investors can keep abreast of trends in the financial markets by reading daily financial reports as well as more in-depth weekly and monthly publications. There is also a wealth of current financial information available online.

TAKE YOUR AGE INTO ACCOUNT

Investors must also be sure to shift strategies as they grow older. Investors in their 30s and 40s can typically recover from losses more easily than retired investors. As you get closer to leaving the workforce, it makes sense to start shifting your investment strategy from growth securities to income-producing securities.

DIVERSIFICATION

Besides flexibility, the best long-term strategy is building a diverse portfolio that includes investments from different sectors of the financial markets. The basic building blocks of any portfolio are stocks, bonds and mutual funds. Typically, you want a healthy mix of all three.

Historically, stocks have outperformed income-oriented investments like bonds, as well as cash investments in bank accounts, over periods of five to ten years or longer. Consequently, investment advisors will recommend that you include stocks in your portfolio if you are investing for the long term.

Between 1976 and 1995, for example, investors in stocks enjoyed annualized total returns of 14.6%, while bonds gained 10.6%. Even so, most financial advisors also recom-

STICK WITH YOUR PLAN

While flexibility is important, it is also important to keep your overall financial goals in perspective. Sticking with your investment strategy means keeping a long-term perspective that enables you to stay on course even when the financial markets are declining. Historical data suggest that a down market will eventually return to profitability.

Widely respected studies consistently show that stock investors who keep their money in the stock market during a declining market will eventually come out ahead of investors who sell off their stock investments. Long-term stock investors also come out ahead of short-term stock investors who bail out temporarily during a falling market, and then switch back when the stock market recovers.

YOUR INVESTMENT GOAL

CHASING HOT STOCK TOO LATE

INFLEXIBLE STRATEGY

Comparing Returns Over 70 Years

Annualized Total Returns Over 70 Years, 1926–1995

Large company stocks	**10.5%**
Long-term corporate bonds	**5.7%**
Treasury bills	**3.7%**

Source: © Computed using data from *Stocks, Bonds, Bills & Inflation 1996 Yearbook*™, Ibbotson Associates, Chicago (annually updates work by Roger G. Ibbotson and Rex A. Sinquefield). Used with permission. All rights reserved.

mend at least a modest investment in bonds for long-term investors. The reason is that bonds carry less risk, and they offer a steady flow of income that non-dividend paying stocks do not offer.

Finally, mutual funds have soared in popularity among investors in recent years. The reason is they offer instant diversity and professional management by pooling the money from a range of investors and reinvesting it in a broad portfolio of stocks, bonds and other securities.

Bang for Your Buck

The greater the risk, the more you stand to gain—or lose.

Risk is inherent in all investments. There's no such thing as absolute safety. There are always factors you can't control—like an oil embargo or high inflation. Or you may have to sell when prices are down if you need the cash.

But some investments are more risky than others. Low-risk investments, like government bonds, guarantee that you'll get your money back, plus interest. But you may not earn enough to offset inflation. Higher-risk investments, like stock in a new company, aren't guaranteed. But if the company succeeds, your investment could someday be worth lots of money.

INVESTMENT STRATEGIES

CONSERVATIVE
Take only limited risks by concentrating on cash, secure stock and fixed-income investments.

MODERATE
Take moderate risks by putting money into growth stocks.

WHAT CAUSES RISK?

Volatility

The more volatile an investment is, the more often it swings in value—from high to low, or the reverse. You can make more profit since there's a bigger spread between what you paid and what you sell it for. But if the price drops by the same amount, you can lose big, too.

Demanding High Yield

When the economy is down or when interest earnings decline, many investors seek investments with the same returns they got in better times. The risk is buying lower quality, often unfamiliar, investments that promise big returns, as "junk" bonds did in the 1980s. But the search for higher returns can result in greater losses as well.

Playing It Too Safe

If you take no chances, you run the risk of coming out short. The more you have in the safest investments like CDs, bank accounts and Treasury bills, the smaller your chance of substantial reward. There's also the risk of outliving your assets because inflation outpaces them.

WHAT IS A RISK RATIO?

One way to measure the relationship of risk vs. reward in the stock market is to balance how much you think a stock is likely to rise against how far it could fall from its current price. If a stock selling for $20 could go up to $50 or fall to $10, its risk ratio is 3:1 (it could go up 30 or down 10). If the price does go up to $45 but could still fall to $10, the ratio is 1:7 (it could go up 5 or down 35), which makes it more risky.

SPECULATIVE
Take major risks on investments with unpredictable results.

OTHER KINDS OF RISK

Beyond investment risk, there are other risks you can't predict but must be prepared for:

Market risk

depends on the state of the overall economy. If the stock market tumbles, your stock will probably decline in value even if the company is profitable.

Currency fluctuation

is increasingly a factor as more people invest in international markets— especially through mutual funds. As the dollar rises in value, the value of overseas investments may decline—and vice versa.

Inflation risk

affects the value of fixed-rate investments like bonds and CDs. The value of these investments declines as inflation rises because the interest rate isn't adjusted to keep pace.

Political turmoil,

like threats to the oil supply, can wreak havoc in an increasingly interdependent global economy.

RISK VS. RETURN: WHAT'S THE TRADE-OFF?

When it comes to investing, trying to weigh risk and reward can seem like throwing darts blindfolded. Investors don't know the actual returns that securities will deliver, or the ups and downs that will occur along the way.

Looking to the past can provide some clues. Over several decades, for instance, investors who put up with the stock market's gyrations earned returns far in excess of bonds and "cash" investments like Treasury bills.

	AVERAGE ANNUAL RETURN* 1926–1995	Best Year	Worst Year
Small company stocks	12.5%	142.9% (1933)	−58.0% (1937)
Large company stocks	10.5%	54.0% (1933)	−43.3% (1931)
Long-term corporate bonds	5.7%	42.6% (1982)	−8.1% (1969)
Cash (Treasury bills)	3.7%	14.7% (1981)	−0.02% (1938)
Price inflation	3.1%	−2.1% (1949)	13.3% (1979)

* Price changes of securities plus dividends and interest income

Source: © Computed using data from *Stocks, Bonds, Bills & Inflation 1996 Yearbook*™, Ibbotson Associates, Chicago (annually updates work by Roger G. Ibbotson and Rex A. Sinquefield). Used with permission. All rights reserved.

The Right Moves

To earn more with your investments, consider what they cost and what they pay.

By using some basic techniques of effective buying, you can build a strong portfolio that minimizes taxes, controls investment expenses, and protects against market ups and downs. Here are three ways to help you get there.

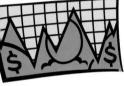

DOLLAR COST AVERAGING

The old adage that the smart-est way to make money is to buy at the lowest price and sell at the highest is easier said than done. If you could do that regularly, funding your retirement—or anything else—would be no problem.

A less dramatic but more reliable strategy is to make regular investments in specific mutual funds, for example $100 every month, or $300 each quarter. It's much less painful to spread your in-vestment over a year rather than to come up with $1,200 all at once. And, over time, you can build a substantial investment.

Using this approach, called **dollar cost averaging**, you can even out the cost of your investment. Since the prices of mutual funds fluctuate, sometimes you'll buy at a higher price, sometimes at a lower one. When the price is low, your $100 buys more. When it's high, it buys less. But you're never paying more than the current worth. Better yet, you don't risk making a major investment just before a major drop in price.

Of course, dollar cost averaging does not guarantee a profit or protect against loss in declining markets.

To use dollar cost averaging for stock purchases, you can enroll in a company-sponsored reinvestment plan that lets you make additional purchases. Many larger companies offer this option. Or you can put a regular amount each month into a special investment account.

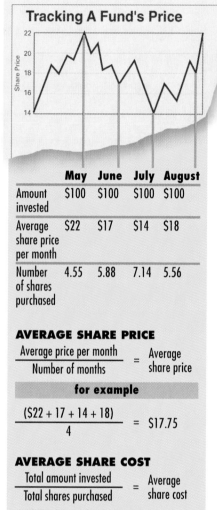

Tracking A Fund's Price

	May	June	July	August
Amount invested	$100	$100	$100	$100
Average share price per month	$22	$17	$14	$18
Number of shares purchased	4.55	5.88	7.14	5.56

AVERAGE SHARE PRICE

$$\frac{\text{Average price per month}}{\text{Number of months}} = \text{Average share price}$$

for example

$$\frac{(\$22 + 17 + 14 + 18)}{4} = \$17.75$$

AVERAGE SHARE COST

$$\frac{\text{Total amount invested}}{\text{Total shares purchased}} = \text{Average share cost}$$

for example

$$\frac{\$400}{4.55 + 5.88 + 7.14 + 5.56} = \$17.29$$

If you have no trouble sticking to a buying schedule, you can write the checks yourself. Or, if it's more convenient, you can arrange for automatic deductions from your account. The advantage of the former is more flexibility, letting you change the amount or skip an occasional month.

INVESTING STYLES

When you **buy and hold**, you keep a stock or bond for the long term. Or you can **trade**, by turning over your portfolio regularly, buying when you think a stock is going to increase in value, and selling when its return meets your expectations.

In general, you make out better following one approach or the other rather than switching back and forth. In the end, most studies show holding for the long term pays off.

AVOIDING THE TAX MAN

Of the two great myths about retirement—that your living expenses will drop dramatically and that you'll owe less income tax—the second is probably the bigger misconception. There's not much you can do to influence the tax rate. But some investing strategies can foil—or at least postpone—the inevitable amount due the IRS.

If you're in one of the higher federal tax brackets and live in a high-tax state, one solution is to do some of your investing in tax-exempt municipal bonds. Often, none of the interest is taxed (though **capital gains**, or any profit you make when you sell, will be). While tax-exempt investments usually pay less interest than taxable investments, you can use the following steps to figure out what you need to earn on a taxable investment to equal the income on a tax-exempt one.

1 Subtract your current **federal tax bracket** from 100. For example, if you're in the 36% bracket, you get 64.

$$100 - 36 = 64$$

2 Divide the yield on the tax-exempt investment by the number you get in step 1. The answer is the taxable yield you need on a taxable investment to equal the tax-exempt yield.

$$\frac{\text{Tax-exempt yield}}{100 - \text{your tax rate}} = \begin{array}{l}\text{Equivalent}\\\text{taxable yield}\end{array}$$

If you are in the 36% tax bracket, you'd need a taxable yield of 9.4% to earn as much as a tax-exempt investment paying 6%.

for example

$$\frac{6}{64} = .09375$$

9.4% THE TAXABLE EQUIVALENT YOU NEED

BUILDING A LADDER

If you're buying bonds or CDs, you can use a technique known as **laddering**. When you ladder, you choose investments with different maturity dates, and split your total investment more or less equally among the different bonds.

As each bond comes due, you have the principal to reinvest. When one bond matures, you buy a new one. If interest rates have dropped, say from 8% to 6% on medium-term bonds, only that part of your total bond investment has to be reinvested at the lower rate. By the time the next bond matures, rates could be up again.

Laddering, in other words, is a way to keep your investments fluid and at the same time protect yourself against having to invest all your money at once if rates are low. Laddered investments can also be used as a regular source of income. As they come due, you can put the money into more liquid accounts to use for living expenses. By planning those cash infusions, you can avoid having to sell off other investments that would continue to produce income, like stocks, longer-term bonds, or mutual funds.

HOW LADDERING WORKS

Purchase three Treasury bonds with varying terms to split up your principal. When each bond matures, reinvest the principal in another bond.

- If interest rates rise, you're able to take advantage of high-yielding investments.

- If interest rates drop, you'll have to reinvest only one-third of your total principal at lower rates.

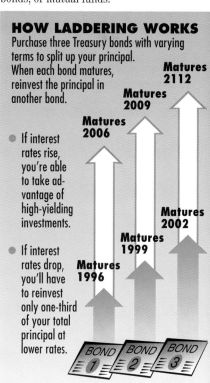

Matures 2112
Matures 2009
Matures 2006
Matures 2002
Matures 1999
Matures 1996

BOND 1 BOND 2 BOND 3

Diversity

If variety is the spice of life, diversity is the heart and soul of investing.

While some of your investments are living up to expectations, others may be in the dumps. If you want your **portfolio**, or list of investment holdings, to produce the income you'll need after you retire, you have to **diversify**, or spread your investment money around.

That's because any time all of your money is concentrated in one place, your financial security depends on the strength of that investment. And no matter how sound an investment may be, there will be times when its price falls or its interest payments don't keep up with inflation.

For example, if your life savings are in CDs paying 3% while inflation is running at 4%, you're facing a loss of buying power. Or if you own hundreds of shares in a company that loses money, cuts its dividend, and drops in the stock market, you'll be short dividend income and even part of your original investment if you sell your shares.

THE FIRST STEPS

Diversifying your investments is no easy matter. For starters, you need enough money to make a variety of investments. And you have to judge each one not only on its own merits, but in relation to the rest of your portfolio.

If you put long-term investment money into **fixed-income investments** like corporate or municipal bonds, you should also make **equity investments** like stocks or stock mutual funds. If some of your short-term investments are Certificates of Deposit (CDs), the rest could be money market funds or U.S. Treasury bills.

THE SECOND STAGE

Diversification also means spreading your investment dollar within a specific type of investment. For example, your stock portfolio is not diversified if you own shares in just one or two companies, or in companies all involved in the same sector of the economy, like health care or utility companies. Neither are your fixed-income

investments diversified if you own only municipal bonds issued by the state in which you live. If you invest in eight mutual funds, but they all track small-growth companies, you're not diversified either.

Increasingly, real diversification calls for international investments. Because the world economies are linked by round-the-clock trading and stimulated by the opening of new markets, many investors—and their professional advisors—believe that putting money into overseas markets is a good way to balance investments at home. Generally, mutual funds provide the simplest way to invest internationally, since the funds handle all of the currency and taxation issues that go along with buying and selling abroad.

HOW DIVERSIFYING CAN BALANCE GROWTH OVER TIME*

1985	GROWTH
STOCKS ONLY	UP 50%
BONDS ONLY	UP 2%
MIX	**UP 31%**

STOCKS ONLY

BONDS ONLY

MIX

Value of your investment

1983   1985

*Source: © Computed using data from *Stocks, Bonds, Bills & Inflation 1996 Yearbook™*, Ibbotson Associates, Chicago (annually updates work by Roger G. Ibbotson and Rex A. Sinquefield). Used with permission. All rights reserved.

THE VALUE OF MUTUAL FUNDS

One of the reasons mutual funds keep cropping up in discussions of diversity is that they are, by definition, diversified. A fund may own hundreds of stocks, bonds and other investments. That way, if some of the holdings aren't performing well, they are offset by others that are doing better. In fact, some funds balance stocks and bonds to provide diversification in different categories of investment and within each of those categories.

Because a fund has so much money to invest, it can achieve a breadth of diversity that no individual can. And because a fund buys and sells in such volume, the cost of diversifying is minimized as well.

ONE MORE THING TO REMEMBER

Diversity is essential for retirement investments. It's especially important if a stock purchase plan is part of your pension plan, because your long-term return will depend on how well that stock does. You'll probably want to balance your dependence on the company's financial health with different investments in your own accounts, including your 401(k) or similar plan.

Diversity is especially important if your company's stock is **cyclical**, that is, a stock strongly influenced by economic conditions. Airline stocks, for example, tend to be depressed in a slow economy because people travel less. If that's the case, you may not want to put too much money into other stocks that behave the same way.

To extend the idea one step further, you may want to think twice about building a portfolio full of stocks and bonds in companies that are in the same business your employer is in. If the pharmaceutical business declines, for example, and all you own are drug company stocks, you'll really need an aspirin.

This simplified chart illustrates the advantages of diversifying your portfolio, in this case by investing 60% in stocks and 40% in bonds. While its total value increases less than the better-performing investment in any year, it never does as poorly as the weaker one.

1990	GROWTH
STOCKS ONLY	DOWN 10%
BONDS ONLY	UP 5%
MIX	**DOWN 4%**

1995	GROWTH
STOCKS ONLY	UP 37%
BONDS ONLY	UP 27%
MIX	**UP 33%**

1990   1995

ASK YOURSELF

Achieving diversity isn't a one-shot deal. In analyzing your portfolio, ask the following questions to measure where you are and what's next:

1 What resources have I committed to buying stocks, bonds, mutual funds, real estate and other money-producing investments?

2 What are those investments worth in relation to each other? How about in comparison to last year? Five years ago? Ten years ago?

3 What investments have I made lately? Are they all basically the same?

4 What am I going to buy next? Why?

DIVERSITY FOR THE LONG HAUL

Diversifying isn't the same as buying randomly. If anything, it's the opposite, because it means buying according to your strategic plan to get the right mix of growth and income in your investments. But there's nothing wrong with achieving diversity gradually. If you decide to expand your equity holdings because the stock market seems poised for steady growth, you can do it and think about beefing up your bond portfolio in the months or years ahead. Taking one from column A doesn't mean you have to add one from column B at the same time.

Allocating Your Assets

The recipe for making the most of your investments calls for measuring your ingredients carefully.

Finding the right investment mix, one that balances risk and reward and achieves diversity, means carefully deciding what you're going to buy. The decision is based on your age, your goals and the overall economy. But since these factors are all fluid, allocating your assets is really an ongoing process.

Who Has the Best Blend?

Performance of asset-allocation blends recommended by 14 major brokerage houses in periods ended June 30, 1996. Figures do not include transaction costs. Houses are ranked by 12-month performance. Also shown is the mix each house now recommends.

BROKERAGE HOUSE	PERFORMANCE 3 MONTHS	1 YEAR	5 YEARS	RECOMMENDED BLEND STOCKS	BONDS	CASH
Goldman Sachs[1]	3.7%	20.0%	87.0%	60%	25%	10%
Lehman Brothers	3.6	19.0	80.3	70	30	0
Dean Witter	3.1	18.0	84.4	60	25	15
CS First Boston	3.3	18.0	NA	60	35	5
PaineWebber	3.1	17.8	83.5	52	38	10
Prudential	3.8	17.7	79.6	60	25	15
Edward Jones	3.1	17.7	NA	65[2]	25	10
Smith Barney	2.9	17.2	78.5	45	40	15
Bear Stearns	3.1	16.9	NA	55	35	10
Raymond James[3]	3.1	16.5	70.2	60	15	15
A.G. Edwards	2.8	15.5	73.9	50	35	15
Merrill Lynch	2.4	15.4	77.2	40	50	10
Everen	2.4	15.1	73.2	63[4]	25	12
Salomon Brothers	2.8	14.7	NA	50	35	15
AVERAGE	3.1	17.1	78.8	57	31	11
BY COMPARISON						
Robot blend[5]	3.1	16.9	78.3			
Stocks	4.8	27.3	109.5			
Bonds	0.9	5.0	51.1			
Cash	1.3	5.7	25.5			

[1] Recommends 5% in commodities
[2] 55% in U.S. stocks, 10% international
[3] 45% in U.S. stocks, 15% international, 10% in real estate
[4] 45% in U.S. stocks, 18% international
[5] Always 55% stocks, 35% bonds, 10% cash

NA= Not applicable (not in study for full period)
Sources: Company documents, Wilshire Associates, Carpenter Analytical Services

KEEPING RECORDS

One complication of a diversified portfolio is keeping track of your investments. If simplicity were your primary goal, you could just keep everything in one savings account. You'd never have to wonder about what your investment was worth or where your money was—although you would have to worry about what you are going to live on as inflation erodes the value of your account.

A hands-off approach that does work is to use one financial institution— a brokerage or a bank—as an administrator for all your investments. They'll send you a consolidated statement each month, detailing your assets and the value of your portfolio. The only extra recordkeeping will be confirmations of what you buy and sell so that you can figure your profit or loss for income tax purposes.

If you're like many investors, with a diversity of accounts as well as a diversified portfolio, you'll need to set aside space and time to keep track of your investments.

What you really want to know is how well each one is doing and what share of your portfolio it makes up.

ALLOCATION MODELS

Asset allocation plans, or models, tend to focus, for the most part, on securities—stocks, bonds and mutual funds—and cash or its equivalents—investments which can be easily liquidated, like CDs and U.S. Treasury bills.

No single model produces the best results in all economic climates, so brokerage houses and other financial institutions suggest different models at different times. And their models tend to differ from each other as well, as this chart from The Wall Street Journal illustrates. Several brokerages are recommending 60% in stocks, including Goldman Sachs, the year's best performer, which also proposes 25% in bonds.

The same allocation also produces different results over different time spans. Prudential's 65-25-15 allocation pro-duced above-average results over one year and the fifth strongest over five years.

Asset allocation models are important for the personal investments you make outside a qualified retirement plan as well as for the money you have in a 401(k) or 403(b) plan. You should develop a sense of how much of your total nest egg should be allocated to each category, and then buy and sell to keep that approximate balance. Your financial advisor will customize a general model to suit your situation, basing it on your age, family situation and financial status.

Experts maintain that asset allocation accounts for 80% of the results you get as an investor. That means having money in stocks when stocks are strong, in bonds when they're hot, and in cash when it's time to wait for a change. The only problem is figuring out when that is!

AVERAGE INVESTMENT RETURNS

10.5% FOR STOCKS

5.7% FOR BONDS

3.7% FOR CASH

WHAT A DIFFERENCE AN ALLOCATION MAKES

Asset allocation can make a real difference in portfolio performance, as these hypothetical examples show.

Here's what you would earn if you allocated a $100,000 portfolio three different ways and figured an annual return using the average return on each investment type—10.5% for stocks, 5.7% for bonds and 3.7% for cash—between 1926 and 1995.

60% stock 30% bond 10% cash	OR	30% stock 60% bond 10% cash	OR	10% stock 30% bond 60% cash
$8,380 earnings		**$6,940 earnings**		**$4,980 earnings**

HELP FROM THE COMPUTER

There are a growing number of computer programs to help you analyze your investments and keep track of how they're performing. Some of the programs produced by software companies are comprehensive tools that incorporate advice with background information and work charts. Mutual fund companies and brokerages are other software sources. You can get reviews of what's available for the type of equipment you have, plus critiques of how effective they are, and how compli-cated to use, regularly in The Wall Street Journal, personal finance magazines and the business section of many newspapers.

INVESTMENT TRACKING SOFTWARE

Asset Allocation Choices

You don't have to reinvent the wheel to plan your asset allocation. It's already been done.

Fortunately, there are some standard ways to split up your assets. If you're a cautious investor, you'll stress bonds and cash. And the more aggressive you are—about investing anyway—the more you'll put into stocks. You might even decide that a small percentage of your assets belongs in higher-risk investments, like futures or gold mines.

CASH IN THE BANK

A cash investment is money you can get your hands on in a hurry—like a money market fund—without risking a big loss in value. For example, while putting your money in a regular savings account has serious limitations as an investment strategy, the logic behind a cash reserve makes a lot of sense. If all your assets are tied up in stocks and long-term bonds, and you need to **liquidate** (turn them into cash quickly), you may take a loss if the market is down. Or, you might miss a great opportunity for new investing.

TAKING STOCK

In an asset allocation model, stocks represent growth. While some stocks pay dividends that provide a regular income, stocks are essential to long-term investment planning because, historically, they

LOOKING AHEAD

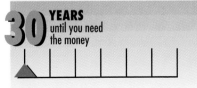

30 YEARS until you need the money

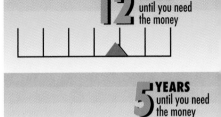

12 YEARS until you need the money

5 YEARS until you need the money

increase in value. While it's possible to lose a lot of money in the stock market in any one year, the longer you stay in the market, the more apt you are to come out ahead.

Financial experts may recommend that you have as much as 80% of your total portfolio in stocks (or stock mutual funds) while you're in your 20s and 30s. That means every time you invest $1,000, $800 of it would go into stocks or stock mutual funds. However, as you get older, say in your 50s and 60s, the percentage of stocks in your portfolio is usually scaled back to 60% or sometimes less. Generally, the greater the risk a particular stock carries, the more suitable it is for long-term investors.

STASHING THE CASH

Option	Advantages
Bank money market account	<ul><li>Instant access</li><li>Better interest than savings account</li><li>May reduce cost of checking account</li><li>Check-writing privileges</li><li>FDIC insured</li></ul>
Money market mutual fund	<ul><li>Easy access; possible overnight electronic transfer</li><li>Interest usually higher than bank money market account</li><li>Check-writing privileges</li><li>SIPC insured</li></ul>
CDs	<ul><li>Money available (with early withdrawal penalty possible)</li><li>Interest rate slightly higher than money market accounts</li><li>Due dates can be staggered for convenience</li><li>Bank CDs FDIC insured</li></ul>
U.S. Treasury bills	<ul><li>Short-term investments (13 to 26 weeks)</li><li>Enough interest to protect against inflation</li><li>Can be sold any time, though at a potential loss</li><li>Extremely safe</li></ul>

INVESTING

**SHIFTING GEARS
FOR SHIFTING GOALS**
As retirement gets closer, you might want to shift
your assets from growth toward income.

STOCKS	BONDS	CASH
80% Aggressive growth fund Small company stocks Growth stocks	**15%** Long-term bonds High-yield municipal bond fund	**5%** Money market account
60% International equity fund Blue chip stocks	**30%** Zero-coupon bonds Intermediate bonds	**10%** Money market account CD
40% Blue chip stocks S&P 500 index fund	**40%** U.S. Treasury notes Municipal bonds	**20%** CD Money market account Treasury bills

THE BOND'S THE THING

Bonds have traditionally been seen as income-producing investments. You buy a bond, hold it to maturity, and receive a regular interest payment every six months or year. Then you get the principal back when the bond matures. As an added plus, bonds issued by the U.S. government, by most state and local governments, and by top-notch corporations are virtually safe from **default**, or failure to pay what's due. That means bonds appeal to investors—often those nearing retirement—who are looking for steady income and don't want to risk losing their investment.

Most experts advise all investors to include bonds—or bond mutual funds—in their portfolios because they balance movement in the stock market. When interest rates are high, for example, the stock market isn't usually as strong as it is when rates are lower. That means that the steady return on a bond could offset falling stock prices. Further, there's an active market in bond trading that you can use to turn a profit. Buying a bond for less than **par**, or face value, and selling it for more than par can result in a substantial profit.

OTHER FIXED INCOME

Corporate and government bonds are the best known—but not the only—fixed-income investments. Mortgage-based investments like relatively conservative **Ginnie Maes**, sold by the Government National Mortgage Association, as well as the riskier **CMOs**, or Collateralized Mortgage Obligations, which derive from a package of mortgages, repay your investment with interest. But what you get back often depends more on the state of the economy than it does with corporate or government bonds. For example, if interest rates drop and lots of people refinance their mortgages, investments based on mortgages reflect the amounts being paid back and the rates at which the new loans are made.

Certain annuities and some life insurance policies also provide regular, or fixed, income, usually after you retire. Unlike bonds, with their established maturity dates, the return is paid out either over your lifetime, or for a period you and the issuer agree on.

Stocks: Sharing a Corporation

Stocks are pieces of the corporate pie. When you buy stocks, or shares, you own a slice of the company.

A corporation's **stockholders**, or **shareholders**—sometimes thousands of people and institutions—all have **equity** in the company, or own a fractional portion of the whole. They buy the stock because they expect to profit when the company profits. Companies issue two basic types of stock: common and preferred.

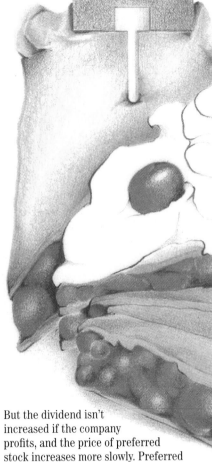

COMMON STOCK

- Owners share in success when company profits
- Owners at risk if company falters

COMMON STOCK

Common stocks are ownership shares in a corporation. They are sold initially by the corporation and then traded among investors. Investors who buy them expect to earn **dividends** as their part of the profits, and hope that the price of the stock will go up so their investment will be worth more. Common stocks offer no performance guarantees, but over time have produced a better return than other investments.

The risks investors take when they buy stocks are that the individual company will not do well, or that stock prices in general will weaken. At worst, it's possible to lose an entire investment—though not more than that. Shareholders are not responsible for corporate debts.

When corporations sell shares, they give up some control to investors whose primary concern is profits and dividends. In return for this scrutiny, they get investment money they need to build or expand their business.

PREFERRED STOCK

Preferred stocks are also ownership shares issued by a corporation and traded by investors. They differ from common stocks in several ways, which reduce investor risk but may also limit reward. The amount of the dividend is paid before dividends on common stock.

But the dividend isn't increased if the company profits, and the price of preferred stock increases more slowly. Preferred stockholders have a greater chance of getting some of their investment back if a company fails.

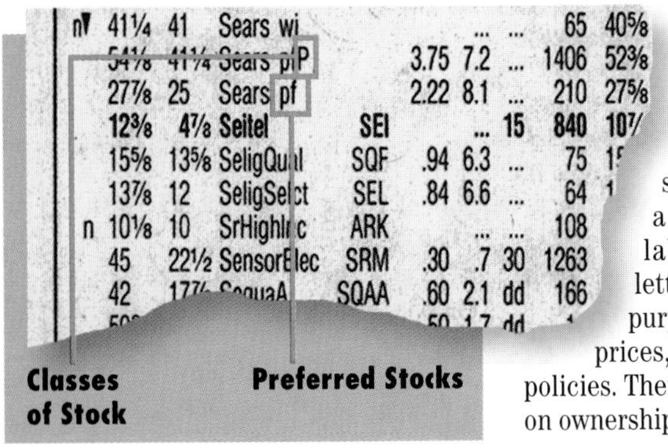

CLASSES OF STOCK

Corporations may also issue different classes of stock. Some, like Sears' preferred P shares, represent ownership in a specific subsidiary. Others—labeled A, B, C or some other letter—have specific investment purposes, sell at different market prices, or have different dividend policies. There can also be restrictions on ownership.

n▼	41¼	41	Sears wi			...	...	65	40⅝
	54⅛	41¼	Sears pfP	3.75	7.2	...	1406	52⅜
	27⅞	25	Sears pf	2.22	8.1	...	210	27⅝
	12⅝	4⅞	Seitel	SEI		...	15	840	10⁷/
	15⅝	13⅝	SeligQual	SQF	.94	6.3	...	75	1⁵
	13⅞	12	SeligSelct	SEL	.84	6.6	...	64	1
n	10⅛	10	SrHighInc	ARK		...	...	108	
	45	22½	SensorElec	SRM	.30	.7	30	1263	
	42	17⅞	SequaA	SQAA	.60	2.1	dd	166	
	5⁰				5⁰	1.7	dd		

Classes of Stock

Preferred Stocks

PREFERRED STOCK

- Dividend payment has priority over common stock dividends
- Dividends don't increase if company prospers

BLUE CHIPS

is a term borrowed from poker, where the blue chips are the most valuable, and refers to the stocks of the largest, most consistently profitable corporations. The list isn't official—and it does change.

AT&T

STOCK SPLITS

When the price of a stock gets too high, investors are often reluctant to buy, either because they think it has reached its peak or because it costs so much. Corporations have the option of splitting the stock to lower the price and stimulate trading. When a stock is split, there are more shares available but the total market value is the same.

Say a company's stock is trading at $100 a share. If the company declares a two-for-one split, it gives every shareholder two shares for each one held. At the same time the price drops to $50 a share. An investor who owned 300 shares at $100 now has 600 at $50—but the value is still $30,000.

The initial effect of a stock split is no different from getting change for a dollar. The only change is there are more shares available to new buyers at a more accessible price.

Stocks can split three for one, three for two, ten for one, or any other combination. Stocks that have split within the last 52 weeks may be identified in newspaper stock columns with an **s** adjacent to the company name.

SPLIT STOCK

- More shares created at lower price per share
- Stockholders profit if price goes up

REVERSE SPLITS

In a **reverse split** you exchange more stocks for fewer—say ten for five—and the price increases accordingly. Reverse splits are sometimes used to raise a stock's price. This discourages small investors who are costly for corporations to keep track of and can attract institutional investors who may refuse to buy stock which costs less than their minimum requirement—often $5.

Exxon

holds the record for the largest number of common shares. As of December 31, 1995, it had

1,813,000,000 shares

The Right to Vote

Owning stock gives you the right to vote on important company issues and policies.

As a stockholder, you usually have the right to vote on major policy decisions, such as whether to issue additional stock, sell the company to outside buyers, or change the board of directors. In general, the more stock you own, the greater your voice in company decisions.

ALL STOCKS ARE NOT EQUAL

Usually, each share of stock gives you one vote. Some companies, especially ones whose founders are active stockholders, issue different classes of stock with different voting privileges. When stocks carry extra votes, a small group of people can control the company while owning less than 50% of the shares.

THE WAY YOU VOTE

Most shareholders vote by **proxy**, an absentee ballot they receive before the annual meeting. Or they have the option of attending the meeting and voting in person.

The mailing includes a **proxy statement**. It's often a jargon-filled legal document that presents information on planned changes in company management that require shareholder approval. By law, it must also present shareholder proposals, even if they are at odds with company policy. The statement also identifies the nominees for the board of directors, and lists the major shareholders.

Security and Exchange Commission rules require proxies to show in chart form the total compensation of the company's top five executives. The proxy must also report stock performance in relation to comparable companies in the industry and to the S&P 500 Index.

The proxy asks shareholders to elect a board of directors and vote on several issues. The directors oversee the operation of the company and set long-term policy goals. You can support them all, vote against them, or vote for some but not others.

The proxy lets shareholders vote Yes or No or Abstain on shareholder proposals and other issues affecting the corporation. The directors want you to vote Yes on the issues they support and No on the others.

X Please mark your votes as in this example.

Unless otherwise specified, proxies will be voted FOR the election of the nominees for directors FOR proposals 2 and 3, and AGAINST proposals 4, 5 and 6.

The Board of Directors recommends a vote FOR election of directors and proposals 2 and 3.

1. Election of Directors (see reverse) — FOR [X] WITHHELD [ ]
FOR, except vote withheld from the following nominee(s):

2. Approval of Amendments to the 1987 Stock Option Plan — FOR [X] AGAINST [ ] ABSTAIN [ ]

3. Appointment of Independent Auditors — FOR [ ] AGAINST [X] ABSTAIN [ ]

The Board of D stockholder pro

4. Stockholder proposal
5. Stockholder proposal
6. Stockholder proposal

SIGNATURE(S) _John Q. Investor_ DATE _4/10/96_
NOTE: Please sign exactly as name appears hereon. Joint owners should each sign. When signing as attorney, executor, administrator, trustee or guardian, please give full title as such.

CHANGING ATTITUDES

For years, senior management assumed, and got, shareholder support. But with a record number of new investors, including more **institutional investors** like big pension and mutual funds that own large blocks of stock, corporate management has had to listen more closely to shareholder concerns. Increasingly, these new investors are more actively engaged in the companies they invest in.

NOTICE and PROXY STATEMENT

Annual Meeting of Stockholders

April 14, 1996

To Stockholders:

You are cordially invited to attend the annual meeting of stockholders of Spellman Inc. (the "Company") to be held at the Hotel duPont, 11th and Market Streets, Wilmington, Delaware, on Wednesday, April 14, 1996, at 10:30 a.m., for the following purposes:

1. To elect three directors comprising the class of directors of the Company to be elected for a three-year term expiring in 1999;

2. To approve amendments to the 1987 Stock Option Plan as set forth and described in the attached Proxy Statement;

3. To approve the action of the Board of Directors in appointing Price Waterhouse as independent auditors for 1996;

4. To act upon three stockholder proposals which are set forth and described in the attached Proxy Statement; and

5. To transact such other business as may properly be brought before the meeting or any adjournment thereof.

The close of business on February 16, 1996, has been fixed as the record date for determination of stockholders entitled to notice of, and to vote at, the annual meeting or any adjournment thereof. The transfer books will not close.

By Order of the Board of Directors

1433

IMPORTANT

review these proxy materials and sign and return your proxy in the enclosed stamped, addressed attend the meeting you may, if you so desire, withdraw your proxy and vote in

Thank you for acting promptly

mends a vote AGAINST d 6.

OR | AGAINST | ABSTAIN

CUMULATIVE VOTING

Shareholders have one vote for each share they own. In regular voting, a shareholder casts that number of votes for each director up for election. In cumulative voting, the number of votes (or shares) is multiplied by the number of openings to give the shareholder a total number of votes. For example, a shareholder with ten shares voting for eight directors would have 80 votes. Those votes can be divided any way the shareholder chooses, giving all 80 to one candidate, 40 to each of two, or any other combination. Some states require companies to use cumulative voting, and most allow it.

The Value of Stock

A stock's value can change at any moment, depending on market conditions, investor perceptions, or a host of other issues.

If investors pour money into a company's stock because they believe the company is going to make a profit, the company's stock will go up in value. But if investors decide the outlook is poor, and don't invest—or sell the stock they already own—the company's stock price will fall.

BUY LOW, SELL HIGH

Investors who buy a stock believe other people will buy as well, and that the share price is going to increase. Investing is always a gamble. A long shot can always win the race even if everyone bets the favorite. In the stock market, the current

THE BLUES AT BIG BLUE

The peaks and valleys in the price of IBM stock dramatically illustrate how value changes.

IBM stock began to climb with the bull market that started in August 1982. The company was a major player in the expanding PC market. In less than a year its price climbed to $134¼.

Despite some setbacks as the competition gained ground and the company introduced new technology, the value of the stock stayed over $100— its gains outstripping the market as a whole. Stockholders earned healthy dividends too.

In the fall of 1987, IBM hit the top and crashed with the rest of the market— falling 70 points, from 174¾ to 104— by the end of the year. Despite a few rallies, the price was headed down.

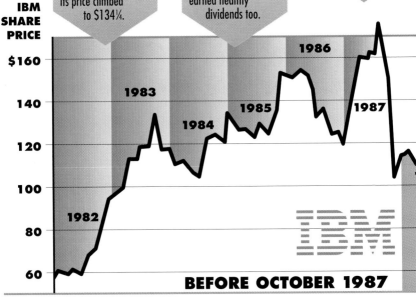

IBM SHARE PRICE — 1982, 1983, 1984, 1985, 1986, 1987, 198... BEFORE OCTOBER 1987

MAKING MONEY WITH STOCKS

Most people buy stocks to make money through **capital gains**, or the profit from selling stock at a higher price than they paid for it.

If you buy 100 shares of Atlas at $50 a share (for a total investment of $5,000), and sell it for $75 a share (for a total of $7,500), you've realized a capital gain of $25 a share, or $2,500. If you've held the stock for more than a year, your profits are long-

term capital gains. Of course, it doesn't all go in your pocket. You owe taxes on the gain as well as commissions to your stock broker for buying and selling the stock.

TIMING IT RIGHT

To make money, you must buy a stock before others want it and sell before they decide to unload. As IBM investors are keenly aware, timing the market is not always easy to accomplish. Historically, popularity of a stock influences the outcome. If lots of investors buy Atlas stock, Atlas's price will go up. The stock becomes more valuable because investors want it. The reverse is also true: If investors sell Zenon stock, it will fall in value. The more it falls, the more investors are likely to sell.

EARNING DIVIDENDS

Some people invest in stocks to get quarterly dividend payments. Dividends are the portion of the company's profit paid out to its shareholders. For example, if Atlas declares an annual dividend of $4 a share, and you own 100 shares, you'll earn $400 a year, or $100 paid each quarter.

A company's board of directors decides how large a dividend the company will pay, or whether it will pay one at all. Usually only large, mature companies pay dividends. Smaller ones reinvest their profits to continue growing.

If you're buying stocks for the quarterly income, you can figure out the **dividend yield**—the percentage of purchase price you get back through dividends each year. For example, if you buy stock for $100 a share and receive $4 per share, the stock has a dividend yield of 4%. But if you get $4 per share on stock you buy for $50 a share, your yield would be 8% ($4 is 8% of $50).

Purchase Price	Annual Dividend	Yield
$100	$4	4%
$ 50	$4	8%

CYCLICAL STOCKS

All stocks don't act alike. One basic difference is how closely a stock's value, or price, is tied to the condition of the economy. **Cyclical stocks** are shares of companies that are highly dependent on the state of the economy. When things slow down, their earnings fall rapidly, and so does their stock price. But when the economy recovers, earnings rise rapidly and the stock's value goes up. Airline and hotel stocks are typically cyclical: People tend to cut back on travel when the economy slows.

Between 1988 and 1991 the price hovered around the $100 to $120 range. By the summer of 1992, when the rest of the market was booming, IBM stock dropped steadily. The company lost $4.97 billion and laid off 40,000 employees by the end of the year.

By mid-1993, IBM had replaced its top leadership, fired another 25,000 employees and cut its dividend. The stock hit a low of $41⅝.

In less than ten years, the price climbed more than a hundred dollars—from $58 to $174¾—and then plummeted. By 1996, the price recovered, topping $125 a share.

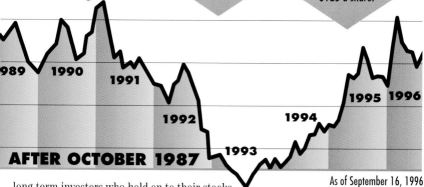

989 1990 1991 1992 1993 1994 1995 1996

AFTER OCTOBER 1987

As of September 16, 1996

long-term investors who hold on to their stocks do as least as well as market-timers. Getting the timing right means you have to pay attention to:

- The rate at which the company's earnings are growing
- Competitiveness of its product or service
- The availability of new markets
- Management strengths and weaknesses
- The overall economic environment in which a company operates

Stocks that pay dividends regularly are known as **INCOME STOCKS**. Those that pay little or no dividend, while reinvesting their profit, are known as **GROWTH STOCKS**.

The Stock Certificate

A stock certificate records all the important information about your shares in a very traditional— and elaborate—format.

Before the era of electronic record-keeping, written proofs of ownership, called **securities**, were needed to track investments. Today, investors often don't get certificates—in fact some brokerage houses charge a fee to issue them. Instead, the information is stored in computer files.

Today, most investors choose to keep their securities in **street name**—which means they are held electronically by their brokerage firm. Transferring stocks is much easier if they are held this way. It's also safer. In 1995, stock, bond and government-issued certificates totaling $5.8 billion were reported lost or stolen.

Still, the certificates have a charm of their own, and rather than abandoning them as outdated, many companies are redesigning them for the '90s, with new images of their identities.

Each corporation's stock certificate is distinctive, but they all share certain identifying features.

SEC registration numbers are assigned to all stock certificates by the Securities and Exchange Commission

as one way to establish their authenticity and ownership. Stock certificates are negotiable, but they're tracked in several ways to make stolen ones more difficult to trade in.

The **corporate seal** of the issuer, with the date and place of incorporation, appears along the bottom of the certificate.

Certificates are designed in several shades of color on specially made paper to ensure that they are difficult to forge. Delicate shades are engraved next to heavy shadows to make the artwork hard to copy. The intricate geometric designs that form the

SCRIPOPHILY
It isn't a dread disease. It's collecting antique stocks, bonds and other securities. The most valuable ones are the most beautiful and those that have some historical significance because of the role the issuing company played in the economy.

borders are created by machines programmed to specific settings. Finally, they're printed on intaglio plates so that the image feels raised. Other printing methods can't reproduce the feel.

The **name of the issuer** appears prominently on the certificate.

A **human figure** with clearly recognizable facial features must appear with at least a three-quarter frontal view on all certificates issued by New York Stock Exchange-listed companies.

The **number of shares** the certificate represents appears several times, in numbers and words.

The **stockholder** is identified on the face of the certificate. To make any changes in the ownership or to sell the shares, the certificate has to be endorsed on the back and surrendered to the corporation or a broker. If a broker holds your stocks for you, they're registered in street name, which is the name of the brokerage house, and aren't issued as certificates.

A **CUSIP number** is a security identification number assigned to every stock certificate. The Committee on Uniform Securities Identification Procedures was established by the American Bankers Association as a way to safeguard the security.

The **par value** on stock certificates—usually from 25¢ to $1—has no relationship to the stock's actual value. In contrast, the par value of a bond, which is also called its face value, is what it's worth—usually $1,000.

Selling New Stock

The first time companies issue stock, it's called **going public**. After that they can raise additional money, or **capital**, by selling more stock.

To take a company public, which means making it possible for investors to buy the stock, the management makes an **initial public offering (IPO)**.

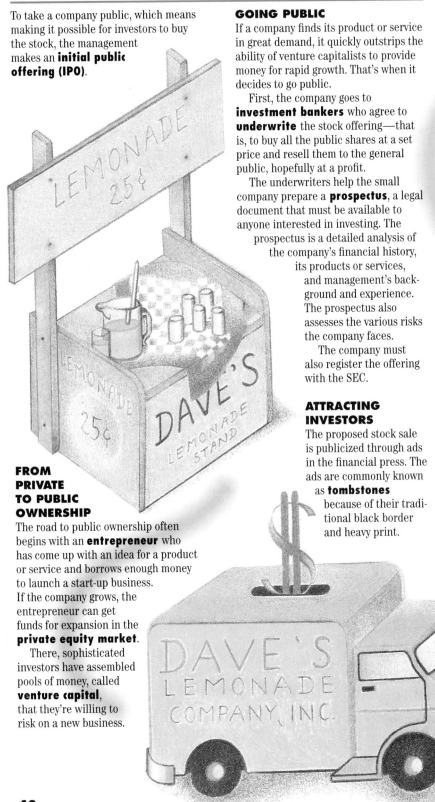

FROM PRIVATE TO PUBLIC OWNERSHIP

The road to public ownership often begins with an **entrepreneur** who has come up with an idea for a product or service and borrows enough money to launch a start-up business. If the company grows, the entrepreneur can get funds for expansion in the **private equity market**.

There, sophisticated investors have assembled pools of money, called **venture capital**, that they're willing to risk on a new business.

GOING PUBLIC

If a company finds its product or service in great demand, it quickly outstrips the ability of venture capitalists to provide money for rapid growth. That's when it decides to go public.

First, the company goes to **investment bankers** who agree to **underwrite** the stock offering—that is, to buy all the public shares at a set price and resell them to the general public, hopefully at a profit.

The underwriters help the small company prepare a **prospectus**, a legal document that must be available to anyone interested in investing. The prospectus is a detailed analysis of the company's financial history, its products or services, and management's background and experience. The prospectus also assesses the various risks the company faces.

The company must also register the offering with the SEC.

ATTRACTING INVESTORS

The proposed stock sale is publicized through ads in the financial press. The ads are commonly known as **tombstones** because of their traditional black border and heavy print.

The underwriters sometimes also organize meetings between the company's management and large potential investors, such as managers of pension or mutual funds. The day before the actual sale, underwriters **price the issue**, or establish the price they will pay for each share. That's the amount the company receives from the stock sale.

When the stock begins trading the next day, the price can rise or fall depending on whether investors agree or disagree with the underwriters' valuation of the new company.

SECONDARY OFFERINGS

If a company has already issued shares, but wants to raise additional money, called **capital**, through the sale of more stock, the process is called a **secondary offering**.

Companies are often wary of issuing more stock, since the larger the supply of stock outstanding, the less valuable each share already issued.

Usually a company issues new stock only if its stock price is high. That helps minimize complaints from existing shareholders that their shares are being diluted. Sometimes, if the company's management thinks the shares are too cheap, it will buy some back to boost the value of the remaining ones.

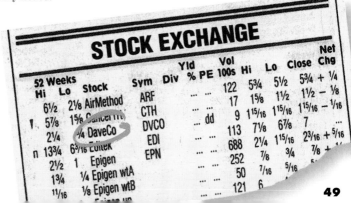

| 52 Weeks | | | | | Yld | | Vol | | | | Net |
Hi	Lo	Stock	Sym	Div	%	PE	100s	Hi	Lo	Close	Chg
			ARF	...	...		122	5¾	5½	5¾	+ ¼
6½	2⅛	AirMethod		...	...		17	1⅝	1½	1½	− ⅛
5⅞	1⅝	Cancer...	CTH		dd		9	1¹⁵/₁₆	1¹⁵/₁₆	1¹⁵/₁₆	− ¹/₁₆
2¼	⁷/₈	DaveCo	DVCO				113	7⅛	6⅞	7	
n 13¾	6⁹/₁₆	Editek	EDI				688	2¼	1¹⁵/₁₆	2³/₁₆	+ ⁵/₁₆
2½	1	Epigen	EPN				252	⁷/₈	¾	⅞	+ ...
1¾	¼	Epigen wtA		...	...		50	⁷/₁₆	⁵/₁₆		
¹¹/₁₆	⅛	Epigen wtB		...	...		121	6			

STOCK EXCHANGE

Stock Buyers

All investors buy stock for the same reason: to make money. But they do their buying differently.

More than 50 million Americans own stocks. The average investor's stock is worth about $14,000, or about 35% of a typical portfolio's value.

While the number of individual investors is growing, the proportion of shares owned by individuals is dropping. That's because institutional investors, including mutual funds and pension funds, have become major players in the market. People with money in such funds have indirect stock investments, but no real role in what's bought and sold.

INSTITUTIONAL INVESTORS

An institutional investor is an organization that invests its own assets or those it holds in trust for others. Typical institutional investors are investment companies (including mutual funds), pension systems, insurance companies, universities and banks. CALPERS, California's $100 billion public pension fund, had $58 billion, or 58% of its assets, invested in stocks in mid-1996.

Because they have so much money to invest, and are committed to making a profit, institutional investors trade regularly and in enormous volume.

A buy or sell order must be 10,000 shares or more to be considered an institutional trade—a small number for a big mutual fund eager to put its investors' money to work.

WHAT IS PROGRAM TRADING?

Some of the big investors speed up the process of buying and selling stock by using program trading techniques that involve placing large orders by computer. The programs are sometimes triggered automatically, when prices hit predetermined levels.

Such sudden buying or selling can cause abrupt price changes or even dramatic shifts in the entire market. The stock market crash of 1987 occurred, at least in part, because of program trading triggered by falling prices. To combat potentially catastrophic program trades in an increasingly electronic market, trading now shuts down in a major sell-off to let things cool down.

SIZE MAKES A DIFFERENCE

Capitalization

BLUE CHIPS ($500 Billion)

MID-CAPS ($100 Billion)

SMALL-CAPS ($10 Billion)

INVESTMENT CLUBS

Investors who want to have more direct say over the way their money is invested but don't have enough money of their own to buy a range of different stocks can—and do—join one of the more than 16,400 investment clubs around the U.S.

These clubs can pay off if their members do their homework. It's a clear example of 10 or 15 heads being better than one when it comes to absorbing all the information about a company that's available. On the other hand, club buying involves making consensus invest-ment decisions, potentially the most difficult problem a group confronts.

Most clubs work more or less the same way, following guidelines from the National Association of Investors Corp. (NAIC, 810-583-6242). Members present their information at regular meetings and vote on proposed trades. The investments themselves, and the commissions, are funded by monthly contributions from members. Since most clubs require modest amounts—often $10 to $100 a month—it's hard to get rich. But often members use what they've learned from the group to bolster their individual holdings—a nice bonus.

Increasingly, many clubs are going online. Visit NAIC's home page at: **http://www.better-investing.org**

BUYING STYLES

Some individual investors look for quick profits in "hot" stocks. Called day traders, they buy stocks whose price they expect to rise dramatically in a short time. When the price goes up, they sell and buy something else. Other investors take a longer-term view, prefer-ring to buy and hold a stock—in some cases for years—until it gains substan-tially in price.

Institutional investors, including those using sophisticated analytical computer programs, also have buying styles that help determine how profitable their stocks have been over time and during particular phases of the economic cycle.

A company's size can be a major factor for investors deciding which stocks to buy. The size not only influences the amount of information they can get hold of—in this case bigger is better—but the ease with which they can buy and sell, and the kinds of risks they take. The chart below summarizes the difference size makes.

Where to Get Information	Volume of Trading	Ease of Trading	Risks and Rewards
Dow-Jones Industrial Average S&P 500 Index	Large	Easy	Often high prices though little risk of company failure
Extensive media and brokerage attention			Usually regular dividends
Companies provide information			Not always high growth potential
Some Indexes	Large	Easy	Potential for growth greater than for larger companies
Mixed media and brokerage attention			
Companies provide information			
Little coverage until price has gone up dramatically	Usually small, but can be heavy	Potentially difficult	Big gains possible
Companies provide information			Higher risk from company failure or poor management

Buying Stocks

Buying stocks isn't hard, but the process has its own rules, its own distinctive language and a special cast of characters.

To buy or sell a stock, you have to go through a **brokerage house**, an investment firm that is registered with the **Securities and Exchange Commission (SEC)** and the **National Association of Securities Dealers (NASD)**. Your deal is handled by a **stockbroker** who has passed an exam on securities law and products, and has registered with the NASD.

WHAT'S IN A NAME?

Though a broker is generally recognized as someone who buys and sells stocks, the financial markets use other, not so widely recognized, job descriptions to identify the various ways securities change hands and the people who get the job done.

Brokers act as agents to execute buy and sell orders from the investing public.

Dealers are people or firms that buy and sell securities as principals rather than agents, making their money on the difference between the cost of buying and the price for selling.

Investment bankers, or underwriters, buy new issues directly from corporations and sell them to individual and institutional investors.

Traders buy and sell for their own accounts. People who buy and sell for broker/dealers or financial institutions are also called traders.

ROUND LOTS

Usually you buy or sell stock in multiples of 100 shares, called a **round lot**. Small investors can buy just a single share, or any number they can afford. That's called an **odd lot**. Brokers often charge more to buy and to sell odd lot orders.

A **broker**, originally, was a wine seller who broached—broke open—wine casks. Today's broker has a less liquid but often heady job as a financial agent.

CUSTOMER

PLACES ORDERS TO BUY AND SELL

CALLING THE SHOTS

When you tell your broker to buy or sell, you're giving an order. A **market order** tells your broker to act now to buy or sell at the price available at the moment. Or you can give your broker more specific guidelines.

If you think the price of a stock you want to buy is going down, you can place a **limit order**. That way your broker will buy only when the price falls to the amount you've named.

Similarly, if you own a stock that's rising in value, you can place a **limit order to sell**. That means your broker will sell only if and when it climbs to the pre-established price.

Finally, if you own a stock that is declining in price, you might want to place a **stop loss order**. That tells your broker to sell if the price falls to a certain level, in order to prevent further losses.

TIMING YOUR ORDERS

Orders can specify time limits as well as price limits. When you give a stop order or a limit order, your broker will ask if you want it to be **Good 'til Canceled (GTC)** or a **day order**. A GTC stands until it is either filled or you cancel it. A day order is cancelled automatically if it isn't filled that day.

WHERE THE COMMISSION GOES
The commission you pay to buy and sell stocks is divided—by prearranged contract—between your broker and the brokerage firm. The commissions and any additional fees are set by the firm, but your broker may be able to give you a break if you trade often and in large volume. Generally, the higher the fee, the more room there is for negotiation.

BROKERAGE FIRM
INITIATES TRANSACTION

STOCK MARKET
COMPLETES TRANSACTION

DIFFERENT BROKERS, DIFFERENT SERVICES

Some brokers spend a lot of time researching investments, helping clients develop goals and giving advice. They are often called **full-service brokers** and charge investors a relatively high **commission**, or fee, for their services.

Other brokers, called **discount brokers**, merely act as the agent for an investor, executing buy and sell orders, but offering no investment advice. But their commissions are usually much lower than a full-service broker's.

Finally, for investors who trade often or in large blocks of stock, there are **deep discount brokers** whose commissions are lowest of all.

THE BROKER'S ROLE

Several different types of stockbrokers get involved in buying or selling stock. You're in touch with the ones who take your orders, either over the phone or in person. Depending on the firm they work for, they're known as account executives, financial consultants, investment executives, portfolio salesmen or something similar.

In a typical stock transaction, brokers either pass the orders to a **floor broker**, who does the actual buying or selling, or simply execute the trade electronically.

If the order reaches the floor of the exchange, the floor broker takes it to a **specialist** in that particular stock, who maintains a post on the exchange floor. At that post, the floor broker who wants to buy a specific stock may meet another floor broker who wants to sell, or vice versa. If not, your order is left with the specialist, who keeps a list of unfilled orders.

As the price of the stock changes, and buy and sell orders flow, the specialist tries to fill your order at the best price. In that sense, the specialist serves as a **broker to the brokers**, charging them a commission for each deal completed.

Selling Short

Investors may not want to sell stocks they don't actually own, but it's a good idea to know the risks and rewards of this kind of trading.

Not all stock trades are straightforward buys or sells. Investors use several different techniques to make money. Many of them—like **selling short** or **buying warrants**—are based on a calculated wager that a particular stock will go up or down in value in the near future.

How Selling Short Works

Selling short is a way to make money in the stock market when you think a stock's price is going to decline. It helps if you have reliable information or good instincts about the future price of the stock you're selling short.

Your broker will borrow shares and sell them for you. The money from the sale serves as collateral, which goes to the stock lender. You must pay your broker 50% of the sale price on margin.

Then you wait, expecting the price of the stock to drop. If it does, you buy the shares at the lower price and repay your broker to settle the loan (plus some interest and commission). For example, you sell short 100 shares of Apple at $50 a share. When the price drops, you buy 100 shares of Apple at $25 a share, give them to your broker, and pocket the $25 a share difference as profit—minus commission. Buying shares back is called **covering the short position**. Because the cost to return the shares is less than what it cost to borrow them, you make a profit.

YOU BORROW 100 SHARES AT $10 PER SHARE FROM YOUR BROKER	YOU SELL THE 100 SHARES AT THE $10 PRICE, GETTING $1,000
	Stock Value **$10**
SHARES YOU OWE YOUR BROKER	**100** Shares
YOUR COST TO PAY BACK THE SHARES	
YOUR PROFIT— OR LOSS	

Short-Interest Highlights reports the number of open short positions that have not been covered by various companies. ("Interest" here means the volume of short sales, or level of interest investors are showing, rather than a fee for using money.) It reports the largest increases and decreases during the month, the latest changes and the stock's average daily volume for the month.

Investors' interest in selling short increases when the market is booming but the economy isn't keeping pace. Sellers believe that a correction has to come, and that stocks will drop in value. They want to capitalize on those losses.

Average daily volume indicates the average number of shares sold short in a day during the month. Investors watch short interest to judge what other investors are thinking. For example, an increase in short selling of a stock means investors expect the price to fall.

% Change shows the percentage rise or fall in short-interest volume from one month to the next. Here, it's down 3%.

The number of shares held by short sellers, or the short interest, in Consolidated Stores was 1,167,693 on February 12, down from 1,203,362 on January 15.

BUYING WARRANTS

Warrants are a way to wager on future prices—though using warrants is very different from selling short. Warrants guarantee, for a small fee, the opportunity to buy stock at a fixed price during a specific period of time. Investors buy them if they think a stock's price is going up.

For example, you might pay $1 a share for the right to buy DaveCo stock at $10 within five years. If the price goes up to $14 and you **exercise** (use) your warrant, you save $3 on every share you buy. You can then sell the shares at the higher price to make a profit ($14 − ($10 + $1) = $3), or $300 on 100 shares.

Companies sell warrants if they plan to raise money by issuing new stock or selling stocks they hold in reserve. After a warrant is issued, it can be listed in the stock columns and traded like other investments. A **wt** after a stock table entry means the quotation is for a warrant, not the stock itself.

If the price of the stock is below the set price when the warrant expires, the warrant is worthless. But since warrants are fairly cheap and have a relatively long life span, they are traded actively.

YOU PROFIT IF STOCK PRICE DROPS

| Stock Value **$7.50** |
| 100 Shares |
| $750 |
| $250 Profit |

YOU LOSE IF STOCK PRICE RISES

| Stock Value **$12.50** |
| 100 Shares |
| $1,250 |
| $250 Loss |

WHAT ARE THE RISKS?

The risks in selling short occur when the price of the stock goes up, not down, or when the process takes a long time. The timing is important because you're paying your broker interest on the stocks you borrowed. The longer the process goes on, the more you pay and the more the interest expense erodes your eventual profit.

A rise in the stock's value is an even greater risk. Because if it goes up instead of down, you will be forced—sooner or later—to pay more to **cover your short position** than you made from selling the stock.

SQUEEZE PLAY

Sometimes short sellers are caught in a squeeze. That happens when a stock that has been heavily shorted begins to rise. The scramble among short sellers to cover their positions results in heavy buying that drives the price even higher.

SHORT INTEREST HIGHLIGHTS

Avg Dly Volume		2/12	1/15	% Chg	Avg Dly Volume	
464,490	Consl Frgh $1.54D/S .	223,825	215,062	4.1	12,730	Goodrich
309,220	Consolidated Ed	2,045,107	1,583,018	29.2	195,810	Goodyear
212,210	Consolidated Freight	547,331	570,099	−4.0	72,815	Grace (W
675,740	Consolidated Nat Gas	511,907	399,204	28.2	94,440	Grainger
197,415	Consolidated Rail	622,516	689,302	−9.7	433,710	Great Atl
646,585	Consolidated Stores ..	1,167,693	1,203,362	−3.0	161,140	Great We
332,660	Continental Bank	268,200	207,388	29.3	256,135	Green Tr
45,875	Continental Corp	208,913	323,873	−35.5	161,985	Grow Gro
121,485	Contl Info Sys Corp ...	226,078	226,078	0.0	2,655	GTE Cor
174,285	Contl Medical Sys	3,553,256	3,041,627	16.8	118,785	Gulf Sts
253,645	Cooper Companies	921,536	928,736	−0.8	51,460	Hadson C
302,490	Cooper Ind Inc	490,176	325,946	50.4	202,410	Haemone
123,075	Cooper Tire & Rub	254,719	321,912	−20.9	130,270	Halliburt
93,660	Corning Inc	802,981	1,156,706	−30.6	467,530	Hancock
7,415	Countrywide Credit ..	4,044,941	3,414,499	18.5	414,265	
	CPC Intl Inc	386,810	544,268	−28.9	312,785	
		200,862	178,090			

Buying on Margin

Buying on margin lets investors borrow some of the money they need to buy stocks.

Investors who want to buy stock but don't want to finance it on their own can **leverage** their purchase by buying on margin. They set up a **margin account** with a broker or another investment professional, sign a margin agreement (or contract) and maintain a minimum balance. Then they can borrow up to 50% of the price of the stock and use the combined funds to make their purchase.

Investors who buy on margin pay interest on the loan portion of their purchase, but don't have to repay the loan itself until they sell the stock. Any profit is theirs. They don't have to share it.

For example, if you want to buy 200 shares of a stock selling for $40 a share, the total cost would be $8,000. Buying on

How It Works

YOU OPEN A MARGIN ACCOUNT—$5,000 OF YOUR MONEY AND $5,000 OF YOUR BROKER'S MONEY

YOU PURCHASE 1000 SHARES AT $10 EACH

YOU PROFIT IF STOCK PRICE RISES

THE VALUE OF YOUR INVESTMENT

Stock Value **$10**

Stock Value **$15**

$10,000

$5,000

YOUR BROKER'S INVESTMENT

$5,000

$5,000

$2,000 MINIMUM

MARGIN MINIMUMS
To open a margin account, you must deposit $2,000 in cash or eligible securities (securities your broker considers valuable). That's the minimum margin requirement. All margin trades have to be conducted through that account, combining your own money and money borrowed from or through your broker.

STOCKS

LEVERAGING YOUR STOCK INVESTMENT

Leverage is speculation. It means investing with money borrowed at a fixed rate of interest in the hope of earning a greater rate of return. Like the lever, the simple machine that provides its name, leverage lets the users exert a lot of financial power with a small amount of their own cash.

Companies use leverage—called **trading on equity**—when they issue both stocks and bonds. Their earnings per share may increase because they've expanded operations with the money raised by bonds. But they must use some of those earnings to repay the interest on the bonds.

margin, you put up $4,000 and borrow the remaining $4,000 from or through your broker.

If the stock price rises to $60 and you decide to sell, the proceeds amount to $12,000. You repay your broker the $4,000 you borrowed and put $8,000 in your pocket (minus interest and commissions). That's almost a 100% profit on your original $4,000 investment.

Had you used all your own money and laid out $8,000 for the initial purchase, you would have made only a 50% profit: a $4,000 return on an $8,000 investment.

YOU LOSE IF STOCK PRICE DROPS

Stock Value **$7.50**

YOUR BREAK-EVEN POINT

MARGIN CALL

$2,500

$5,000

MARGIN CALLS

Despite its advantages, buying on margin can be very risky. For example, the stock you buy could drop so much that selling it wouldn't raise enough to repay the loan to your broker. To protect themselves in cases like this, brokers issue a **margin call** if the value of your investment falls below a set percentage of its original value. That means you have to put additional money into your margin account. If you don't want to **meet the call**, or can't afford to, you must sell the stock, pay back the broker in full and take the loss even if you think the stock will rise again.

Brokerage firms in the U.S. may set their own margin levels, but they can't be less stringent than the limit required by the Federal Reserve and regulatory bodies. The Federal Reserve Board's Regulation T limits the leveraged portion of any margin purchase to 50%.

During crashes, and dramatic price decreases in the market, investors who were heavily leveraged because they'd bought on margin sometimes couldn't meet their margin calls. The result was panic selling to raise cash, and further declines in the market.

To protect themselves from margin calls, investors should consider safeguards such as stop loss limits and portfolio diversification.

Sifting Stock Information

Investors can find out everything they want to know about stocks and the companies that issue them—and more.

Although the stock tables are the logical place to start, there is a lot of other information investors and investment professionals can use to evaluate stocks.

WHAT THE NUMBERS TELL

Four pieces of financial information are useful indicators of the shape a company's in—and whether its stock is a good investment. These figures are reported regularly in the financial press, and are also available from brokerage firms.

- **The book value** is the difference between the company's assets and liabilities. A small or low book value from too much debt, for example, means that the company's profits will be limited even if it does lots of business. Sometimes a low book value means that assets are underestimated; experts consider these companies good investments.
- **The earnings per share** are calculated by dividing the number of shares into the profit. If earnings increase each year, the company is growing.
- **The return on equity** is a percentage figured by dividing a company's earnings per share by its book value.
- **The payout ratio** is the percentage of net earnings a company uses to pay its dividends. The normal range is 25% to 50% of its net earnings. A higher ratio means the company is struggling to meet its obligations.

DARTBOARD ANALYSIS

For several years The Wall Street Journal has carried a monthly column in which professional managers' stock picks are pitted against choices reporters make by throwing darts at the stock pages. So far, the professionals are doing twice as well as the dart throwers.

THE ST. MARK COMPANIES
Consolidated Financial Highlights

For the Year
Revenues ....
Operating earnings ....
Operating earnings per common share ....
Net income ....
Net income per common share ....
Dividends paid per common share ....

At Year-End
Total investments ....
Total assets ....
Common shareholders' equity ....
Book value per common share ....

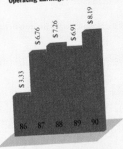

Operating Earnings Per Common Share

$3.33 — 86
$6.76 — 87
$7.26 — 88
$6.91 — 89
$8.19 — 90

Return 15.2%

Record per share 1996 operating earnings (excluding realized investment gains) exceeded the previous high year by 13%.

Contents

USING THE INFORMATION

Different investment professionals use various methods to analyze the information that's available.

Fundamental analysis studies a company's financial condition, management and competitive position in its industry.

Technical analysis uses charts based on past performance to identify price trends and cyclical movements of particular stocks, industries or the whole market. Some experts argue that research is over-rated because unforeseen events at a company or in the overall economy can radically alter any stock's prospects.

	1996	1985	Percent Change
	$ 4,005,237,000	$ 3,788,648,000	5.7
	$ 385,458,000	$ 338,267,000	14.0
	$ 8.19	$ 6.91	18.5
	$ 391,270,000	$ 398,158,000	(1.7)
	$ 8.31	$ 8.12	2.3
	$ 2.35	$ 2.15	9.3
	$ 8,467,668,000	$ 8,106,756,000	4.5
	$12,203,990,000	$11,030,066,000	10.6
	$ 2,196,371,000	$ 2,349,254,000	(6.5)
	$ 52.00	$ 47.65	9.1

Dividends Paid Per Common Share

16.8% 16.1%

89 90

$1.50 $1.695 $1.94 $2.15 $2.235

86 87 88 89 90

ulated by
g earnings
vidends) by
year
lders' equity.

We have paid a common share dividend for 119 consecutive years.

A NOTE OF CAUTION:
Most annual reports are prepared by the company's public relations department and are intended to show the company in the best possible light.

WHAT THE COMPANY TELLS

Publicly traded companies are required by law to keep shareholders up to date on how the business is doing. That information can be very valuable in keeping tabs on your investment.

The most complete information the company provides is included in its **annual report**. You also get **quarterly reports**, with concise summaries of the company's current performance.

An annual report summarizes the company's operations for the past year. Often quite elaborately designed and illustrated, it usually begins with a letter from the company's chairman touching on the highlights of the past year and offering some broad predictions for the coming one.

A typical annual report includes:

● A section outlining the company's **philosophy** or some insight into how it does business.
● Detailed reports on each segment of the company's **operations**. The reports can reveal weaknesses in the management structure or the products or services the company offers.
● Financial information, including the profit-and-loss statement for the year, and the **balance sheet**, showing the company's assets and liabilities at the end of the fiscal year compared to previous years. Footnotes attached to the financial summaries can sometimes reveal problems, such as lawsuits against the company or proposed government regulations that might influence profitability.
● An **auditor's letter** reassuring shareholders that outside accountants have examined the company's financial statements to ensure that they are fair and accurate.

Evaluating Companies

Reports of company earnings and dividend payments tell investors more than what has already happened. They're a reliable guide to what's in store.

The rising prices and big dividends that make investors happy with a stock's performance are tied directly to the financial health of the company. When a company's earnings are up, investor confidence increases and the price of the stock usually rises. If the company is losing money—or not making as much as it expected to make—the stock price usually falls.

Reports of corporate earnings and dividend payments, combined with feature stories on various industry groups and individual companies, provide the background material for investors' buy and sell decisions.

DIGEST OF EARNINGS REPORTS

Newspapers often publish a scorecard of company earnings and profits, reported four times a year. Shown below is an example from The Wall Street Journal.

The **name** of the company is listed, followed by a **code** for the stock market where the company is traded. (Most frequently used are **N** for the New York Stock Exchange, **A** for the American Stock Exchange and **O** for the Nasdaq Stock Market.) Earnings for the current quarter (past 13 weeks) are compared with those a year ago.

Gross income is listed as **sales** for manufacturing companies and **revenues** for service companies.

Net income is the company's profit for the current quarter.

Share earns is the net income divided by the number of shares.

Year-to-date information is given for companies reporting their second, third and fourth quarter profits.

In this example, **Orafill Corporation**, traded on Nasdaq, had revenues of $472,615,000— up $112,387,000 from the year before. Its net income was $69,110,000 or 47¢ per share. For the year to date, net earnings were 67¢ per share.

Consumer Services had a net loss of 47¢ per share for the year ending March 31, 1996. (Numbers indicating loss appear in parentheses.)

DIGEST OF EARNINGS REPORTS

AUDIO CORP. (A)

Quar May 31:	1996	1995
Sales	$95,510,000	$82,971,000
Income	2,757,000	1,194,000
aExtrd cred	1,066,000	509,000
Net income	3,823,000	1,703,000
Shr earns:		
Income	.31	.13
Net income	.42	.19
6 months:		
Sales	187,330,000	160,202,000
Income	5,209,000	1,859,000
aExtrd cred	1,951,000	863,000
Net income	7,160,000	2,722,000
Shr earns:		
Income	.58	.21
Net income	.79	.30

a-Tax benefit from tax-loss carry-forwards.

AUTO INC. (O)

Quar May 31:	1996	1995
Revenues	$5,214,740	$4,289,941
Net income	497,266	350,949
Avg shares	7,349,974	7,361,404
Shr earns (com & com equiv):		
Net income	.07	.05
Year:		
Revenues	19,296,575	13,339,130
Income	1,736,198	1,085,269
...red	...6,198	a134,277
		1,219,546
		7,319,720

ORAFILL CORP. (O)

Quar May 31:	1996	1995
Revenues	$472,615,000	$360,228,000
Net income	69,110,000	28,768,000
Avg shares	147,511,000	144,579,000
Shr earns:		
Net income	.47	.20
Year:		
Revenues	1,502,768,000	1,178,496,000
Income	a141,726,000	61,510,000
Acct adj	b(43,470,000)	....
Net income	98,256,000	61,510,000
Avg shares	146,476,000	142,769,000
Shr earns:		
Income	.97	.43
Net income	.67	.43

a-Includes a charge of $24,000,000 related to settlement of litigation. b-Cumulative effect of an accounting change.
Figures in parentheses are losses.

CONSUMER SVCS (O)

Year Mar 31:	1996	1995
Revenues	$2,460,000	$1,026,000
Net income	(1,502,000)	a(2,526,000)
Avg shares	3,189,041	2,900,000
Shr earns:		
Net income	(.47)	(.87)

a-Includes a loss of $276,000 on sale of equipment.
Figures in parentheses are losses.

CONTINENTAL

FIND IT ON THE INTERNET

The Internet is a useful new tool to help investors find information about companies and their financial performance. In addition to home pages for individual companies, investors can visit financial forums which allow users to discuss investor topics online. One place to start is the Internet home page of the Securities and Exchange Commission. They publish a daily online newsletter, along with information on hundreds of companies.

The Internet address is: **http://www.sec.gov**

CORPORATE DIVIDEND NEWS

Dividends, like earnings, often have a direct influence on stock prices. When dividends are increased, the message is that the company is prospering. That often stimulates added interest in the stock.

When dividends are cut, the opposite message is sent. A dividend cut is usually anticipated in the financial press before it happens—and one sign of impending trouble is often falling stock prices.

The names of companies announcing dividends are listed in alphabetical order.

A **pf** following the name indicates a dividend on preferred stock and a **clA** or **clB** shows different classes of stock.

Q indicates a quarterly dividend—the most common type.

M indicates a monthly dividend.

S indicates a semi-annual dividend. A few stocks pay dividends irregularly.

The dollar amount of the dividend per share appears in the first column, called Period Amount.

The payable date, when the dividend will be paid, is followed by the **record date**. Dividends will be paid to shareholders of record on that date.

In this example, **Chittenden Corporation** has declared a regular quarterly dividend of 6¢ per share, with a record date of August 4, that it will pay on August 20.

Dividend News also provides information on companies that have recently split their stock (see page 41), increased or decreased their dividends, or issued them for the first time.

DIVIDEND NEWS

Dividends Reported July 22

Company	Period	Amt.	Payable date	Record date
REGULAR				
Alcan Aluminium	Q	.07½	9—20	8—20
Alltel Corp pfC	Q	.51½	9—15	8—24
Amity Bancshares	S	n.15	8—20	8—5
n-Change in payment schedule from quarterly to semi-annual.				
Arco Chemical Co	Q	.62½	9—3	8—13
Bando McGlocklin	Q	.22	8—15	8—5
Bank of Boston	Q	.10	8—27	8—2
Bay State Gas Co	Q	.35½	9—1	8—18
Bearings Inc	Q	.16	8—31	8—16
Brown-Forman clA	Q	.68	10—1	9—4
Brown-Forman clB	Q	.68	10—1	9—4
Brown-Forman 4%pf	Q	.10	10—1	9—4
Calif Fedl Bk pfA	Q	.484⅜	8—16	8—5
Callaway Golf	Q	.02½	8—23	8—2
Castle (AM) & Co	Q	.10	8—20	7—30
Chittenden Corp	Q	.06	8—20	8—4
IRREGULAR				
BayBanks Inc	—	.25	9—1	8—14
MNB Bancshares	—	.06¼	8—13	8—2
Midwest Bancshares	—	.10	8—20	8—6
Republic Sec Finl	—	.01	8—16	8—2
TransTechnology	—	.06	9—1	8—15

FUNDS · REITS · INVESTMENT COS · LPS

* * *

Stocks Ex-Dividend July 26

Company	Amount	Company	Amount
ACM Govt Secs	.08	Mellon Bank pfH	.65
Aetna Life & Cas	.69	Mellon Bank pfI	
AgricultMinLP pref	.60½	Mellon	
AmerFirst PrepFd?	.13½		

EX-DIVIDEND means **without dividend**, or that a dividend has been declared within the last four days. An investor who buys during the ex-dividend period does not receive a dividend until the next time one is paid—usually three months.

The Traditional Stock Market

Wall Street—home of the two major U.S. exchanges—is the financial center of the world.

The first stock exchange in America was organized in Philadelphia in 1790. But by the time the traders who met every day under the buttonwood tree on Wall Street adopted the name **New York Stock Exchange** in 1817, New York had become the center of market action. It still is.

The rival **New York Curb Exchange** was founded in 1842. Its name said it all: trading actually took place on the street until it moved indoors in 1921. In 1953, the Curb Exchange became the **American Stock Exchange**.

A STREET BY ANY OTHER NAME

Wall Street, which got its name from the stockade built by early settlers to protect New York from attacks from the north, was the scene of New York's first organized stock trading. Now it lends its name to the financial markets in general—though lots of traders never set foot on it.

OTHER U.S. MARKETS

Stocks listed on the NYSE or AMEX may also be traded on one of the five **regional exchanges** located in other cities. These smaller exchanges, including the Pacific in San Francisco, the Chicago, Boston and Philadelphia, are linked with the two in New York but trading is faster and cheaper.

Trading results for stocks listed on both the NYSE and regional exchanges are combined at the end of every business day into the NYSE **Composite Trading** columns. Some small regional companies, like Canton Corporation, however, are listed only on one of the smaller regional exchanges. The most actively traded are listed in **U.S. Regional Markets** published in daily newspapers.

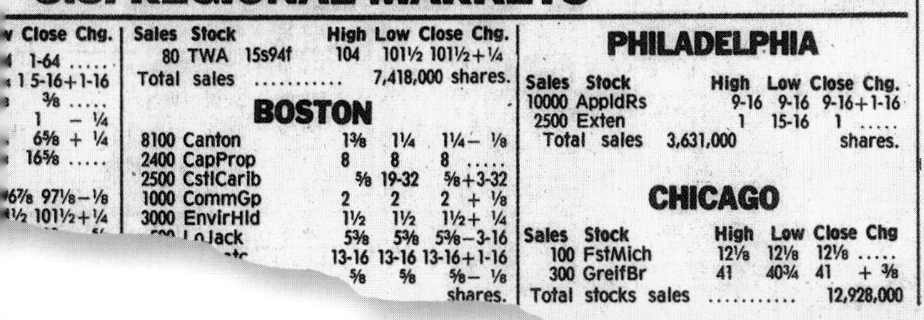

U.S. REGIONAL MARKETS

Close	Chg.
1-64	.....
1 5-16	+1-16
3/8	.....
1	− 1/4
6 5/8	+ 1/4
16 5/8	.....
97 1/8	−1/8
101 1/2	+1/4

Sales	Stock	High	Low	Close	Chg.
80	TWA 15s94f	104	101 1/2	101 1/2	+ 1/4
Total sales	....			7,418,000 shares.	

BOSTON

Sales	Stock	High	Low	Close	Chg.
8100	Canton	1 3/8	1 1/4	1 1/4	− 1/8
2400	CapProp	8	8	8	.....
2500	CstlCarib	5/8	19-32	5/8	+3-32
1000	CommGp	2	2	2	+ 1/8
3000	EnvirHld	1 1/2	1 1/2	1 1/2	+ 1/4
	LoJack	5 3/8	5 3/8	5 3/8	−3-16
		13-16	13-16	13-16	+1-16
		5/8	5/8	5/8	− 1/8
				shares.	

PHILADELPHIA

Sales	Stock	High	Low	Close	Chg.
10000	AppldRs	9-16	9-16	9-16	+1-16
2500	Exten	1	15-16	1	.....
Total sales	3,631,000			shares.	

CHICAGO

Sales	Stock	High	Low	Close	Chg
100	FstMich	12 1/8	12 1/8	12 1/8	.....
300	GreifBr	41	40 3/4	41	+ 3/8
Total stocks sales	....			12,928,000	

THE ROLE OF THE SEC

In the wake of the Great Depression and the stock-trading scandals that it exposed, the U.S. government created the **Securities and Exchange Commission** (**SEC**) in 1934. Its mission is to regulate the activities of stock traders and protect investors.

The President appoints five commissioners who oversee a staff of attorneys, accountants and investigators. Their job is to ensure that the securities markets operate honestly and fairly. When necessary, the SEC enforces securities law with various sanctions. Simply put, the SEC's role includes:

- Seeing that investors are fully informed about securities being offered for sale
- Preventing misrepresentations, deceit and other types of fraud in securities transactions

INSIDER TRADING

The SEC also monitors insider trading, which occurs when corporate officers or others buy or sell stock in their own company. Their trading decisions are influenced by what they know about the company's inner workings and its prospects.

It is perfectly legal for corporate officials to buy and sell their company's stock as long as they follow certain rules and report their trading activity (as shown below). In fact, tracking legitimate insider trading can be a valuable indicator of which way a stock price is heading.

But corporate officers—or their legal or financial advisors or others involved in a merger or acquisition—can be aware of potential problems or events that could affect the price of the company's stock. If they engage in trading to profit from the information before it is released to the investing public, that trading is illegal. So are efforts to hide trading by having a third party—such as a relative—buy or sell for them, or failing to report insider trading to the SEC.

SEATS, AT A PRICE

The NYSE and AMEX are private associations which sell memberships, or seats. The NYSE has 1,366 members and the AMEX has 661. Generally, the value of a seat rises as stock prices and trading volume rise. But when there is turmoil in the markets, or when competition increases and commissions decrease, the price fluctuates.

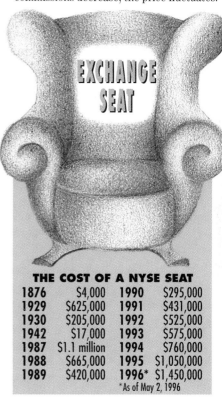

THE COST OF A NYSE SEAT

1876	$4,000	1990	$295,000
1929	$625,000	1991	$431,000
1930	$205,000	1992	$525,000
1942	$17,000	1993	$575,000
1987	$1.1 million	1994	$760,000
1988	$665,000	1995	$1,050,000
1989	$420,000	1996*	$1,450,000

*As of May 2, 1996

INSIDER TRADING SPOTLIGHT

Biggest Individual Trades
(Based on reports filed with regulators last week)

COMPANY NAME	EXCH.	INSIDER'S NAME	TITLE	$ VALUE (000)	NO. OF SHRS. IN TRANS. (000)	% OF HLDNG.	TRANSACT▶ DATES
BUYERS							
Weldotron	A	M. Siegel	CB	508	225.6	117.00	6/4
Churchill Downs	O	J. D. Grissom	D	307	6.0	148.00	6/18
Newell	N	R. L. Kate x	D	165	5.0	6.00	6/8
SELLERS							
Bristol-Myers Squibb	N	R. L. Gelb	CB	5,920	100.0	7.00	6/10
DSC Comm	O	J. M. Nolan	D	2,678	60.0	41.00	6/3
Schering-Plough	N	R. J. Kogan	P	2,115	31.1	58.00	6/15

Trading on the New York Stock Exchange

A stock exchange is both the activity of buying and selling and the place where those transactions take place.

The New York Stock Exchange provides the facilities for stock trading and the rules under which trading takes place. It has no responsibility for setting the price of a stock. That is the result of supply and demand, and the trading process.

Stock trading on the NYSE occurs **auction style**: In each transaction, stock is sold to the highest bidder and bought for the lowest offer.

THE TRADING FLOOR is where buy and sell orders are executed.

1 The trading day begins (at 9:30 am EST/EDT) and ends (at 4:00 pm) when the bell is rung from **the podium**.

8 Confirmation is made when the floor broker sends the successful trade details back to the branch office where the order originated.

7 After every deal, a reporter uses a hand-held wireless device to record the stock symbol, the price and the initiating broker. The device transmits the information within seconds to the Exchange's electronic tape. It also begins an **audit trail** in the event that something about the trade is suspicious.

COMPUTERIZED TRADING
Market orders of up to 30,099 shares can be processed through a computerized system called SuperDOT. An average of 85% of all orders reach the floor this way.

6 **Post Display Units** show the day's activity at the post. They report the stocks traded, the last sale price and order size.

Action on the floor often occurs at a furious pace. People wear differently colored jackets to indicate they're doing specific jobs:

Light blue jackets with orange epaulets for messengers

Green jackets for floor supervisors or traders

Navy jackets for reporters

2 The Exchange rents **booths** to brokerage houses. Each booth is home base for a firm's floor brokers. When an order is received from one of its brokerage offices, a floor broker takes the order to the appropriate **specialist** post to carry out the transaction.

3 The Exchange rents space to **specialist** firms—the brokers to brokers. A specialist keeps a list of unfilled orders in an electronic **book**. As buy and sell orders move in response to price changes, the specialist facilitates transactions.

The specialist's other job is to maintain an orderly market in a stock. If the **spread** between the **bid** and **ask** (the gap between the highest price offered by a buyer and the lowest price asked by a seller) becomes too wide, specialists turn into dealers themselves, who buy and sell stock. This narrows the spread and stimulates trading—a good thing for the vitality of the exchange.

4 Various stocks or groups of stocks are traded at **trading posts** near the specialists' positions. Each company's stock trades at only one post on the floor of the exchange, so the trading can be tracked accurately. However, the stock of several different companies may be traded at the same post. The number of companies assigned depends on the combined volume of business they generate.

5 Floor brokers can use a specialist if they choose. But many trades actually occur between two floor brokers who show up at the post at the same time.

On a typical day a floor broker walks an average of

12 MILES,
crisscrossing the floor.

The Electronic Stock Market

Thousands of stocks are traded electronically—using computers and telephones—on the Nasdaq Stock Market.

A sophisticated electronic network run by the **National Association of Securities Dealers** lets brokers trade from their offices all over the country. Continuously updated prices are carried on their computer screens, while they buy and sell over the telephone. **Nasdaq** lists 5,500 companies—from small, emerging firms to corporate giants like Microsoft, Apple Computer and Intel. Many of the Nasdaq listings in every size category are in technology, telecommunications, banking, retail and other growth sectors.

OVER-THE-COUNTER TRADING

Stocks in more than 28,000 small and new companies are traded in the **over-the-counter** market. The term originated at a time when you actually bought stock over the counter from a local broker.

Some OTC stocks are so low-priced or traded so infrequently that they aren't quoted regularly. Brokers receive daily results, called the **pink sheets**, for these stocks, or subscribe to an electronic service, called the OTC Bulletin, which provides selected quotes.

NASDAQ NATIONAL MARKET ISSUES

Net se Chg	52 Weeks Hi	Lo	Stock	Sym	Div	Yld %	PE	Vol 100s	Hi	Lo	Close	Net Chg	52 Weeks Hi	Lo	S
								107	1	1	1		18	12¾	In
	1½	¼	GtLksBcp wt					53	28	27⅝	27¾	+ ¾	15	9⅝	In
	32	23½	GtSoBcp	GSBC	.36	1.3	12	101	6	5¾	5¾	− ³⁄₁₆	6½	3⅛	In
½ + ½	6⅞	1¾	GtrNYSvg	GRTR			38	5	21	20	20	− ⅛	6	1⅞	In
½ − ¼	21⅛	15	GreenAp	APGI			cc	2	11¼	11¼	11¼		16¾	8⅞	In
1¼ + ¼	13	7	GreenwFnl	GFCT	.28b	2.5	10	528	4⅜	4⅛	4⅛	− ⅛	9⅜	8¼	In
1¼ ...	12½	3¾	GreenwPhar	GRPI			dd	26	22¾	22½	22½	− ⅛	32⅜	13½	
6½ − ⅛	25¼	15¼	GrenadaSun	GSSC	.68f	3.0	11	415	8¼	7¾	7¾	− ½	13⅝	6⅞	
2 + ¼	s 14⅛	5¼	GristMill	GRST			13	430	3⅛	2⅞	3⅛	+ ⅛	n 8¼	7	
5⅛	4⅞	2⅞	Grossman	GROS			39	337	6⅞	6½	6¹¹⁄₁₆	+ ¹⁄₁₆	12½	5¾	
5¼ − 1½	9⅝	4¾	GroundRound	GRXR			15	76	13	12½	12½	− ¼	12	8⅛	
9 + ³⁄₁₆	24¾	12⅝	GrndwtrTech	GWTI			16	4	8½	8½	8½	− ½	5⅝	3½	
7¼ + ¾	▼ 20¾	9	Groupl	GSOF			8	60	14¼	14	14	+ ½	7½	4½	
15 − ¼	16¾	10¾	GroveBk	GROV	.48f	3.4	8	183	8¾	8¼	8¾	+ ⅛	8½	4⅜	
12⅝ − ⅛	9¼	4⅞	GuestSply	GEST			25	2861	18	16	17½	+1½	6	2¼	
¹⁵⁄₁₆ + ¹⁄₁₆	n 35¼	14½	GuptaCp	GPTA				13	28	26¾	26¾	+ ¼	21	15	
19¾ +1	x 28¼	18½	GwinnetBcshr	GBSI	.60	2.2	13	291	43½						

READING NASDAQ TABLES

The largest and most actively traded Nasdaq stocks are listed in the **Nasdaq National Market Issues** and are published every trading day. Because they are either small or start-up companies which need to put earnings back into the business, many Nasdaq companies pay no dividends.

National Market Issues use a format similar to the listings for NYSE and AMEX stocks (see page 68). But the trading symbols for Nasdaq stocks have four or five letters, unlike the NYSE and AMEX exchanges, which use symbols of one to three letters.

For example: **GristMill** had a high of 14⅛ and a low of 5¼ during the past year. In other words, its price is fairly volatile, having dropped 8.875 points, or about 63% during the year, because of a stock split indicated by the **s** in the margin.

The company paid no dividend, and its **price/earnings ratio** (see page 69) is 13. There were **sales** of 41,500 shares on the trading day before this column appeared. During that day, the **high** was 8¼ ($8.25), the **low** 7¾ ($7.75). Since the **closing price** was 7¾, the **net change** was ½ point (50¢) lower than on the previous day.

NASDAQ SMALL-CAP ISSUES

ue	Div	Vol 100s	Last	Chg	Issue	Div	Vol 100s	Last	Chg	Issue	Div	Vol 100s	Last
xA Fd g		1245	2⁷/₁₆	+ ¹/₁₆	Camelot		668	⅞	...	FarmT wt		201	½	−
ON		435	1³/₁₆	...	Camiz		267	9½	...	FarmT un		20	1⁵/₁₆	−
R		24	¹³/₁₆	+ ¹/₃₂	Candie un		80	6	− ⅝	Fibchm		105	1⁵/₁₆	+
S Ent		605	17¼	+ 1	CandBk		20	5	− ¼	FnBenA t		7	2⅜	+
TV		291	6¼	− ⅛	CndyTor		40	2½	− ⅜	Fd SVP		10	1⁵/₁₆	
M Tr		4586	⁹/₁₆	+ ¹/₁₆	CaptlGm		2933	11½	− ½	Firetct s		2	1¼	+
		200	2³/₃₂	+ ¹/₃₂	CapG wt		25	19½	+ ¾	Firetc un		35	3²¹/₃₂	+
g		340	1⅛	− ³/₁₆	CapMult		86	12¼		FAmHlt		64	5¼	+
wt		13	³/₃₂	...	CapMl wt		6	7¼		FtLbty pf1.94		22	29¼	+
Co		190	3		Capucin		24	¹³/₃₂	− ¹/₃₂	FtNtFlm		441	1¹⁵/₁₆	−
		33	2¼	− ⅛	CarMrt		62	6½	+ ⅛	FRegBc		103	2⅝	−
		60	2¾	− ¼	CarMt wt		831	2⅝		FUtBG pf2.12		1000	48⅝	+
		411	5¾	− ³/₁₆	CareCon		142	2¾	+ ¼	FUtdSv .20e		26	15	+
		10	⅜	− ⅛	Caretnd		469	1¾	− ¹/₁₆	FFFn pfA1.75		22	36	
				...	CaroFt pf2.08					FschWt		50	¹³/₃₂	+
												108	4	+

NASDAQ SMALL-CAP ISSUES
Smaller, emerging companies—Nasdaq's specialty—are listed in the **Nasdaq Small-Cap Issues**. The table concentrates on current volume and price, since many of the companies are too new to have established a financial track record, including a P/E ratio.

Some of the companies do pay dividends, though, especially on preferred stock offerings, so that information is also reported.

In this example, 293,300 shares of **Capital GM** stock sold on the trading day before this column appeared, at 11½ ($11.50), down ½ (50¢) from the previous closing price.

REQUIREMENTS FOR STOCK MARKET LISTING

To be traded on the NYSE, AMEX or Nasdaq Stock Market, companies must meet the size and earning requirements of that market.

Traditionally, a company is traded on only one of the three major markets although it may also be traded on regional exchanges.

Exchange	Requirements	Type of Company	Number Listed
NYSE New York Stock Exchange	Pre-tax earnings of $2.5 million; 1.1 million shares held with $18 million minimum market value	Oldest, largest, best-known companies	2,755
NASDAQ The Nasdaq Stock Market	Nasdaq National Market: 500,000 publicly held shares minimum; $3 million minimum market capitalization. Nasdaq Small-Cap Market: 100,000 publicly held shares minimum; $1 million market capitalization	Large, mid-sized and small growth companies	5,500
AMEX American Stock Exchange	500,000 publicly held shares minimum; minimum market capitalization of $3 million	Mid-sized growth companies	796
OTC Over-the-Counter	Minimal or none	Smallest and newest companies or companies with few shares available for trade	28,000+

Reading the Stock Tables

The stock tables keep investors up to date on what's happening in the markets.

Highest and lowest prices for the past 52 weeks are reported daily. When there's a new high or low, it's indicated with an arrow in the margin like the one next to Deere in the second column of this example. The range between the prices is a measure of the stock's volatility, or price movement. (The more volatile a stock is, the more you can make or lose within a relatively short time.) The stock with the most volatile price here is Chrysler, where the range of movement is from 18⅞ to 47⅞, about 150%.

Percent yield is one way to evaluate the stock's current value. It tells you how much dividend you get as a percentage of the current price. For example, the yield on Chrysler is 1.4%.

Percent yield also lets you compare your earnings on a stock with earnings on other investments. But it doesn't tell you your total return, which is the sum of your dividends plus increases (or decreases) in stock price. When there's no dividend, yield can't be calculated, so the column is left blank.

NEW YORK STOCK EXCHANG

Net ose Chg		52 Weeks Hi	Lo	Stock	Sym	Div	Yld %	PE	Vol 100s	Hi	Lo	Close	Net Chg
39% + ⅝		47⅞	18⅞	Chrysler	C	.60	1.4	8	12256	43¾	43⅛	43¼	− ⅛
91¼ + ⅛		96⅜	73½	Chubb	CB	1.72	1.9	13	763	93	92¼	92¾	+ ⅛
16⅛ − ⅛		35¾	23⅝	Church&Dwt	CHD	.44f	1.9	16	240	24¼	23¾	23¾	...
17½ + ⅛		1¼	½	Chyron	CHY	...	...		1526	½	½	½	− ⅛
38⅞ + ⅝		43¾	37	Cilcorp Inc	CER	2.46	5.8	18	12	42⅝	42⅜	42⅝	+ ⅛
34⅜ − ⅛		24⅜	15⅜	CincBell	CSN	.80	4.1	28	513	19¾	19¼	19⅝	− ⅛
57⅝ +1¾	S	28⅝	23¼	CincGE	CIN	1.66	6.0	14	974	27⅝	27⅜	27⅝	..
28⅜ − ¼		62	50½	CincGE pfA		4.00	6.7	...	z110	59½	58	59½	+1¼
48 +2		29⅝	12⅝	CinciMacron	CMZ	.36	1.5	32	1384	24⅝	23⅜	24⅝	+1¼
19⅝ + ½		3⅝	1⅛	CineplxOde	CPX	...	dd		493	2¾	2½	2⅝	..
51 + ¼	S	33⅞	14⅛	CircuitCty	CC	.08	.3	22	5653	27⅝	26¾	27	− ⅛
8⅛ − ⅛	S	41½	27½	Circus	CIR		26	3003	30¼	37⅛	37¾	− ¼
38¼ + ¼		33⅝	14⅜	Citicorp	CCI	...	14	9615	32⅝	32¼	32⅝	− ⅛
19½ ...		89¼	68¼	Citicorp pf		6.00	6.8						+ ¼
27 + ¼		100½	80¼	Citicorp pfA		27⅝							
26⅛ + ¼													
25¼ + ⅜													

Cash dividends per share is an estimate of the anticipated yearly dividend per share in dollars and cents. Notice that the prices of stocks that pay dividends tend to be less volatile than the prices of stocks with no dividend. Chubb's yearly dividend is estimated at $1.72 a share. If you owned 100 shares, you'd receive $172 in dividend payments, probably in quarterly payments of $43.

Corporations are listed alphabetically—sometimes in shortened versions of the actual name—and followed by their trading symbol. Some symbols are easy to connect to their companies, like OAT for Quaker Oats, but others can be more cryptic. That often happens when companies have similar names or the logical abbreviation has already been used.

MOVING AVERAGE
A moving average is created by charting 52 weeks of weekly average stock prices. It's moving because the chart is updated every week by dropping the oldest number and adding the newest one. The result is a smoother curve than you would get by recording the daily ups and downs of the market.

Price/earnings ratio (P/E) shows the relationship between a stock's price and the company's earnings for the last four quarters. It's figured by dividing the current price per share by the earnings per share—a number the stock table doesn't provide as a separate piece of information. Here, for example, Dayton Hudson's P/E ratio of 14 means its price is 14 times its annual per-share earnings.

Since stock investors are interested in earnings, they use P/E ratios to compare the relative value of different stocks. But the P/E ratio isn't foolproof. It reports past earnings, not future potential. Two companies with a P/E of 12 may face very different futures: one on its way to posting higher earnings and the other headed for a loss.

There's no perfect P/E ratio, though some investors avoid stocks if they think the ratio is too high. A small company growing rapidly can have a high P/E, yet still be an attractive investment. On the other hand, a mature company in a declining industry could have a low P/E and be a poor investment.

Volume refers to the number of shares traded the previous day. Unless a **Z** appears before the number in this column, multiply by 100 to get the number of shares. (The Z indicates the actual number traded.) An unusually large volume, indicated by underlining, usually means buyers and sellers are reacting to some new information. In this example, 827,800 shares of Data General were traded in this session.

OMPOSITE TRANSACTIONS

52 Weeks Hi	Lo	Stock	Sym	Div	Yld %	PE	Vol 100s	Hi	Lo	Close	Net Chg	52 Wee Hi	L
36⅝	21⅛	Danaher	DHR	.06e	.2	25	536	35⅝	35¼	35⅝	...	s 45	2
14¾	10½	Daniellnd	DAN	.18	1.2	43	112	14¾	14⅝	14¾ + ¼		18½	1
13⅞	7⅝	DataGen	DGN	...		dd	8278	8¼	8	8¼ + ¼		s 40¾	2
2⅝	⅞	DataDsgn	DDL	...		dd	196	2⅜	2¼	2¼	...	50½	3
7⅜	1⅜	Datapoint	DPT	...		dd	540	6⅜	6	6⅜ + ¼		33½	3
9⅛	6⅛	Datapoint pfA		1.00	12.5	...	66	8⅛	8	8	...	24⅜	1
7¼	5	DavisW&W	DWW	...		cc	17	6¼	6⅛	6⅛ − ⅛		10½	
85	61⅛	DaytnHud	DH	1.60	2.3	14	1429	69⅛	68⅛	68⅝ + ⅝		8⅛	
29⅞	23⅛	DeanFood	DF	.64f	2.3	16	457	27⅝	27⅜	27½ − ⅛		8	
9½	8¾	DeanWtGvTr	GVT	.72	7.9	...	804	9⅛	9⅛	9⅛ − ⅛		14⅜	
39¼	30⅝	DeanWtDscvr	DWD	.10p	.3	...	3622	38⅜	37¼	37¼ −1		49	3
67½	36¾	Deere	DE	2.00	3.0	cc	3073	67⅝	66⅞	67⅛ + ⅜		34½	2
2⅝	⁹⁄₁₆	DelValFnl	DVL	...		dd	107	1⅜	1⅜	1⅜ − ⅛		n 18	1
15⅛	13%	DelGpDivInco	DDF	1.06	7.4	...	276	14½	14⅜	14⅝ + ⅛		▲ 3⅝	
24½	21½	DelmarPL	DEW	1.54	6.3	15	2501	24½	24¼	24½ + ⅛		34⅞	1

High, low and **close** report a stock's highest, lowest and closing price for the previous day. Usually the daily difference is small even if the 52-week spread is large. One of the largest spreads here is for Deere, which was as high as 67⅝ and as low as 66⅞ before closing at 67⅛.

Net change compares the closing price in the chart with the previous closing price. A minus (–) indicates a lower price, and a plus (+) means it's higher. Here, Dayton Hudson closed at 68⅝, up ⅝ point from the day before. Prices that change 5% or more are in **boldface**, as CincMilacron is here.

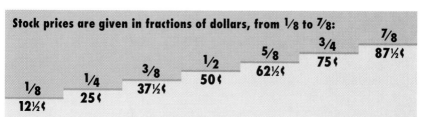

Stock prices are given in fractions of dollars, from 1/8 to 7/8:

1/8	1/4	3/8	1/2	5/8	3/4	7/8
12½¢	25¢	37½¢	50¢	62½¢	75¢	87½¢

Market Cycles

Stock market ups and downs can't be predicted accurately, but they often can be explained logically—most of the time in hindsight.

The market goes up when investors put their money into stocks. It falls when investors sell. A number of factors influence whether people buy or sell stocks—as well as when and why they do so.

Changing market direction doesn't always mirror the state of the economy. The crash of 1987 occurred in a period of economic growth, and the bull market of the early 1990s kept rising despite a stubborn recession. But most of the time the strength or weakness of the stock market is directly related to economic and political forces.

INFLUENCES ON INVESTMENT

Economic, social and political factors affect investment. Some factors encourage it and others make investors unwilling to take the risk.

Positive factors	Negative factors
Ample money supply	Tight money
Tax cuts	Increased taxes
Low interest rates	High interest rates offering better return in less risky investments
Political stability or domestic expectation of stability	Political unrest, turmoil
High employment	International conflicts
	Pending elections

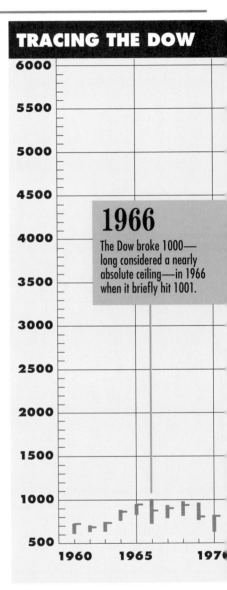

TRACING THE DOW

1966

The Dow broke 1000—long considered a nearly absolute ceiling—in 1966 when it briefly hit 1001.

MOVING WITH THE CYCLES

While pinpointing the bottom of a slow market or the top of a hot one is almost impossible—until after it's happened—investors who buy stocks in companies that do well in growing economies, and buy them at the right time, can profit from their wise decisions (or their good luck).

The strength of the underlying company is probably as important to its performance as the state of the economy. One characteristic of expanding companies is their ability to raise prices as inflation and the demand for their products and services increases. Higher productivity, increased sales and rising prices usually mean more profits for the company, and increased dividends and higher stock prices for the investor.

But since no economic cycle repeats earlier ones exactly, it's impossible to predict with precision that what happened in one growth or recovery period will happen in another. And while some types of companies do poorly in a slump, it's hard to be certain which ones will take the biggest hits or find it hardest to recover.

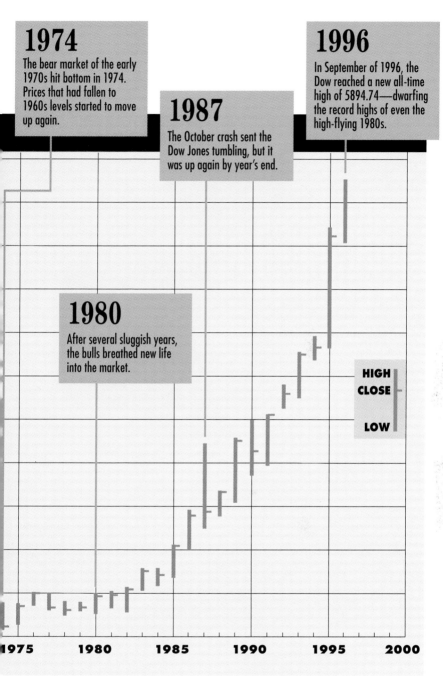

1974
The bear market of the early 1970s hit bottom in 1974. Prices that had fallen to 1960s levels started to move up again.

1987
The October crash sent the Dow Jones tumbling, but it was up again by year's end.

1996
In September of 1996, the Dow reached a new all-time high of 5894.74—dwarfing the record highs of even the high-flying 1980s.

1980
After several sluggish years, the bulls breathed new life into the market.

HIGH
CLOSE
LOW

1975   1980   1985   1990   1995   2000

BULL AND BEAR MARKETS

The stock market moves up and down in recurring cycles, gaining ground for a period popularly known as a **bull market**. Then it reverses and falls for a time before heading up again. A falling market is called a **bear market**. Generally, the market has to fall 15% before it's considered a bear. Sometimes market trends last a long time, even years. Overall, bull markets usually last longer than bear markets.

That doesn't mean, though, that markets usually rise farther than they fall. It just means that drops in the market tend to

UP

INVESTMENT ACTIVITY

DOWN

happen quickly while rises tend to take a long time. It's much like the law of gravity—it takes a lot longer to climb 1,000 feet than it takes to fall that distance.

71

Crash!

The bottom has fallen out of the stock market twice in the 20th Century: in October 1929, and almost 60 years later, in October 1987.

October is the cruelest month for American stock markets. The two great market crashes of the 20th Century—in 1929 and 1987—both came in October.

The crashes, or sudden collapses in the value of stocks which sent the Dow Jones Industrial Average (DJIA) into a tailspin, were triggered by too-high (or overvalued) stock prices and problems in the economy. Afraid of losing everything, investors rushed to sell, compounding the problem by driving the prices lower and lower. In 1987, the volume was intensified by the sell orders resulting from computerized **program trading** (see page 50).

WHICH WAS THE GREATER LOSS?

October 29, 1929

% Loss **12.8%**
$ Loss **$14 BILLION**

October 19, 1987

% Loss **22.6%**
$ Loss **$500 BILLION**

TRACKING THE COLLAPSE

The dramatic loss of value that characterized both market crashes is illustrated in these graphs, which index the weekly closing prices of the Dow Jones Industrial Average for 1929 and 1987. They use December 31 of 1928 and 1986 as the **index point**, or base, and show a parallel pattern of increasing prices and stunning drops—12.8% in 1929 and 22.6% in 1987.

Using an index, which gives figures in terms of an agreed-upon base, instead of the actual Dow Jones Industrial Average—which closed at 230.07 in 1929 and 1738.34 in 1987—makes it possible to compare the two events.

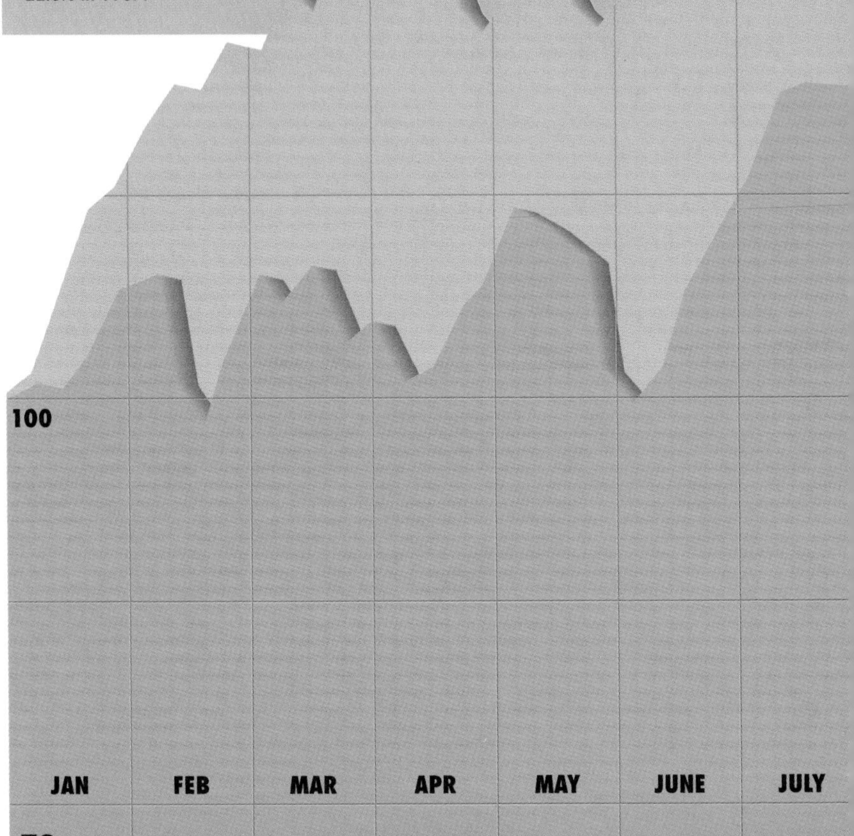

100						
JAN	**FEB**	**MAR**	**APR**	**MAY**	**JUNE**	**JULY**

HOW BLUE CHIP COMPANIES FARED IN THE TWO GREAT CRASHES

1929	opening price	closing price	loss	% loss
AT&T	266	232	−34	−12.7
Eastman Kodak	222⅞	181	−41⅛	−18.7
Sears Roebuck	127	111	−16	−12.5
1987	opening price	closing price	loss	% loss
AT&T	30	23⅝	−6⅜	−21.2
Eastman Kodak	90⅛	62⅞	−27¼	−30.2
Sears Roebuck	41½	31	−10½	−25.3

LEARNING FROM THE PAST

In 1987, in part because of government regulations and trading limitations that had been put in place after 1929, the market recovered much more quickly and the long-term effect on the economy was modest in comparison to the worldwide depression of the 1930s.

In the wake of '87, efforts to prevent yet another crash led to restrictions on computer-generated program trading and the introduction of a mechanism to shut down trading when the market falls too far in one session. If the DJIA falls 250 points, the NYSE closes for a half hour. If the drop hits 400 points from the previous day's close, it shuts down for one hour. The financial futures markets close down when stocks drop about 160 points.

That means a crash would almost certainly be drawn out over several days. Since investor panic makes any crash worse, slowing down the pace of the fall should help deter hasty sell decisions.

RECORD TRADING VOLUMES

Trading Date	NYSE Shares Traded
10/24/29	12.9 million
10/29/29 **CRASH**	16.4 million
10/30/29	10.7 million
1/23/87	302.4 million
10/19/87 **CRASH**	604.3 million
10/20/87	608.1 million

On an average day in 1996, 418 million shares were traded on the NYSE, while 561 million shares changed hands on Nasdaq.

International Investing

In the new economy, investors looking for ways to diversify their portfolio have a world of opportunity.

For many years investors from some countries, such as England, have been comfortable putting money into other nations' stocks. But Americans shied away from investing overseas, satisfied with the opportunities they had at home.

Now American investors are increasingly aware that a truly diversified portfolio often includes international investments. As foreign nations have moved to open their markets in recent years, investment opportunities have proliferated. Since foreign markets often operate in different financial cycles than U.S. markets, international investments can make gains while domestic markets are flat or declining. Consequently, savvy global investors venture into foreign markets to protect themselves from a downturn at home.

REWARDS...

Buying international stocks can produce rich returns. In the best of all possible worlds, investors win three ways:

- The stock rises in price, providing **capital gains**.
- The investment pays **dividends**.
- The country's **currency rises against the dollar**, so that when investors sell they get more dollars.

...BUT ALSO RISKS

Buying stocks abroad is no less risky than buying at home. Prices do fall and dividends get cut. Plus, there may be hidden traps that can catch unwary investors. Here are some of the common ones:

- Tax treatments of gains or losses differ from one country to another.
- Accounting and trading rules may be different.
- Converting dividends into dollars may add extra expense to the transaction.
- Some international exchanges require less information about a company's financial condition than U.S. exchanges do, so investors need to be wary.
- Giving buy and sell orders can be complicated by distance and language barriers.

- Unexpected changes in overseas interest rates or currency values can cause major upheavals.
- Political risk may be higher and major government policy changes more common.

The Currency Risk—and Its Reward

The greatest variable in calculating the risks and rewards of international investing hinges on changes in currency values. If the dollar shrinks in value, U.S. investors make more when they sell at a profit. But just the opposite happens if the dollar gets stronger.

STOCK PRICE IN MARKS

BUY
- Dollar is strong

One Share
DM **50**

SELL
- Stock rises
- Dollar weak

One Share
DM **60**

SELL
- Stock rises
- Dollar is strong

One Share
DM **60**

SELL
- Stock drops
- Dollar weak

One Share
DM **45**

SELL
- Stock rises
- Dollar very strong

One Share
DM **60**

SELL
- Stock drops
- Dollar very strong

One Share
DM **45**

ANOTHER PERSPECTIVE

Overseas investors make money in U.S. stocks when the dollar is strong against their currency and stock prices are climbing. If the dollar weakens, though, the value of their investment drops as well.

WAYS TO INVEST

There are several ways for a U.S. investor to buy international stocks:

- Big U.S. brokers with branch offices abroad can buy stocks directly.
- Many international and multinational companies list their stocks directly on U.S. markets.
- Many mutual fund firms offer international funds that invest overseas.
- The stocks of some of the largest companies are sold as **American Depositary Receipts (ADRs)** on U.S. markets.

Although trading information on ADRs, like Glaxo or Mitsubishi, is reported in newspapers' U.S. stock tables, the ADRs are certificates representing a set number of shares held in trust for the investor by a bank. The bank converts the dividends it receives into dollars, and takes care of withholding taxes plus other paperwork.

In this example, a U.S. investor buys a German stock for 50 marks per share. A year later, the investor sells for 60 marks per share. Clearly that's a profit, but how much?

Since the price has gone up 10 marks per share, from 50 to 60, there's a gain of 20%. That's also what a German investor would have made on the deal. But the revaluation of the currency also affects the return. If the dollar were worth less—say $1.50 per mark instead of $1.80—an American investor would have a greater gain.

But if the dollar had gained ground against the mark, and was worth 2.25 marks, the U.S. investor would have a net loss despite selling the stock for a profit in marks.

To figure the stock price, divide the price per share by the exchange rate.

$$\frac{\text{price per share}}{\text{exchange rate}} = \text{stock price}$$

To figure the gain or loss, divide the difference between the sale price and the initial cost by the initial cost.

$$\frac{\text{sales price} - \text{initial cost}}{\text{initial cost}} = \text{gain or loss}$$

EXCHANGE RATE	STOCK VALUE IN DOLLARS
Dollar = DM **1.80**	**$27.78**
Dollar = DM **1.50**	**$40.00**
Dollar = DM **1.80**	**$33.33**
Dollar = DM **1.50**	**$30.00**
Dollar = DM **2.25**	**$26.67**
Dollar = DM **2.25**	**$20.00**

GAIN OR LOSS

44% GAIN The double advantage of a higher stock price and a lower dollar produced a $40 sale price, for a $12.22—or 44%—per share profit.

20% GAIN Because the stock price increased and there was no change in the exchange rate, the $33.33 sale price was $5.55 more than the purchase price, a 20% gain.

8% GAIN Investors can make money on a dropping share price if the value of the dollar also drops. In this example the price drops to $45 but there's a $2.22—or 8%—profit.

4% LOSS American investors often lose money when the dollar increases in value if they bought when it was worth less. Here, the $27.11 sale price means a 4% loss.

28% LOSS The biggest losses occur when the value of the dollar increases and the share price drops. Here a return of $20 a share represents a 28% loss.

Tracking International Markets

As investors buy more global stocks, they want to know more about how those markets are doing.

With global markets increasingly open to all investors, and electronic media capable of providing up-to-the-minute reports on what's happening around the world, investors' appetites are being met with a steady stream of information.

The performances of 21 major global stock markets are reported daily in The Wall Street Journal and tracked by many online services, including those provided by some firms. These statistical composites, which are similar to the S&P 500, include the day's close and the net change from the previous day, as well as the change expressed as a percentage.

Here, for example, the **Nikkei** closed at 19,688.67, down 32, or .16%, from trading on July 7, the previous trading day.

Stock Market Indexes

EXCHANGE	7/00 CLOSE	NET CHG	PCT CHG
Tokyo Nikkei Average	19688.67	− 32.0	− 0.16
Tokyo Topix Index	1590.93	+ 6.55	+ 0.40
London FT 30-share	2227.8	− 6.3	− 0.28
London 100-share	2845.9	− 2.4	− 0.08
London Gold Mines	229.5	− 9.8	− 4.10
Frankfurt DAX	1783.7	+ 63.94	+ 3.72
Zurich Swiss Market	2397.9	+ 24.9	+ 1.05
Paris CAC 40	1980.37	+ 36.64	+ 1.89
Milan Stock Index	1200	+ 22.0	+ 1.37
Amsterdam ANP-CBS General	231.7	+ 2.2	+ 0.96
Stockholm Affarsvarlden	1106.6	+ 8.7	+ 0.79
Brussels Bel-20 Index	1285.21	+ 8.89	+ 0.70
Australia All Ordinaries	1782.5	+ 8.7	+ 0.49
Hong Kong Hang Seng	7122.39	− 18.72	− 0.26
Singapore Straits Times	1802.28	− 0.21	− 0.01
Johannesburg J'burg Gold	1971	− 121.0	− 5.78
Madrid General Index	258.77	+ 1.11	+ 0.43
Mexico I.P.C.	1694.67	+ 37.11	+ 2.24
Toronto 300 Composite	3920.86	− 51.86	− 1.31
Euro, Aust, Far East MSCI-p	904.1	− 2.5	− 0.28

p-Preliminary
na-Not available

DAILY NUMBERS
The daily numbers on a particular exchange have meaning only in relation to what has happened on that exchange in the past. For example, the Nikkei index here reports only what has happened in that market; it is unrelated to Frankfurt's 1783.7, Paris's 1980.37, or Singapore's 1802.28.

WORLDWIDE STOCK MARKET PERFORMANCE
The **worldwide stock market performance** can be compared by looking at the **percentage change**: knowing that London's Financial Times 100 share, or FTSE (pronounced footsie), is down .08% means more to investors than saying it was down 2.4 points.

About half the markets were up on July 8—and about half were down. That's because the political and economic situations at home have a major influence on stock performance, despite what's happening in the world at large.

PICKING A MARKET

Financial analysts tend to evaluate overseas markets from a top-down perspective, focusing on a country's or a region's financial environment rather than on the prospects of individual companies. Among factors that make a country's stocks attractive to investors are the underlying strength and stability of its economy, the value of its currency and its current interest rate. Growing economies, strengthening currencies and flat or falling interest rates are generally good indicators of economic growth. Conversely, countries whose currencies are weak, interest rates high and economies in recession don't attract equity investors.

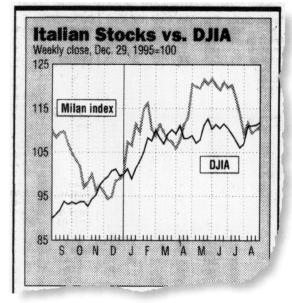

Italian Stocks vs. DJIA
Weekly close, Dec. 29, 1995=100

The financial press regularly tracks foreign markets in comparison with the benchmark Dow Jones Industrial Average.

In this example, the activity of the Dow seems placid when compared with the volatile Milan Stock Index.

FOREIGN MARKETS

Wednesday, September 1

LONDON
(in pence)

	Close	Prev. Close
Abbey National	393	400
Argyll Group	332	341
Assoc Brit Fds	511	518
BAA PLC	827	833
Barclays	498	499
Bass	498	502
Blue Circle	265	266
Body Shop	193	195
Boots	490	489
British Airwys	359	360
British Gas	331.5	

PARIS
(in French francs)

	Close	Prev. Close
Accor	673	675
Air Liquide	771	780
Alcatel Alstm	761	767
AXA Group	1618	1627
BSN-Gervais	936	952
Carrefour	3007	3040
Club Med	405.1	436.1
Dassault Avitn	496	487
Elf Aquitaine	435.7	445.9
Elf Sanofi	996	1009

FRANKFURT
(in Marks)

	Close	Prev Clo
AEG	169	16
Allianz	2545	25
Asko	740	
BASF	254.9	25
Bayer	299.6	30
Byr Vereinsbk	510	5
BMW	565.5	5
Commerzbank	315.5	3
Continental	228	2
Daimler Benz	739.5	7
Degussa	367	

FOREIGN MARKETS

Some of the most actively traded stocks on foreign exchanges are listed in the Foreign Markets column daily. Their closing prices and previous close are given in local currency. For example, on the London Exchange, Abbey National closed at 393 pence (£3.93), down from the previous day's 400.

Many of the corporations whose stocks are listed in their home country's exchanges are also traded on U.S. markets or over-the-counter as ADRs (see page 75) or as U.S. subsidiary companies. Of those listed here, Barclays, Bass and Club Med all trade on the NYSE. Other foreign companies, like Japan's Canon and Sweden's Volvo, are traded on Nasdaq. Until 1993, no German corporations had their stocks traded in the U.S. But on October 4, Daimler Benz joined the list.

Because prices are quoted in different currencies and the markets are influenced by different forces, there's no easy formula to compare the yields on international investments. But stock market performances around the globe are increasingly interrelated, so that a boom or bust in one market affects what happens in all markets.

Bonds: Financing the Future

Bonds are loans that investors make to corporations and governments. The borrowers get the cash they need while the lenders earn interest.

Americans have always invested heavily in the bond market. One of the major appeals is that bonds pay a set amount of interest on a regular basis. (That's why they're called **fixed-income securities**.)

Another attraction is that the issuer promises to repay the loan in full and on time. So bonds seem less risky than investments that depend on the ups and downs of the stock market.

Every bond has a fixed **maturity date** when the bond expires and the loan must be paid back in full, at **par value**. The interest a bond pays is also set when the bond is issued. The rate is competitive, which means the bond pays interest comparable to what investors can earn elsewhere. As a result, the rate on a new bond is usually similar to current interest rates, including mortgage rates. Municipal bond rates are an exception because their yields are free from federal taxes.

TYPES OF BONDS

Investors can buy bonds issued by U.S. companies, by the U.S. Treasury, by various cities and states and various federal, state and local government agencies. Many overseas companies and governments also sell bonds to U.S. investors. When those bonds are sold in dollars rather than the currency of the issuing country, they're sometimes known as **yankee bonds**. There is an advantage for individual investors: they don't have to worry about currency fluctuations in figuring the bond's worth.

ISSUERS PREFER BONDS

When companies need to raise money to invest in growth and development, they can issue stock or sell bonds. They often prefer bonds, because issuing more stock can **dilute**, or lessen, the value of shares investors already own. Bonds may also provide income-tax advantages.

Unlike companies, governments aren't profit-making enterprises and can't issue stock. Bonds are the primary way they raise money to fund capital improvements like roads or airports. Money from bond issues also keeps everyday operations running when other revenues (like taxes, tolls and other fees) aren't sufficient to cover their costs.

ISSUING A BOND

When a company or government wants to raise cash, it tests the waters by **floating a bond**. That is, it offers the public an opportunity to invest for a fixed period of time at a specific rate of interest. If investors think the rate justifies the risk and buy the bond, the issue floats.

THE INDIVIDUAL AS LENDER

INVESTORS WILLING TO LEND MONEY

INVESTOR GETS PAR VALUE AT MATURITY

INVESTOR GETS INTEREST PAYMENT AT SPECIFIC INTERVALS

THE LIFE OF A BOND

The life, or **term**, of any bond is fixed at the time of issue. It can range from **short-term** (usually a year or less), to **intermediate-term** (two to ten years), to **long-term** (ten to thirty years). Generally speaking, the longer the term, the higher the interest rate that's offered to make up for the additional risk of tying up money for so long a time. A graph of the interest rates paid on short-term and long-term bonds is called the **yield curve**.

MAKING MONEY WITH BONDS

Traditionally, investors use bonds to earn a steady income. They buy a bond when it's issued and hold it, expecting to receive regular, fixed interest payments until the bond matures. Then they get the principal back to reinvest.

When interest rates fluctuate widely, investors try to make money by trading bonds rather than holding them. Bonds that are issued when interest rates are high become increasingly valuable when interest rates fall. That's because investors are willing to pay more than par value for a bond with a 10% interest rate if the current rate is 7%.

In this way, an increase in the price of a bond, or capital appreciation, often produces more profits for bond sellers than holding the bonds to maturity.

But there are also risks in bond trading. If interest rates go up, buyers may lose money because the bonds they hold don't pay as well as the newer ones being issued. And if they sell before maturity, they won't be able to get back the full amount that they've paid for the bond (see page 82).

The other risk bondholders face is rising inflation. Since the dollar amount they earn on a bond investment doesn't change, the value of that money can be eroded by inflation. For example, if an investor has a 30-year bond paying $5,000 annual interest, the money bought less in 1993 than it did in 1973.

THE INSTITUTION AS BORROWER

CORPORATE BONDS

Corporations use bonds
- To raise capital to pay for expansion, modernization
- To cover operating expenses
- To finance corporate take-overs or other changes in management structure

U.S. TREASURY BONDS

The U.S. Treasury floats debt issues
- To pay for a wide range of government activities
- To pay off the national debt

MUNICIPAL BONDS

States, cities, counties and towns issue bonds
- To pay for a wide variety of public projects: schools, highways, stadiums, sewage systems, bridges
- To supplement their operating budgets

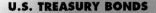

BOND MATURES

HOW BONDS ARE SOLD

For corporations, issuing a bond is a lot like making an initial public offering. An investment firm helps set the terms and underwrites the sale by buying up the issue. In cooperation with other companies, the investment firm then offers the bonds for sale to the public.

When bonds are issued, they are sold at **par**, or face value, usually in units of $1,000. The issuer absorbs whatever sales charges there are. After issue, bonds are also traded in the **secondary market**, which means they are bought and sold through brokers, similar to the way stocks are. The company gets no money from these secondary trades.

Government bonds (U.S. Treasury bills, notes and bonds) are available directly to investors through a Federal Reserve Bank or through brokers. Most agency bonds and municipal bonds are sold through brokers, who often buy large denomination bonds ($25,000 or more) and sell pieces of them, usually in units of $5,000, to individual investors.

The Bond Certificate

A bond is an IOU, a record of the loan and the terms of repayment.

Unlike stockholders, who have **equity**, or part ownership, in a company, bondholders are **creditors**. The bond is an IOU, or a record of the money they've lent and the terms on which it will be repaid.

Until 1983, all bondholders received certificates that detailed this information. **Bearer bonds** had coupons attached to the certificate; when it was time to collect an interest payment, the investor (or bearer) detached the coupon and redeemed it. That's why a bond's interest rate is known as its **coupon rate**.

Though new bonds aren't usually issued in certificate form, there are thousands of investors still holding bond certificates. Today most new bonds are registered and stored electronically, like stock purchases. They're called **book-entry bonds**.

OLD DEBTS NEVER DIE

A determined group of bondholders—or more accurately their descendants—is still trying to collect principal and interest to the tune of $13.8 million on $1.5 million worth of bonds dating back to the 1830s. The bonds, issued in Mississippi by banks that folded in 1837, have been moldering since the interest dried up in 1841. The group is determined to collect, but not vindictive, so they're not asking for compound interest. Figuring 152 years at a simple 6% is complicated enough.

Bonds are registered by the issuer and carry an **identifying number**. The owner's name also appears.

The issuer is the corporation, government or agency that issues the bond. It is identified by name and often by a symbol or logo. Its **official seal** authenticates the bond's validity. When a company issues bonds, the documents have the same design as the company's stock certificates. And they are protected against counterfeiting in the same way, with special paper, elaborate borders and intaglio printing (see page 46).

FOR FEDERAL INCO AMOUNT OF THE ORIGINA IS $55 PER $100 FACE AMO 1992, THE TAX YIELD TO MA SEMI-ANNUALLY USING SHOULD BE AWARE TH PURPOSES THIS NOTE IS DISCOUNT AND THE AMO DISCOUNT MUST BE RE HOLDER OVER A PERIOD ENDING ON JUNE 6,1999. FOR PURPOSES OF BELOW, THE AMOUNT OF THE NOTE IS $55 PER $10 TO MATURITY IS 11.74%.

ZERO COUPO
SUBORDI
DU

DUE 1999

NUMBER
R

SEAL
1974
CUC INTERNATIONAL INC.
CORPORATE
DELAWARE

American Bank Note Company

Interest rate is the percentage of par value that is paid regularly to the bondholder. For example, a $1,000 bond that pays 9.5% yields $95 a year. If the original buyer holds the bond to maturity, the **yield** (or return on investment) is also 9.5% a year. However, if the bond is traded, the yield could change even though the interest rate stays the same. For example, if an investor buys the bond for $1,100 in the secondary market, the interest will still be $95 a year, but the yield will be reduced to 8.6%, because the new owner paid more for the bond (see page 83, about figuring yield).

Par value, or the dollar amount of the bond at the time it was issued, appears several times on the face of the bond. Par value is the amount originally paid for the bond and the amount that will be repaid at maturity. Most bonds are sold in multiples of $1,000.

A **baby bond** has a par value of less than $1,000. Bonds of $500, or even less, can be issued by municipal governments to involve a larger number of people in the fund-raising process.

Maturity date is the date the bond comes due and must be repaid. A bond can be bought and sold in its lifetime for more or less than par value, depending on market conditions. Whoever owns the bond at maturity is the one who gets par value back.

---

2 2 2 2 2

REGISTERED

CUSIP 220210 AA 0
SEE REVERSE FOR CERTAIN DEFINITIONS

OSES ONLY, THE
NT ON THE NOTE
E DATE IS JUNE 6,
% COMPOUNDED
THOD. HOLDERS
AL INCOME TAX
ORIGINAL ISSUE
NCOME BY THE
JUNE 6, 1992 AND

E DEFERRED TO
E DISCOUNT ON
F AND THE YIELD

RTIBLE
OTE

INTERNATIONAL INC.

national Inc.. a Delaware corporation (the "Issuer"), for value received hereby promises to pay to

JOHN B. HOLDER

DUE 1999

DOLLARS

urpose in New York, New York on June 6, 1999 in such coin or currency of the United States of America as at the time of payment shall be legal tender for the payment of public and private debts. I not bear interest except in the case of a default in payment of principal upon acceleration, redemption or at maturity and in such case the overdue principal of this Security shall bear interest at the e payment of such interest shall be legally enforceable), which shall accrue from the date of such default in payment to the date payment of such overdue principal has been made or duly provided e basis of a 360-day year of twelve 30-day months. Interest on any overdue principal shall be payable on demand. Payment of the principal of and any such interest on this Security will be made at the e for that purpose in New York, New York.

ovisions set forth on the reverse hereof including without limitation provisions subordinating the payment of principal of and interest on overdue principal, if any, on the Securities to the payment in denture dated as of May 25, 1992 (the "Indenture") between the Issuer and Morgan Guaranty Trust Company of New York, as Trustee (the "Trustee"), and provisions giving the holder hereof the on Stock, par value $.01 per share ("Common Stock"), of the Issuer on the terms and subject to the conditions and limitations referred to on the reverse hereof, as more fully specified in the

all purposes have the same effect as though fully set forth at this place. obligatory until the certificate of authentication hereon shall have been duly signed by the Trustee acting under the Indenture.

Whereof, the Issuer has caused this instrument to be duly executed under its corporate seal.

International Inc.

AUTHENTICATION
s described in the within-mentioned
ST COMPANY OF NEW YORK,
as Trustee

Attest:

By:

Authorized Officer

Secretary

Chairman of the Board

The 30-year Treasury bond is popularly known as the long bond. But the longest bonds around are the 100-year corporate bonds that were introduced in 1993 by Disney Corporation. The first ones come due in 2093.

Figuring a Bond's Worth

The value of a bond is determined by the interest it pays and by what's happening in the economy.

A bond's interest rate never changes, even though other interest rates do. If the bond is paying more interest than is available elsewhere, investors will be willing to pay more to own it. If the bond is paying less, the reverse is true.

Interest rates and bond prices fluctuate like two sides of a seesaw. As the table below illustrates, when interest rates drop, the value of existing bonds usually goes up. When rates climb, the value of existing bonds usually falls.

Several factors—including **yield** and **return**—affect whether a bond turns out to be a good investment.

PAR FOR THE COURSE

If the bond investor buys at par, and holds the bond to maturity, **inflation** (or the shrinking value of the dollar) is the worst enemy. The longer the maturity of the bond, the greater the risk that at some point inflation will rise dramatically and reduce the value of the dollars that the investor is repaid.

If the bond pays more than the rate of inflation, the investor comes out ahead. For example, if a bond is paying 8% and the annual rate of inflation is 3%, the bond produces real earnings of 5%. But if inflation shoots up to 10%, the interest earnings won't buy what they once did. And in either case, the dollar amount of the bond itself also shrinks in value.

UNDER (AND OVER) PAR

But many bonds, particularly those with maturities of five or more years, aren't held by one investor from the date of issue to the date of maturity. Rather, investors trade bonds in the secondary market. The prices fluctuate according to the interest rate the bond pays, the degree of certainty of repayment and overall economic conditions—especially the rate of inflation—which influence interest rates.

SELLERS

BUYERS

6% Prevailing interest rate

At Issue

Original bond issuer is selling bond
AT PAR VALUE

Par Value:	$1,000
Term:	10 Years
Interest Rate:	6%

BUYING AT PAR VALUE

- Pay par value at issue and keep till maturity
- Receive ten annual interest payments of $60
- Receive par value—$1,000—at maturity

8% Prevailing interest rate

2 Years Later

If bondholder sells two years after issue when interest rates are high, the bond is
SELLING AT A DISCOUNT

Market Value	$800
Interest (x2)	+ 120
	920
Less Original Cost	− 1,000
LOSS	**$80**

BUYING AT A DISCOUNT

- Pay $200 less than par value
- Receive eight annual interest payments of $60
- Receive par value—$1,000—at maturity

3% Prevailing interest rate

3 Years Later

If bondholder sells three years after issue when interest rates are low, the bond is
SELLING AT A PREMIUM

Market Value	$1,200
Interest (x3)	+ 180
	1,380
Less Original Cost	− 1,000
RETURN	**$380**

BUYING AT A PREMIUM

- Pay $200 more than par value
- Receive seven annual interest payments of $60
- Receive par value—$1,000—at maturity

HOW IT WORKS

Generally, when inflation is up, interest rates go up. And conversely, when inflation is low, so are interest rates. It's the change in interest rates that causes bond prices to move up or down.

If DaveCo Corporation floats a new issue of bonds offering 6¾% interest, it seems like a good deal; so you buy some bonds at the full price (par value) of $1,000 a bond.

Three years later, interest rates are up. If new bonds costing $1,000 are paying 8% interest, no buyer will pay you $1,000 for a bond paying 6¾%. To sell your bond you'll have to offer it at a **discount**, or less than you paid. If you must sell, you might have to settle for a price that wipes out most of the interest you've earned.

But consider the reverse situation. If new bonds selling for $1,000 offer only a 5½% interest rate, you'll be able to sell your 6¾% bonds for more than you paid—since buyers will agree to pay more to get a higher interest rate. That **premium**, combined with the interest payments for the last three years, makes a tidy profit.

The fluctuations in interest rates, and therefore in bond prices, produce much of the trading that goes on in the bond market as investors try to get out of low-interest-rate bonds or try to make profits on high-interest-rate bonds.

CHANGING YIELD

Yield is what you actually earn. If you buy a 10-year $1,000 bond paying 6% and hold it until it matures, you'll earn $60 a year for ten years—an annual yield of 6%, or the same as the interest rate.

But if you buy in the secondary market, after the date of issue, the bond's yield may not be the same as its interest rate. That's because the interest rate stays the same, but the price you pay may vary, changing the yield.

Most bond charts express current yield as a percentage. For example, if a bond's yield is given as 6%, it means your interest payments will be 6% of what you pay for the bond today—or 6% back on your investment. Investors use the yield to compare the relative value of bonds.

Return is what you make on the investment when the par value of the bond, and profit or loss from trading it, and the yield are computed.

RETURN   YIELD

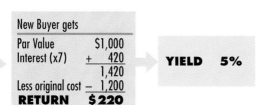

Original Buyer gets

Par Value	$1,000
Interest (x10)	+ 600
	1,600
Less original cost	− 1,000
RETURN	**$600**

YIELD   6%

New Buyer gets

Par Value	$1,000
Interest (x8)	+ 480
	1,480
Less original cost	− 800
RETURN	**$680**

YIELD 7.5%

New Buyer gets

Par Value	$1,000
Interest (x7)	+ 420
	1,420
Less original cost	− 1,200
RETURN	**$220**

YIELD   5%

HOW TO FIGURE A BOND'S YIELD

$$\frac{\text{annual interest}}{\text{price}} = \text{yield}$$

for example

$$\frac{\$60}{\$1,000} = 6\%$$

YIELD TO MATURITY

There's an even more precise measure of a bond's value called the **yield to maturity**. It takes into account the interest rate in relation to the price, the purchase price vs. the par value and the years remaining until the bond matures. If you paid $200 less than par value for a bond, that discount will be added to your interest in calculating the yield to maturity. Yield to maturity is a way to predict return over time.

Yield to maturity is calculated by a complicated formula—and it isn't often stated in bond tables. Brokers have access to the information, and some hand-held computers can be programmed to provide it.

Rating Bonds

Investors want to know the risks in buying a bond before they take the plunge. Rating services measure those risks.

Bond investors want to be reasonably sure that they'll get their interest payments on time and their principal back at maturity. It's almost impossible for an individual to do the necessary research. But rating services make a business of it.

The best-known services are **Standard and Poor's** and **Moody's**. These companies carefully investigate the financial condition of a bond issuer rather than the market appeal of its bonds. They look at other debt the issuer has, how fast the company's revenues and profits are growing, the state of the economy and how well other companies in the same business (or municipal governments in the same general shape) are doing. Their primary concern is to alert investors to the risks of a particular issue.

Issuers rarely publicize their ratings, unless they are top of the line. So investors need to get the information from the rating services themselves, the financial press or their brokers.

WHAT BONDS GET RATED?

The rating services pass judgment on municipal, corporate and international bonds. U.S. Treasury bonds are not rated—the assumption is that they're absolutely solid since they're obligations of the federal government, backed by its full faith and credit. This means the government has the authority to raise taxes to pay off its debts.

Rating a Bond: A Key to the Code

Moody's	Standard & Poor's
Aaa	AAA
Aa	AA
A	A
Baa	BBB
Ba	BB
B	B
Caa	CCC
Ca	CC
C	C
•	D

RANKINGS INFLUENCE RATES

As the chart to the left shows, a credit rating not only indicates an issuer's ability to repay a bond, but it also influences the yield on a bond. In general, the higher the bond's rating, the lower its interest rate will tend to be. For example, issuers of highly rated bonds don't need to offer high interest rates; their credibility does part of the selling for them.

But issuers of low-rated bonds need to offer higher rates to entice investors. Junk bonds, for example, pay high interest, since they are rated very low because of their risk.

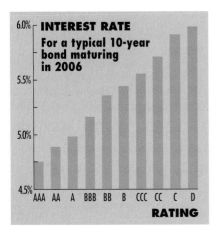

INTEREST RATE For a typical 10-year bond maturing in 2006

6.0% — 4.5%, RATING: AAA AA A BBB BB B CCC CC C D

THE RISK OF DOWNGRADING

One danger bondholders face—and one they can't anticipate—is that a rating service may **downgrade** its ratings of a company or municipal government during the life of a bond, creating a **fallen angel**. That happens if the issuer's financial condition deteriorates, or if the rating service feels a business decision might have poor results. If downgrading occurs, investors instantly demand a higher yield for the existing bonds. That means the price of the bond falls in the secondary market. It also means that if the issuer wants to float new bonds, the bonds will have to be offered at a higher interest rate to attract buyers.

The rating systems of the two major services are similar, but not identical, in the ways they label bond quality. Both services also make distinctions within categories Aa/AA and lower. Moody's uses a numerical system (1,2,3) and Standard & Poor's uses a + or − .

Meaning

Meaning		
Best quality, with the smallest risk; issuers exceptionally stable and dependable	**INVESTMENT GRADE BONDS**	**Investment grade generally refers to any bonds rated Baa or higher by Moody's, or BBB by Standard & Poor's.**
High quality, with slightly higher degree of long-term risk		
High to medium quality, with many strong attributes but somewhat vulnerable to changing economic conditions		
Medium quality, currently adequate but perhaps unreliable over long term		
Some speculative element, with moderate security but not well safeguarded		
Able to pay now but at risk of default in the future		
Poor quality, clear danger of default		
Highly speculative quality, often in default	**JUNK BONDS**	**Junk bonds are the lowest-rated corporate bonds. There's a greater-than-average chance that the issuer will fail to repay its debt.**
Lowest-rated, poor prospects of repayment though may still be paying		
In default		

The highly publicized mergers and takeovers of the 1980s were financed with junk bond issues. Corporations sold high risk bonds to the public. Investors were willing to take the risk because the yields were so much higher than on other, safer bonds.

YIELD COMPARISONS

Based on Merrill Lynch Bond Indexes, priced as of afternoon Eastern time.

	8/12	8/11	—52 Week— High	Low
Agencies 1-1yr	5.34	5.34	6.22	5.24
10+ yr	6.79	6.78	8.01	6.78
Corporate				
1-10 yr High Qlty	5.79	5.82	7.00	5.72
Med Qlty	6.21	6.24	7.31	6.16
10+yr High Qlty	7.28	7.29	8.31	7.28
Med Qlty	7.04	7.00	8.74	7.04
Yankee bonds(1)	6.73	6.75	7.97	6.73
Current-coupon mortgages (2)				
GNMA 6.50%	6.57	6.61	7.97	6.51
FNMA 6.50%	6.57	6.58	7.98	6.53
FHLMC8.00%	6.25	6.22	7.95	6.14
High-yield corporates	9.81	9.81	11.43	9.80
New tax-exempts				
10-yr G.O. (AA)	4.75	4.85	5.85	4.65
20-yr G.O. (AA)	5.35	5.45	6.60	5.30
30-yr revenue (A)	5.75	5.85	6.80	5.75
rated AAA-AA; medium quality				

TIME IS MONEY

In this example, 10-year high quality corporate bonds are earning 5.79% while 10-year plus bonds of the same quality are earning 7.28%.

Tracking Bond Performance

Corporate bonds are listed on the New York and American Stock Exchanges. Details about trading are reported daily.

The **name** is the company issuing the bond. The abbreviations can differ from those used for the same companies in the stock tables. Some are easy to decipher (like duPnt for duPont) and some are fully spelled out (Dow and Exxon). You may need help to figure out the others, like McDnlDg (McDonnell Douglas).

The **s** which sometimes appears after the interest rate doesn't mean anything. It's used to separate the interest rate figure from the following numbers. Usually, it shows up when the interest rate doesn't include a fraction and may be confused with the maturity date. Dow's 6.7% bond maturing in 1998 is a typical example.

A **zr** written where the interest rate should be means that the bond is a zero-coupon bond—like this Eastman Kodak bond maturing in 2011. Zero-coupons pay no periodic interest because interest accumulates until maturity.

NEW YORK EXCHANGE BONDS

ose	Net Chg.	Bonds	Cur Yld	Vol	Close	Net Chg.	Bonds
		CnNG 7¾96	7.7	10	101¼	+ ¼	Maxus 8½08
		ConNG 7¼15	cv	5	120	+ ¼	vjMcCro 7⅝s97f
		CnPw 8⅝07	8.3	10	103¾	...	McDInv 8s11
¾	− 1½	CoopCo 10⅝05	cv	19	62	+ 1	McDnl 9¾99
¼	− ¼	CrayRs 6⅛11	cv	46	82¾	− ¾	McDnlDg 7⅞97
	...	Dana dc5⅞06	cv	50	108	+ 1	McDnlDg 8⅝97
⅛	+ ¾	DataGn 01	cv	50	94	− 1½	McDnlDg 9¼02
¼	+ ¾	Datpnt 8⅞06	cv	44	77	− 1½	McDnlDg 9¾12
	...	Dow 6.70s98	6.7	20	100⅜	− ⅛	Mead 6¾12
½	+ ¼	Dow 7⅝s03	7.6	15	100⅛	− 3⅜	Medplx 11¾02
¼	− ¾	duPnt dc6s01	6.0	241	99¼	− ¼	Melln 8.6s09
¼	+ 1	duPnt 8½16	8.0	10	106	+ ¼	Melln 7¼99
⅞	− ½	EKod zr11	...	95	30⅞	+ ⅛	MerLyStkMk 97
⅜	− ½	EmbSuit 10½97	10.3	5	102⅛	− ⅞	MesaC 12s96f
¼	+ ½	EBP 6¾06	cv	137	68	...	MichB 7¾11
½	...	EngStr 02	...	20	111¾	− 1¾	MKT 5½33f
¾	− ¼	Exxon 6s97	5.9	35	101⅛	...	MKT 5½33fr
½	+ ¼	Exxon 6½98	6.4	20	101¾	− ⅛	MPac 5s45f
⅞	+ ⅞	FairCp 12¼96	12.1	5	101	+ ¼	Motrla zr09
	+ ¼	FairCp 13⅛06	13.5	6	97¼	+ ¼	MtSTI 7¾13
½	...	FairCp 13s07	13.4	76	97⅜	+ ⅛	NBD 7¼06
¾	− ¼	Farah 5s97	cv	20	97⅝	+ 1	[illegible]
¼	+ ⅛	FdMog 8¾96	8.4	47	100		

The **last two digits** show the year in which the bond principal will be paid off, or **mature**. It's understood that the first two digits are either 19 or 20. For example, the Embassy Suite 10½% bond will mature in 1997, and the Exxon 6½% in 1998.

Close is the price at which the bond closed on the previous trading day. When a bond is traded it usually sells for more or less than its par value. The price moves in relation to the bond's interest rate, its yield to maturity and the bond's rating.

The **current yield** is the percentage of interest an investor would earn if buying the bond at its current price. If the price is lower than par, the yield is higher than the stated rate; if the price is higher, the rate will be lower.

UNDERSTANDING BOND PRICES

Corporate bond prices are quoted in increments of points and eight fractions of a point, with a par of $1,000 as the base. The value of each point is $10, and of each fraction $1.25, as the chart shows:

⅛ = $1.25	⅜ = $3.75	¾ = $7.50
¼ = $2.50	½ = $5.00	⅞ = $8.75
	⅝ = $6.25	

So a bond quoted at 85½ would be selling for $855, and one quoted at 105⅞ would be selling for $1058.75.

Bond volumes report the dollar value of the previous day's trading, in thousands of dollars. To get the actual amount, add three zeroes. Thus, $18,000 of Mead bonds were traded—small in comparison to the $628,000 worth of 10½% Sequa.

The first number is the **interest rate**. This Safeway bond, for example, pays 10% interest. Bonds issued at different times have different rates, as Safeway's five different issues do. Bond interest always refers to a percentage of the **par value**, which is the amount the issuer will repay the bondholder when the bond comes due. The par value of most corporate bonds is $1,000. Thus, the annual interest payment on a 10⅛% bond will be $101.25.

Cur Yld	Vol	Close	Net Chg.
8.6	10	99¼	+ ⅛
...	2	37	– 1⅛
cv	36	107	...
8.7	2	112	...
7.8	97	100⅜	– ⅛
8.2	27	105¼	– ⅝
8.8	55	105⅛	+ ⅛
9.2	48	106	– ½
cv	18	104¼	– ¾
10.8	25	108⅞	+ 1⅛
8.2	2	105	+ 1⅜
6.3	6	116	...
...	15	99¾	...
...	52	102¼	– ⅛
7.6	34	102⅜	– ¼
...	30	56	– ½
...	10	56	...
...	85	63	– ¼
...	31	79⅝	+ ½

Bonds	Cur Yld	Vol	Close	Net Chg.
Rowan 11⅞01	10.7	137	111⅜	+ ⅝
Safwy 10s01	9.1	105	110	+ ½
Safwy 9.65s04	9.0	50	107	+ ⅛
Safwy 9.35s99	8.8	110	106	+ ⅜
Safwy 9.3s07	8.7	6	107½	+ ½
Safwy 9⅞07	9.2	30	107½	– ¼
Sears 9½99	8.2	10	115¼	+ ⅛
Sequa 10½98	10.2	628	103¼	– ⅛
SvceCp 6½01	cv	11	120½	...
SvcMer 9s04	8.7	55	102⅞	...
ShrLehm 10¾96	9.6	44	112½	– ½
ShellO 8s07	7.8	13	102¾	– ¼
SoCnBel 8¼15	7.9	10	104⅝	+ ⅛
SouBell 5s97	5.0	40	99¼	– ⅝
SouBell 4⅜03	5.0	25	87	– ¾
SouBell 6s04	6.1	15	98¾	+ ¾
SouBell 7⅜10	7.2	77	102¼	– ¾
SouBell 8s14	7.7	45	103⅜	+ ⅛
SouBell 8¼16	7.9	20	104	– ⅛

Compare Southern Bell's 4⅜ bond yielding 5% (it's selling at a discount for $870, or $130 less than par) with Mediplex's 11¾% bond yielding only 10.8% (it's selling at a premium for $1,088.75, or $88.75 above par).

Net change is the difference between the closing price given here and the closing price given in the table the previous day. It's always stated as a fraction, and is based on the **par value** of the bond. For example, Southern Bell's 8% bond was **up ⅛ point**, which means that the closing price is ⅛% of par value greater than the closing price on the previous day. To figure out the previous close, you subtract $1.25 (⅛% of its $1,000 par value) from this close of $1033.75, to get $1032.50.

Net price changes almost always reflect interest rate changes. If bond prices are down from the previous day you can conclude that interest rates rose or seemed likely to rise. When most bond prices are up, you can be fairly sure that interest rates fell or seemed likely to fall. When they're evenly split, as they are here, there's uncertainty about interest rates.

Municipal Bonds

The not-so-secret charm of municipal bonds is their federal tax-exempt status. Investors don't have to share their earnings with the IRS.

The interest paid on most corporate bonds is considered income, so it's taxed. To encourage investors to lend money to cities, towns and states to pay for public projects—like schools, highways and water systems—Congress exempts municipal bond interest from federal income taxes.

If an investor were considering both a corporate bond and a municipal bond that paid 6% interest, the obvious choice would be the municipal bond. But the choices are seldom that simple. High-rated municipal bonds usually have a much lower yield than corporate bonds, because they have a tax advantage. Thus, municipal bonds,

commonly called **munis**, usually appeal most to investors in high tax brackets, where the tax exemption provides the biggest tax savings.

In some states, municipal bond interest is also exempt from state tax (and city tax where it applies) for investors who live in the state where the bond is issued. An Ohioan, for example, would pay no Ohio income tax on bond interest earned on a Cincinnati bond. But someone from Kentucky who bought the Cincinnati bond would have to pay Kentucky tax on the interest income. Neither investor, however, would pay federal tax on the interest.

TAX-EXEMPT BONDS

Representative prices for several active tax-exempt revenue and refunding Changes rounded to the nearest one-eighth. Yield is to maturity. n-New. Sour

ISSUE	COUPON	MAT	PRICE	CHG	BID YLD	ISSUE
Alameda Ca Ref 1993-n	5.700	12-01-14	97⅜	— ⅝	5.92	Mt Sterling Ky Ser
Calif Poll Ctrl Ser92B	6.400	12-01-24	102⅜	— ½	6.23	NC Eastern Muni P
Fla St Bd of Ed	5.875	06-01-23	98⅝	— ½	5.97	NC Eastern Muni P
Gainesville Fla Util	5.500	10-01-13	95¼	— ¾	5.90	Nebraska Pub Pwr
Hawaii Dept Bdgt & Fin	6.550	12-01-22	102	— ¾	6.40	NJ Genl Obligation
Hudson Co Imp Auth NJ	6.000	12-01-25	99⅞	— ½	6.01	Northrn Ca Transm
Indpls Lcl Pub Imprvmt	5.900	01-10-14	97⅞	— ⅝	6.08	NY Lcl Gvt Asst Ser
Indpls Lcl Pub Imprvmt	6.000	01-10-18	98½	— ⅝	6.12	NYS Med Care Fac
Intermntn Pwr Utah	5.500	07-01-20	92⅞	— ⅝	6.03	Okla Bldg Bds 92 Se
Jacksonville Elec Fla	5.250	10-01-21	90⅜	— ⅜	5.95	Orange Co Hlth Fac
Jacksonville Elec Fla	5.500	10-01-13	95	— ⅝	5.92	P R Various G O
Kenton Co Airport Ky	6.300	03-01-15	100¼	— ½	6.28	Phoenix Civic Ariz
LA Dept Wtr & Pwr-n	5.875	09-01-30	98¼	— ½	5.99	San Antonio Texas
Mass Bay Trnsp Auth	6.000	03-01-12	98⅜	— ⅝	6.14	Snohomish Co PUD
Mass Bay Trsp Auth	6.100	03-01-23	98¾	— ⅜	6.19	Snohomish Co PUD
Mass Tpke Auth	5.125	01-01-23	89½	— ⅞	5.87	South Central Corn
Massachusettes HFA	6.300	10-01-13	97⅞	— ½	6.31	Southrn Calif Pub P
Massachusettes HFA	6.375	04-01-21	99¾	— ½	6.39	Wamego Kans PC
Metro Seattle WA	6.300	01-01-23	100⅝	— ⅞	6.26	Wash Hlth

READING MUNI STATISTICS

There are hundreds of thousands of munis in the market. The Wall Street Journal quotes price information for some of the largest bonds that are being actively traded.

The **name** of the issuing municipal government or government agency is listed, along with a series number, if it applies.

Coupon rate is the interest rate, given as a percentage of par value. The bond issued by Gainesville Fla Utilities pays 5.50% of par value in interest, or $55 per $1,000. It does not take into account any discount or premium in the purchase price of the security.

Maturity date is the date the bond matures and will be paid off. This Mass Bay Transportation Author-

ity bond comes due on March 1, 2012.

Munis are often long-term bonds, 20 to 40 years; all of the ones in this list mature between 2012 and 2033.

Price is the amount the bond sold for at the end of the previous trading day, given as a percentage of par. Nebraska's Public Power District's price of 99⅞ means it closed at $998.75.

MUNICIPAL BOND INDEXES

Each week The Wall Street Journal prints a Municipal Bond Index of the average interest issuers would have to pay to sell investment quality long-term bonds. In the week ending February 2, for example, the average interest was 6.16%, flat from the week before.

Specific figures are given for the two main categories of municipal bonds.

Revenue bonds are backed by the revenues a specific project or agency generates. New York State Thruway revenue bonds, for example, are repaid by the money paid for tolls. **General obligation bonds** are backed by the **full faith and credit** (meaning the taxing power) of the issuer. Because revenue bonds generally have longer terms and are somewhat riskier, they pay slightly higher rates overall.

Municipal Bond Index
Merrill Lynch 500
Week ended February 2

The following index is based on yields that about 500 major issuers, mainly of investment grade, would pay on new long-term tax-exempt securities. The securities are presumed to be issued at par; general obligation bonds have a 20-year maturity and revenue bonds a 30-year maturity. The index, prepared by Merrill Lynch, Pierce, Fenner & Smith Inc., is calculated using yields on major outstanding bonds in the market. Yields are obtained from an internal source.

—500 MUNICIPAL BOND INDEX—
6.16   +0.00

—REVENUE BONDS—
Sub-Index   6.18   +0.00

—25-YEAR REVENUE BONDS—	02-02	Change In Week	
AAA-Guaranteed ...			
Airport	6.12	+	0.04
Power	6.72	−	0.02
Hospital	6.01	+	0.00
Housing-	6.21	+	0.02
Single Family			
Housing-	6.48	+	0.02
Multi Family			
Miscellaneous	6.38	+	0.01
Pollution Control/	6.31	+	0.02
Ind. Dev.			
Transportation	6.20	−	0.08
Water	5.93	+	0.01
Advance Refunded	6.17	+	0.01
	4.58	−	0.03
—20-YEAR GENERAL OBLIGATIONS—			
Sub-Index	6.09	−0.01	
Cities			
Counties	6.29	+	0.05

based on institutional trades. Bond Buyer.

ON	MAT	PRICE		CHG	BID YLD
200	03-01-18	98⅞	−	⅝	6.29
000	01-01-18	99⅜	−	¾	6.05
250	01-01-23	101¼	−	¾	6.16
125	01-01-15	99⅞	−	½	6.13
000	02-15-13	102	−	⅝	5.83
250	05-01-20	91⅞	−	½	5.84
250	04-01-18	100⅞	−	¼	6.18
800	08-15-22	98¼	−	·½	5.93
200	07-15-16	92¾	−	1	5.77
000	11-01-24	99⅜	−	¾	6.04
000	07-01-14	99	−	½	6.08
125	07-01-23	99¼	−	⅝	6.1.
750	08-01-13	97¼	−	⅝	
000	01-01-13	99¼			

Change is the difference between the price quoted here and the previous day's closing price. It is quoted as a percentage of par value, just as corporate bonds are. New Jersey's General Obligation's price was down ⅝ of a point, or $6.25. So if this price is $1,020.00, the previous one was $1,026.25. You can use the table on page 87 to find the dollar value of each percentage point, or figure it out by multiplying the percentage change by $1,000.

Yield is the time value of money. When a bond sells for more than par value, the yield is higher than the interest rate. If it sells for less than par, the yield is more.

BOND OFFERINGS

When states, cities or towns want to offer new bonds, there are two ways to get them to market. They can negotiate an arrangement with a securities firm to underwrite the bond, or they can ask for competitive bids.

A competitive bid means the issuer works with the lowest bidder to sell the bonds. A negotiated agreement takes other factors into account.

Since the mid-1980s, most offerings—up to 80%—have been negotiated. The main advantage is a guaranteed presale. The potential problems are the opportunity for manipulating the deal to the advantage of the underwriter at the expense of the taxpayer who foots the interest bills, and the possibility of political kickbacks. Competitive bids are free of those problems, but may rule out developing a strong working relationship that could benefit the issuer.

U.S. Treasury Bonds, Notes and Bills

The U.S. Treasury offers three choices: bonds, bills and notes. A key difference is their term, from 13 weeks to 30 years.

Since investors consider the U.S. government the most reliable borrower in the world, they refer to the latest 30-year Treasury bond as the **benchmark** against which all other bonds are measured. Bonds, notes and bills issued by the Treasury almost always yield less than any other debt of the same maturity—despite the fact that interest on Treasuries is federally taxable. The exception is municipal bonds, which usually yield less because they are tax-exempt.

Treasury bills with maturities of 13 and 26 weeks (three and six months) are auctioned every Monday, so investors can buy new issues at any time. Notes, bonds and twelve-month bills are sold less frequently, usually quarterly, and are announced well in advance.

Like other bonds, Treasuries are traded in the secondary market after issue. Treasury bond prices are measured in 32nds rather than 100ths of a point. The value of each point is $10. Each $1/32$ equals 31.25 cents and the fractional part is dropped when quoting a price. For example, if a bond is at 100:2 (or 100 + $2/32$), the price translates to $1,000.62.

READING THE TABLES

Trading information on representative Treasury bonds and notes, listed in order of maturity, appears in a daily table in most financial publications.

TREASURY BONDS

GOVT. BONDS & NOTES

Rate	Maturity Mo/Yr	Bid	Asked	Chg.	Ask Yld.
7 1/4	Jul 96n	100:05	100:07	....	1.12
6 5/8	Jul 96n	100:09	100:11	....	2.50
8	Aug 96n	100:19	100:21	− 2	2.51
8 5/8	Aug 96	100:21	100:23	− 1	2.61
8 3/4	Aug 96n	100:21	100:23	− 1	2.73
7 1/8	Aug 96n	101:02	101:04	− 1	2.48
6 3/8	Aug 96n	100:17	100:19	....	2.66
6 1/8	Sep 93n	100:23	100:25	....	2.88
8 1/4	Sep 96n	101:08	101:10	....	2.82
7 1/8	Oct 96n	101:03	101:05	− 1	3.01
6	Oct 96n	100:28	100:30	....	3.09
7 3/4	Nov 96n	101:20	101:22	− 1	3.10
8 5/8	Nov 96	101:30	102:00	....	3.12
9	Nov 96n	102:03	102:05	....	3.06
11 3/4	Nov 96n	103:03	103:05	− 1	3.07
5 1/2	Nov 96n	100:29	100:31	....	3.11
5	Dec 96n	100:27	100:29	....	3.14
7 5/8	Dec 96n	102:04	102:06	....	3.13
7	Jan 96n	101:30	102:00	....	3.21
4 7/8	Jan 96n	100:28	100:30	....	3.23
	Feb 96n	102:04	102:06		

Rate	Maturity Mo/Yr	Bid	Asked	Chg.	As Yl
7	Apr 02n	108:22	108:24	− 2	5.2
8 1/2	May 97-02	104:03	104:11	....	3.3
9 1/8	May 02n	119:13	119:15	− 3	5.2
6 3/8	Jul 02n	105:18	105:20	− 2	5.2
8	Aug 02n	113:30	114:00	− 3	5.3
6	Oct 02n	103:15	103:17	− 3	5.3
7 7/8	Nov 02n	113:19	113:21	....	5.3
6 3/8	Jan 03n	105:12	105:14	− 3	5.3
7 7/8	Feb 98-03	105:20	105:24	− 5	4.1
8 1/2	Feb 03n	117:05	117:07	− 4	5.3
5 1/2	Apr 03n	100:13	100:15	− 3	5.4
8 7/8	May 03n	119:20	119:22	− 2	5.4
8 3/8	Aug 98-03	108:08	108:12	+ 1	4.2
8 3/4	Aug 03n	119:05	119:07	− 3	5.4
8 1/2	Nov 03n	117:31	118:01	− 3	5.4
7 3/4	Feb 04n	113:18	113:20	− 3	5.4
11 3/4	Feb 04	138:14	138:18	− 1	5.4
8	May 04n	115:10	115:12	− 2	5.5
13 1/8	May 04	147:22	147:26	− 3	
7 7/8	Aug 04n	114:21	114:23	− 1	5.5
		109:18	109:22	− 4	4.6

Rate is the percentage of par value paid as annual interest. The bond maturing in July 1996 pays 7¼% interest.

Maturity date is the month and year the bond or note comes due. An **n** after the month means it is a note rather than a bond.

Prices for Treasury issues are quoted as **bid** and **asked** instead of as a closing price. That's because Treasury issues are traded over-the-counter in private, one-on-one telephone transactions

BONDS

STRIPS AND BILLS

Trading in **U.S. Treasury Strips** (zero-coupons) and **Bills** are reported in separate sections of the table. They're also listed by maturity date, and provide information on prices and yield.

Because strips are sold at **deep discount**, or a fraction of their par value, the ones with distant maturity dates sell for very little money, while the ones coming due are sold for close to par value. Compare the 99:19 bid price on the strip maturing in August '96 with the 88:02 bid for the strip maturing in May 1999.

Bid and **asked** prices for T-bills are stated in such small numbers because they're sold at discount, a price lower than par value. T-bills

don't pay periodic interest, but repay full par value at maturity. The difference between the discount price paid and the par value received equals the interest. For example, if an investor pays $9,500 for a $10,000 T-bill, that's 5% less than the payback—or 5% interest.

Dealers trade in T-bills by bidding and asking discount percents. For example, for the bill due on July 22, the highest bid was 2.80—meaning that someone offered to buy the bill at a 2.80% discount. That is, the offer

was to pay $9,720 to buy a $10,000 bill, yielding $280 in interest.

Yield is the **time value of money**. As with bonds and notes, it represents the relative value of the issue. The figure that gives the most accurate sense of what an investor makes on a T-bill is the **coupon equivalent yield**, or the percentage return resulting from dividing the dollar return by the amount paid. For example, a $10,000 bill sold for $9,600 has a coupon equivalent yield of 4.16% (see box above).

NOTES & BILLS

U.S. TREASURY STRIPS

Mat.	Type	Bid	Asked	Chg.	Ask Yld.
ug 96	ci	99:19	99:20	....	3.22
ov 96	ci	98:26	98:26	....	3.25
b 97	ci	97:31	97:31	....	3.32
a) 97	ci	97:02	97:02	....	3.44
ug 97	ci	96:04	96:05	....	3.53
ov 97	ci	95:04	95:05	....	3.66
v 97	np	95:02	95:03	– 1	3.71
b 98	ci	93:28	93:30	....	3.90
b 98	np	93:31	94:00	– 1	3.85
a) 98	ci	93:00	93:01	....	3.90
a) 98	np	92:28	92:30	– 1	3.96
ug 98	ci	91:29	91:31	– 1	3.99
g 98	np	91:28	91:30	– 1	4.00
ov 98	ci	90:21	90:23	– 1	4.16
ov 98	np	90:25	90:27	– 1	4.09
b 99	ci	89:11	89:14	– 1	4.31
h 99	np	89:11	89:14	– 1	4.31
a) 99	ci	88:02	88:04	– 2	4.45
a) 99	np	88:03	88:05	– 2	4.44
ug 99	ci	86:24	86:26	– 2	4.58

TREASURY BILLS

Maturity	Days to Mat.	Bid	Asked	Chg.	Ask Yld.
Jul 08 '96	6	2.66	2.56	– 0.17	2.60
Jul 15 '96	13	2.81	2.71	....	2.75
Jul 22 '96	20	2.80	2.70		2.74
Jul 29 '96	27	2.79	2.69	– 0.05	2.73
Aug 05 '96	34	2.84	2.80	– 0.04	2.85
Aug 12 '96	41	2.88	2.84	– 0.02	2.89
Aug 19 '96	48	2.91	2.87	– 0.03	2.92
Aug 26 '96	55	2.93	2.89	– 0.02	2.94
Sep 02 '96	62	2.98	2.96		3.02
Sep 09 '96	69	3.01	2.99	+ 0.01	3.05
Sep 16 '96	76	3.02	3.00	+ 0.01	3.06
Sep 23 '96	83	3.05	3.03	– 0.01	3.09
Sep 30 '96	90	3.03	3.01	....	
Oct 07 '96	97	3.05	3.03		
Oct 14 '96	104				
Oct 21 '96	111				
Oct 28 '96					
Nov					

instead of on the major exchanges. So it's not possible to determine the exact price of the last transaction. The best information that's available is the highest bid (price offered) by buyers and the lowest price asked by sellers at 4 pm Eastern time.

For example, the bond paying 8% that matures in August 2002, had a bid price of 113.30 and an asked price of 114. The .30 in the price refers to $^{30}/_{32}$nds of a point, or $9.375. So the bid price was $1139.375 and the asked price was $1140.

Bid change represents the change in the bid price given here and the bid price given in the tables for the previous trading day. The change is stated as a percent and preceded by a "+" if it went up and a "−" if it went down. For example, the bid price on the July 29 bill is .05% of a point lower than on the previous day.

A Bond Vocabulary

Though some people insist that their word is their bond, the words we use to describe bonds have very specific meanings.

Like the word **security**, which once meant the written record of an investment, the word **bond** once referred to the piece of paper which described the details of a loan transaction. Today the term is used more generally to describe a vast and varied market in debt securities.

The language of bonds tells potential investors the features of the loan: the time to maturity, how it's going to be repaid, and whether it's likely to be repaid ahead of schedule.

How Bonds Are Backed Up

ASSET-BACKED BONDS, created in the mid-1980s, are secured, or backed up, by specific holdings of the issuing corporation, such as equipment or real estate. An asset-backed bond can be created when a securities firm **bundles** some type of debt, like mortgages, and sells investors the right to receive the payments that consumers are making on those loans.

DEBENTURES are the most common corporate bonds. They're backed by the credit of the issuer, rather than by any specific assets. Though they sound riskier, they're generally not. The debentures of reliable institutions are often more highly rated than asset-backed bonds.

PRE-REFUNDED BONDS are corporate or municipal bonds, usually AAA rated, whose repayment is guaranteed by the funds from a second bond issue. Proceeds from the secondary issues are usually invested in safe U.S. Treasury securities.

MORTGAGE-BACKED BONDS are backed by a pool of mortgage loans. They're sold to brokers by government agencies and private corporations, and the brokers resell them to investors. Mortgage-backed bonds are **self-amortizing**. That means each payment an investor gets includes both principal and interest, so that there is no lump-sum repayment at maturity.

COLLATERALIZED MORTGAGE OBLIGATIONS (CMOs) are newer, more complex versions of mortgage-backed bonds. Although they are sold as a reasonable alternative to more conventional bonds, evaluating their risks and rewards requires specialized skills.

Bonds With Conditions

A SUBORDINATED BOND is one that will be paid after other loan obligations of the issuer have been met. **Senior** bonds are those with stronger claims. Corporations sometimes sell senior and subordinated bonds in the same issue, offering more interest and a shorter term on the subordinated ones to make them more attractive.

FLOATING-RATE BONDS promise periodic adjustments of the interest rate—to persuade investors that they aren't locked into what seems like an unattractively low rate.

CONVERTIBLE BONDS give investors the option to convert, or change, their corporate bonds into company stock instead of getting a cash repayment. The terms are set at issue; they include the date the conversion can be made, and how much stock each bond can be exchanged for. The conversion option lets the issuer offer a lower initial interest rate, and makes the bond price less sensitive than conventional bonds to changes in the interest rate.

A SINKING FUND, established at the time a bond is issued, is a cash reserve set aside to finance periodic bond calls.

Bonds With Strings Attached

CALLABLE BONDS don't always run their full term. The issuer may **call** the bond—pay off the debt—before the maturity date. It's a process called **redemption**. The first date a bond is vulnerable to call is named at the time of issue. Call, or redemption, announcements are published regularly in financial newspapers.

Issuers may want to call a bond if interest rates drop. If they pay off their outstanding bonds, they can float another bond at the lower rate. (It's the same idea as refinancing a mortgage to get a lower interest rate and make lower monthly payments.) Sometimes only part of an issue is redeemed, rather than all of it. The ones that are called are chosen by lottery.

Callable bonds are more risky for investors than non-callable ones because an investor whose bond has been called is often faced with reinvesting the money at a lower, less attractive rate. To protect bondholders expecting long-term steady income, call provisions usually specify that a bond can't be called before a certain number of years, usually five or ten.

REDEMPTION NOTICES

The following is a listing of securities called for partial or complete redemption during the week ended April 2, 1996. The notices are taken from advertisements appearing in editions of The Wall Street Journal, and are not meant to be definitive. Inquiries regarding specific issues should be directed to the paying agent or, if none is listed, the issuer.

MUNICIPALS

BEXAR COUNTY HEALTH FACILITIES DEVELOPMENT CORP. will redeem, on May 1, 1996, the following hospital revenue bonds, series 1983: $325,000 principal amount of its 9.5% bonds due 1997; $360,000 of 9.6% due 1998; $395,000 of 9.65% due 1999; $435,000 of 9.7% due 2000; $485,000 of 9.7% due 2001; and $17,880,000 of 9.75% due 2016. All bonds are due on May 1 of their respective years. Frost National Bank of San Antonio is paying agent.

CENTRAL MICHIGAN UNIVERSITY will redeem, on May 1, 1999, $40,000 principal amount of ... revenue bonds ... term ... Michigan...

Popular Innovations

ZERO-COUPON BONDS are a popular variation on the bond theme for some investors. Since **coupon**, in bond terminology, means interest, a zero-coupon by definition pays out no interest while the loan is maturing. Instead, the interest **accrues** (builds up) and is paid in a lump sum at maturity.

Investors buy zero-coupon bonds at **deep discount**, or prices far lower than par value. When the bond matures, the accrued interest and the original investment add up to the bond's par value.

Organizations like to issue zeros because they can continue to use the loan money without paying periodic interest. Investors like zeros because they can buy more bonds for their money, and time the maturities to coincide with anticipated expenses. Zeros have two drawbacks: they are extremely volatile in the secondary market, so investors can't be sure how they'll make out if they need to sell; and, except in the case of municipal zeros, investors have to pay taxes every year on the interest they *would have received* had a payment been made.

TAX-FREE ZEROS
One tax break is for purchasers of tax-free zeros, such as municipal zero-coupon bonds.

This announcement is under no circumstances to be construed as an offer to sell or as a solicitation of an offer to buy any of these securities. The offering is made only by the Prospectus.

$575,000,000

...le Worldwide Corporation

...iquid Yield Option™ Notes due 2016
(Zero Coupon – Senior Secured)
...changeable for Shares of Common Stock of

Cole

...he Cole Company, Inc.

Price 24.067%

...ay be obtained in any State or jurisdiction in which this announcement is circulated ...r dealers or brokers as may lawfully offer these securities in such State or jurisdiction.

...Co., Inc.

Buying and Trading Bonds

Investors can buy bonds from brokers, banks or directly from certain issuers.

Newly issued bonds and those trading in the secondary market are available from stockbrokers and some banks. Treasuries, though, are sold at issue directly to investors without any intermediary—or any commission.

The Federal Reserve Banks handle transactions in new Treasury issues—bonds, bills and notes. To buy through the Federal Reserve, an investor establishes a **Treasury Direct** account, which keeps records of the transactions and pays interest directly into the investor's bank account. When the Treasury issue is held to maturity, the par value is repaid directly as well. However, investors can't use Treasury Direct to sell before maturity; bonds bought directly must be transferred into a brokerage account before they are traded. For more information on this, call the U.S. Treasury at 202-874-4000 or visit their home page at http://www.ustreas.gov.

Activity in the bond trading room is every bit as intense as a busy day on the floor of the NYSE.

THE PRICE OF BONDS

Price is a factor that keeps individual investors from investing heavily in bonds. While par value of a bond is usually $1,000, bonds are often sold in bundles, or packages, that require a much larger minimum investment. High individual bond prices also limit the amount of diversification an investor can achieve. As a result, many people prefer bond funds (see page 101), and many of the bonds themselves are bought by large institutional investors. Remember, bond funds never mature, so there is no guarantee that the principal will be repaid in full.

HOW TRADING WORKS

Most already-issued bonds are traded **over the counter** (OTC)—a term that really means over the phone. Bond dealers across the country are connected via electronic display terminals that give them the latest information on bond prices. A broker buying a bond uses a terminal to find out which dealer is currently offering the best price and calls that dealer to negotiate.

Brokerages also have inventories of bonds that they want to sell to clients looking for bonds of particular maturities or yields. Sometimes investors make out better buying bonds their brokers already own—or **make a market in**—as opposed to bonds the brokers have to buy from another brokerage.

The New York Stock Exchange and American Stock Exchange, despite their names, also list a large number of bonds. Their **bond rooms** are the scene of the same kind of brisk auction-style trading that occurs on a stock exchange trading floor.

THE COST ISSUE

While many newly issued bonds are sold without commission expense to the buyer—because the issuer absorbs the cost—all bond trades incur commission costs. The amount an investor pays to buy an older bond depends on the **commission** earned by the stockbroker involved—full-service or discount—and the size of the **markup** that's added to the bond.

A broker should reveal the markup, if asked. Or you can figure it out by finding out the current selling price of the bond and subtracting the buying price. The difference is the markup.

However, investors who trade bonds to take advantage of fluctuating interest rates may find that their profit outweighs the costs of trading.

MONDAY

9AM *T-bills on offer every Monday*

10AM

1 The U.S. Treasury offers 13-week and 26-week T-bills for sale every Monday.

2 Across the country, institutional investors (like pension funds and mutual funds planning to buy at least $500,000 worth of T-bills) buy up a major part of the issue by submitting competitive bids. Their bids must arrive at the Federal Reserve Bank by 1:00 pm Monday, the auction deadline, and state how much less than $10,000 they'd be willing to pay for each T-bill. For example, one fund might offer $9,800 and another $9,600.

11AM

NOON

3 At the same time, individual investors can submit a noncompetitive tender, or offer, by filling out a Treasury Direct form available at local banks. Investors indicate how many T-bills they want to buy and enclose a check for that number times $10,000. For example, someone wanting three bills would enclose a check for $30,000.

1PM *Deadline for all bids!*

2PM

4 All tenders, competitive and non-competitive, received by the Federal Reserve before the deadline are forwarded to the Treasury Department.

5 The Treasury accepts bids beginning with those closest to $10,000 until its quota is filled. That way, they raise the most possible revenue with the least possible debt.

3PM

Cut-off announcement

4PM

6 On Monday afternoon the Treasury announces the cut-off point, perhaps $9,700. News services report the information, and some bidders learn that they've bought T-bills, while others find out they bid too little.

5PM

7 The Treasury computes the average of the accepted bids and sells T-bills to all noncompetitive bidders for that price. It refunds to investors the difference between the $10,000 par value and the price paid. For example, if the price was $9,850, the refund would be $150 per bill or $450 for three.

8 When the bill matures, the buyers get back the full value—$10,000—of each bond they bought.

Other Bonds, Other Choices

Variety is the hallmark of the bond market—there's something for everyone.

Government agencies and government-sponsored enterprises issue bonds to fund specific projects or ongoing operations like mortgage lending, economic development, or flood control.

Agency bonds have a double appeal for investors. They pay higher interest than Treasuries, yet they're almost as safe. They're issued by full-fledged government agencies, like the Federal Housing Administration or the Federal Farm Credit Bank, or by agencies formerly operated by the government that are now public corporations like Fannie Mae (Federal National Mortgage Association).

READING THE TABLES

Government agency and similar issues are reported regularly, in tables that resemble those for Treasury issues. Mortgage-backed issues are included, as well as bonds sold by the World Bank, the Resolution Trust Company and the Tennessee Valley Authority.

MORTGAGE-BACKED BONDS

Mortgage-backed bonds are among the best known agency bonds. They're backed by pools of mortgages and issued by different organizations.

GINNIE MAES (GNMAs)

are bonds issued by the Government National Mortgage Association.

FREDDIE MACS (FHLs)

are bonds issued by the Federal Home Loan Mortgage Corporation.

FANNIE MAES (FNMAs)

are bonds issued by the Federal National Mortgage Association.

A number of states also have mortgage loan corporations that sell bonds.

GOVERNMENT AGENCY & SIMILAR ISSUES

Wednesday, April 7

Over-the-Counter mid-afternoon quotations based on large transactions, usually $1 million or more. Colons in bid-and-asked quotes represent 32nds; 101:01 means 101 1/32.

All yields are calculated to maturity, and based on the asked quote. * -- Callable issue, maturity date shown. For issues callable prior to maturity, yields are computed to the earliest call date for issues quoted above par, or 100, and to the maturity date for issues below par.

Source: Bear, Stearns & Co. via Street Software Technology Inc.

FNMA Issues

Rate	Mat.	Bid	Asked	Yld.
10.75	5-96	100:21	100:29	0.00
8.80	6-96	100:30	101:06	1.37
5.10	6-96	100:11	100:15	2.73
8.45	7-96	101:11	101:19	2.00
7.75	11-96	102:13	102:21	3.06
7.38	12-96	102:20	102:28	2.94

Federal Home Loan Bank

Rate	Mat.	Bid	Asked	Yld.
7.55	4-96	100:06	100:12	0.00
8.13	5-96	100:20	100:26	1.27
8.90	5-96	100:22	100:26	1.51
9.13	5-96	100:		

GNMA Mtge. Issues   a-Bond

Rate	Mat.	Bid	Asked	Yld.
6.50	30Yr	97:18	97:26	7.28
7.00	30Yr	100:13	100:21	6.99
7.50	30Yr	102:30	103:06	7.05
8.00	30Yr	105:08	105:16	6.97
8.50	30Yr	106:20	106:28	6.83
9.00	30Yr	107:29	108:05	6.55
9.50	30Yr	109:02	109:10	6.22
10.00	30Yr	110:18		
10.50	30Yr			
11.00	30			
11.50				

Rate	Mat.	Bid	Aske
7.55	4-96	100:06	100:1
8.13	5-96	100:20	100:2
8.90	5-96	100:22	100:2
9.13	5-96	100:24	100:3
10.75	5-96	100:30	101:0
7.08	6-96	100:25	100:2
7.00	7-96	101:01	101:0
7.75	7-96	101:10	101:1
9.00	7-96	101:22	101:2
11.70	7-96	102:16	102:2
6.22	8-96	101:03	101:0
7.45	8-96	101:17	101:2
8.18	8-96	101:25	102:0
11.95	8-96	103:08	103:1
6.21	9-96	101:11	101:1
7.95	9-96	102:04	102:
8.30	9-96	102:10	102:
6.09	10-96	101:13	101:
7.88	10-96	102:1	

Prices are quoted as **bid** and **asked**. The second Federal Home Loan Bank issue quoted here had a high bid of 100:20 ($1006.25). The lowest price asked was 100:26 ($1008.25). Like Treasuries, the decimals after the colon refer to 32nds.

This bond's **yield to maturity** is 1.27%—less than the bond's stated interest rate of 8.13%. Because the maturity date is just a month away (this chart is dated April 7), the buyer will receive almost no interest before the bond is retired. And even though the purchase price is more than par, only $1,000 will be repaid at maturity.

BONDS

U.S. SAVINGS BONDS

U.S. Savings Bonds are unique among bonds on several counts. Unlike other bonds discussed in this chapter, savings bonds aren't marketable—that is, they can't be traded among investors. People buy them for themselves or as gifts, and usually hold them until maturity, or even longer. Savings bonds go on paying interest, sometimes as long as 40 years after the date of issue.

In one way, savings bonds are the original zero-coupon bonds: they're sold at a **discount** from par (or face) value and are worth the full amount at maturity. The cost and maturity periods vary, based on the series of the bond and the interest being paid. Series EE bonds are sold in denominations of $50 to $10,000. They can be redeemed at maturity, or exchanged for Series HH.

Savings bonds are sold directly by the U.S. Treasury, and are tax-deferred from federal taxes until maturity. They're exempt from state and local taxes. When they mature, they can be redeemed at local banks.

BONDS FOR BAD TIMES

Bonds have been used throughout U. S. history to foot the cost of waging war. The first bonds the government ever authorized—in 1790—were to pay off the debts of the Revolution. And while income taxes helped pay for the Civil War and the two World Wars, **war bonds** played a big role in raising money—and popular support for the war effort.

Liberty Bonds, as World War I bonds were called, raised $16 million—an enormous sum for the time—and were traded on the New York Stock Exchange. Many people held onto their bonds after the war, for sentimental or patriotic reasons, a bonus for the government because they didn't have to be repaid.

During World War II, war bonds were big business, not only raising huge sums of money but generating a mini-industry to market and publicize them. Dramatic war bond posters publicized the sales effort.

Department stores featured bonds in window displays and made change in war stamps. Schools sold them—at a nickel a week. Radio stations produced special programming, and the entertainment industry was mobilized. Nothing on quite that scale ever happened before—or since.

te	Mat.	B
92	9-97*	100
25	11-98	11(
67	1-99*	9'
30	1-99	11(
60	6-99	11
45	7-99	1'
60	8-99	1
38	10-99	
60	1-	

Savings bonds are bearer bonds, which means that the person who has them can cash them. But they're also registered in the name of the person whose name appears on the front. That means lost bonds can be replaced by writing to: The Bureau of Public Debt, P.O. Box 1328, Parkersburg, West Virginia 26106-1328.

Mutual Funds: Putting It Together

A mutual fund is a collection of stocks, bonds or other securities owned by a group of investors and managed by a professional investment company.

Most investment professionals agree that it's smarter to own a variety of stocks and bonds than to gamble on the success of a few. But diversifying can be tough because buying a portfolio of individual stocks and bonds may be expensive. And knowing what to buy—and when—is a full-time job.

Mutual funds offer one solution: when investors put money into a fund, that amount is pooled with money from other investors to create much greater buying power than they would have investing on their own.

Since a fund can own hundreds of different securities, its success isn't dependent on one or two holdings. And the fund's managers keep constant tabs on the markets, adjusting the portfolio for the strongest possible performance.

How Mutual Funds Work

A LARGE NUMBER OF PEOPLE WITH MONEY TO INVEST BUY SHARES IN A MUTUAL FUND

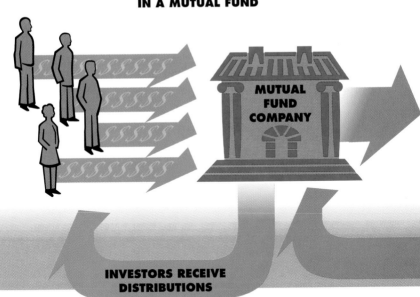

MUTUAL FUND COMPANY

INVESTORS RECEIVE DISTRIBUTIONS

PAYING OUT THE PROFITS

A mutual fund makes money in two ways: by earning dividends or interest on its investments and by selling investments that have increased in price. The fund pays out, or distributes, its profits (minus fees and expenses) to its own investors.

Income distributions are from the money the fund earns on its investments. **Capital gain distributions** are the profits from selling investments. Different funds pay their distributions on different schedules—from once a day to once

a year. Most funds offer investors the option of reinvesting all or part of their distributions in the fund.

Fund investors pay taxes on the distributions they receive from the fund, whether the money is reinvested or paid out in cash. But if a fund loses more than it makes in any year, it can offset future gains. Until profits equal the accumulated losses, distributions aren't taxable, although the share price may increase to reflect the profits.

A mutual fund company decides on an investment concept.

Then it issues a prospectus.

Finally, it sells shares.

CREATING A FUND

Mutual funds are created by investment advisors, brokerage houses and banks. The number of funds a mutual fund sponsor offers varies widely, from as few as two or three to as many as 200. At the time of publication, there were 400 fund groups, offering more than 6,000 different funds. In 1980 there were fewer than 600.

Each new fund has a professional manager, an investment objective and a plan, or investment program, it follows in building its portfolio. The funds are marketed to potential investors with ads in the financial press, through direct mailings and press announcements, and in some cases with the support of brokers or investment advisors who earn commissions selling them.

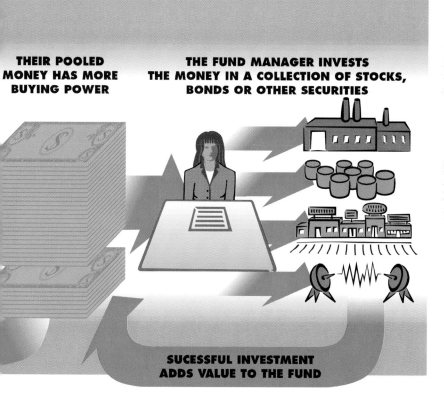

THEIR POOLED MONEY HAS MORE BUYING POWER

THE FUND MANAGER INVESTS THE MONEY IN A COLLECTION OF STOCKS, BONDS OR OTHER SECURITIES

SUCESSFUL INVESTMENT ADDS VALUE TO THE FUND

OPEN- AND CLOSED-END FUNDS

Most mutual funds are **open-end funds**. That means the fund sells as many shares as investors want. As money comes in, the fund grows; if investors sell, the number of outstanding shares drops. Sometimes open-end funds are closed to new investors when they grow too large to be managed effectively—though current shareholders can continue to invest money. When a fund is closed this way, the mutual fund company often creates a similar fund to capitalize on investor interest.

Closed-end funds more closely resemble stocks in the way they are traded. While these funds do invest in a variety of securities, they usually raise money only once, offer only a fixed number of shares, and are traded on an exchange (hence the name **exchange-traded** funds) or over-the-counter. The market price of a closed-end fund fluctuates in response to investor demand and to changes in the value of its holdings.

The Mutual Funds Market

Mutual funds never invest at random. Different funds buy in different markets, looking for particular products.

Most funds diversify their holdings by buying a wide variety of investments that correspond to the type of fund they are. A typical stock fund, for example, might own stock in 100 or more companies providing a range of different products and services. The advantage of diversity is that losses from some stocks will almost always be offset—or overshadowed—by gains in others.

On the other hand, some funds are extremely focused. For example:

- Precious metal funds trade chiefly in mining stocks.
- Sector funds buy shares in a particular industry like health care or electronics.
- High-yield bond funds buy risky bonds, to produce high income.

The appeal of focused funds is that when they're doing well, the return can be outstanding. The risk is that a change in the economy or in the sector can result in a large loss.

FUND TYPES

Mutual funds fall into three main categories:

- Stock or equity funds
- Bond funds
- Money market funds

Funds with specialized investment goals are introduced regularly. Some make a big splash in the market and then disappear, as equity option funds did in the late '80s.

STOCK FUNDS

The name says it all: Stock funds invest primarily in stocks. But their portfolios vary, depending on the fund's investment objective. For example, some stock funds invest in well-established companies that pay regular dividends. Others invest in young, high-technology firms or companies that have been operating below expectation for several years.

Like individual investors, funds buy **blue chip stocks** for income and safety; **growth stocks** for future gains; **value stocks** for stability and growth; and **cyclical stocks** to take advantage of economic booms. The major difference in buying a fund rather than individual stocks is the diversity an investor can achieve for the same amount of money.

There are several different types of stock, or equity, funds. A key distinction among them is that some stress growth, some income, and some a combination of the two. Some funds involve more risk to capital than others because they buy stock in emerging companies. The profits on all stock fund distributions are taxable, but no tax is due on the increased value of a fund until it's sold.

FIRST MUTUAL FUND

The first mutual fund company, called The Massachusetts Investors Trust, was created in Boston in 1924 as a private investment firm for its founders. It's still in business and operating seven funds that are open to all investors. By the company's estimate, $10,000 invested in 1924 would be worth $38 million today.

By 1996, there were more than 6,000 funds in the marketplace, with investments totaling more than $3 trillion.

BOND FUNDS

Like bonds, bond funds produce regular income. Unlike bonds, however, these funds have no maturity date and no guaranteed repayment of the amount you invest. On the plus side, though, the dividends can be reinvested in the fund to increase the principal. And buyers can invest a much smaller amount of money than they would need to buy a bond on their own—and get a diversified portfolio to boot. You can often start investing in a fund for $1,000, and make additional purchases for even smaller amounts.

Bond funds come in many varieties, with different investment goals and strategies. There are investment grade corporate bond funds and riskier junk bonds often sold under the promising label of high-yield funds. You can choose long- or short-term U.S. Treasury bond funds, funds that combine issues with different maturities, and a variety of municipal bond funds, including some limited to a particular state.

IT'S ALL IN THE FAMILY

Mutual fund companies usually offer a variety of funds—referred to as a family of funds—to their investors. Keeping your money in the family can make it easier to transfer money between funds, but like most families, some members do better than others.

MONEY MARKET FUNDS

Money market funds resemble savings accounts, although they don't have federal deposit insurance and they aren't guaranteed. For every dollar you put in, you can expect to get a dollar back, plus the interest your money earns from the investments the fund makes. Since these funds are low-risk, some investors prefer them to stock or bond funds. But the interest the funds pay is low when interest rates are low, and returns may fall behind those of long-term bonds and stocks. As an added appeal, most money market funds let investors write checks against their accounts. There's usually no charge for check-writing—although there may be a per-check minimum.

The two main categories of bond funds are **taxable** and **tax-free**. Distributions earned on corporate and U.S. government funds (including Treasuries and agency funds) are taxed. There's no federal tax on municipal bond fund distributions, and no state or local taxes for investors who live in the municipality that issues the underlying bonds. New York City residents, for example, can buy **triple tax-free** New York funds and keep all their earnings.

Money market funds also come in two varieties, **taxable** and **tax-free**. Taxable funds buy the best yielding short-term corporate or government issues available, while tax-free funds are limited to buying primarily municipal debt. Taxable funds pay higher dividends than tax-free funds, but investors must pay tax on any distributions they receive. In either case, the rate a fund pays tends to be higher than money market accounts or CDs.

Targeted Investments

Mutual funds aim at particular targets. To hit them, the funds make certain types of investments.

INVESTMENT OBJECTIVE

Every mutual fund—stock, bond or money market—is established with a specific investment objective that fits into one of three basic goals:

- **Current income**
- **Future growth**
- **Both income and growth**

To achieve its objective, the fund invests in securities it believes will produce the results it wants.

For example, a Government National Mortgage Association (GNMA) fund is designed to produce regular current income and return of capital. To do that, it buys bonds backed by a pool of government-insured home mortgages that have different maturity dates. The income the fund gets as the underlying mortgages are paid—and paid off—is the source of shareholder distributions.

THE RISK FACTOR

There is always the **risk** that a fund won't hit its target. Some funds are, by definition, riskier than others. For example, a fund that invests in small new companies takes the chance that some of their investments will do poorly because they believe some, at least, will do very well. A GNMA fund runs a risk, too, that the interest rates will drop and many mortgage holders will refinance their loans. Repaid loans and smaller payments mean less income for the fund. For most investors, rising interest rates will decrease your investments' value.

Risk is measured both by **volatility**, or how much the return on a fund and its per-share value can change in the short term, and by **predictability** of overall results.

FUNDS TAKE AIM

These charts group funds in three categories by investment objective. They also illustrate the correlation between a fund's objective and the risks it faces.

LITTLE RISK

investment objective	kind of fund	fund characteristics	what the fund buys
steady income	U.S. Treasury bond and agency bond	safe government-backed securities; only risks are interest rate changes and inflation	U.S. Treasury bonds and bonds issued by government agencies
steady income	high-rated corporate bond	steady income and little risk	corporate bonds, with maturities dependent on type of fund
tax-free income	high-rated municipal bond	steady, slightly higher income and little risk	municipal bonds in various maturities
income	short/intermediate-term taxable and tax-free bond	small risk of loss and steady, if less, income; less influenced by changes in interest rate	different types of bonds in 1-10 year maturities, depending on type of fund
income and currency gains	international money market	risk tied to changes in currency value; expectation of higher return than U.S. money markets	Non-U.S. CDs and short-term government securities
safety and some income	taxable and tax-free money market	low risk to capital; income based on current interest rates	CDs and very short-term government, corporate and municipal debt

MODERATELY RISKY

investment objective	kind of fund	fund characteristics	what the fund buys
strong growth plus some current income	growth and income	growth and current income; average risk of loss	stocks that pay high dividends and show good growth
moderate income and good growth	equity income	income and good growth; average risk of loss	blue chip stocks and utilities that pay high income
income and growth	balanced	reasonable income and growth; limited risk of losses	part stocks and preferred stocks (usually 60%) and part bonds (40%)
primarily income	income	income, but with a little growth; limited risk of losses in down market	primarily bonds, but some dividend-paying stocks
high income	international and global bond	high income; better yield when dollar is weak and worse when dollar is strong	bonds in overseas markets (international funds) and overseas plus U.S. markets (global funds)
good income and regular return of capital	Ginnie Mae	income and return of capital, though value and return dependent on changes in interest rates	securities backed by a pool of government-insured mortgages
imitate the stock market	index	average gains and losses for the market the index tracks	stocks represented in the index the fund tracks

RISKY

investment objective	kind of fund	fund characteristics	what the fund buys
above average long-term gains	aggressive growth funds, also called capital appreciation funds	very volatile and speculative; risk of above-average losses to get above-average gains; small, if any, dividends	stocks of new or under-valued companies expected to increase in value
long-term gains	small company growth	very volatile and specula-tive; risk of above-average losses to get highest gains	stocks in small companies traded on the stock markets or over-the-counter
hedge against turmoil in financial markets	gold and precious metals	extremely volatile and spec-ulative, with big risk of loss	stocks in gold and other precious metal mining companies and some bullion
growth	sector	extremely volatile funds dependent on right market timing to produce results	stocks in one particular industry, like energy or transportation
international growth	international equity	volatile; gains and losses depend on stock prices and currency fluctuation	stocks in non-U.S. companies
above average growth	growth	volatile; risk of larger losses to get higher gains	stocks in mid-sized or large companies whose earnings are expected to rise quickly
world growth	global equity	risk of larger losses in falling markets to capture gains in rising ones; risk of changes in currency values	stocks in U.S. and non-U.S. companies
high current income	high-yield bond (taxable and tax-free)	very high income from high-risk bonds in danger of default	low-rated and junk corporate (taxable) and municipal (tax-free) bonds
responsible growth	conscience	average growth with risk of higher losses because of restrictions on investment	stocks in companies that meet the ethical standards of the fund

Special Purpose Funds

Mutual fund companies have expanded their horizons—and the opportunities they offer to investors—by developing specialty funds.

Stock and bond funds are the oldest and most enduring mutual funds. But as mutual funds have grown in popularity, a greater variety of funds has become available. Most of these newer, specialized funds have been developed to appeal to people who are looking for very specific investments, such as getting tax-free returns or putting money into ethically sound businesses.

SPECIAL INVESTMENT OBJECTIVES

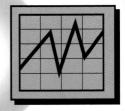

INDEX FUNDS

Index funds are designed to produce the same return that investors would get if they owned all the stocks in a particular index—like the S&P 500. While this diversity would be overwhelming for an individual, it's all in a day's work for an index fund. There are currently more than 140 funds—tracking almost every known index for large, mid-cap and small companies, as well as bond market indexes and several international equity indexes.

Index funds are popular because the performances of the major stock and bond indexes often surpass the returns that professional mutual fund money managers achieve by following a particular investment theory. Investing in an index fund can eliminate having to decide among specific stock or bond funds. It can also provide a balance to other investments.

But there are some limitations. In certain economic cycles, individual fund performance can leave index funds in the dust.

EFFICIENT MARKETS

An efficient market isn't one that works quicker or smarter. Rather, it's the object of constant, intensive analysis, and the information is available to everyone, almost immediately. Inefficient markets, conversely, aren't as widely analyzed and can offer enormous opportunity for profit to savvy fund managers who track them.

QUANT FUNDS

The name comes from their quantitative investment style—they aim to beat the index funds they imitate by relying on statistical analysis to decide which securities will top the benchmarks. Instead of buying all the stocks in the S&P 500, they buy comparable stocks which their numbers tell them will turn a higher profit.

APPEALING TO INVESTORS

Mutual funds provide a variety of investing opportunities designed to make investing easier. Here are some of the advantages:

- Allow purchase of fractional shares
- Provide liquidity (easy access to money)
- Are explicit about investment goals
- Offer simple reinvestment options
- Fund information is easy to get

- You get professional management
- Don't have to accumulate large sums to invest
- Can get money easily in an emergency, although perhaps losing some capital
- Can choose fund to meet goal
- Can build investment through automatic deposits

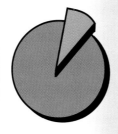

TAX-FREE FUNDS

Although all stock funds (also known as **equity** funds) and most bond funds are taxable, it's possible to invest in a variety of mutual funds that pay tax-free distributions. Tax-free income is particularly appealing to people in the highest tax brackets, since they may come out ahead at tax time even if they've earned the slightly lower yield that's typical of tax-free funds.

The biggest tax savings occur when a person who lives in a high-tax state—like California—buys a fund that specializes in bonds issued there. The interest is free of state and federal taxes. And when a fund buys bonds issued by a municipality like New York City, the interest is triple tax-free for residents who invest in the fund.

The dilemma that many funds face is finding enough high-quality investments to meet investor demands. This can be especially hard for tax-free funds, and even harder for single state funds.

SECTOR FUNDS

Sector funds focus on the stocks of a particular industry or segment of the economy, like technology, health care or financial services. In that sense, they are out of step with the underlying principle behind mutual funds—diversity. While a sector fund is more diversified than a single stock, there is nothing in the fund portfolio to offset a downturn in the sector.

Since sectors are highly volatile, they offer an opportunity for big profits to investors who ride the right wave. However, one year's hot sector may be dead the next. An example is the sharp downturn in pharmaceuticals in 1993, or high-tech stocks in 1996, after a period of substantial growth.

Precious metal funds resemble sector funds since all their money is invested in mining stocks and bullion, but they're more predictable. When inflation is high or there's political turmoil, precious metal funds tend to do well because they are a hedge against instability.

GREEN AND OTHER CONSCIENCE FUNDS

Mutual fund companies have also created funds to attract investors whose strong political or social commitments make them unwilling to invest in companies whose business practices are at odds with their beliefs. A green fund might avoid tobacco companies, companies with poor environmental records, or those that sell certain products in underdeveloped countries. While green funds rarely make it to the top of performance charts because of the restrictions on what they can buy, many have posted at least average growth.

Unlike other specialty funds, green funds aren't treated as a special category in mutual fund tables or by Lipper Analytical Services. Investors who feel strongly about where their money goes may have to do extra research to find a fund they're comfortable with. Some special interest groups sponsor their own funds or recommend particular funds.

Inside a Mutual Fund

The work of a mutual fund goes around the clock, managing the fund and serving the investor.

A mutual fund company, called a **fund sponsor**, has two distinct yet intertwined businesses: providing services to its clients and making a profit. Each fund, or closely related group of funds, is run by a professional manager responsible for both its day-to-day operations and for its successful performance. In fact, the skill of the manager is so closely linked to the success of a fund that many experts advise investors to pick a fund based on the manager—and even to drop a fund if a star manager leaves.

A typical fund depends on a team of employees, including financial analysts, accountants, traders and sales people, plus support staff. Equally crucial are the programs, computers and other electronic equipment—and the people who keep them running.

Managing the Fund

Each fund buys and sells securities in specific financial markets. A stock fund, for example, buys and sells shares through brokers on the stock markets and over-the-counter. Because they trade in large volumes, mutual funds are known as **institutional traders** (see page 50).

While clients may not be able to talk to a telephone representative at the fund until around 8:00 am local time, reports on the fund's previous day's performance are available in the papers and on computer services well before then.

Every day the fund's manager and analysts digest how the markets did the day before, where the fund stands in relation to other funds and the benchmark indexes, and what economic news is affecting the fund's value.

Serving the Investor

Funds are never static. Money moves in and out constantly—in staggering amounts. In 1995, for example, $164 billion poured into stock and bond funds. At the rate of approximately three million sales transactions a day, U.S. mutual fund companies act on 780 million orders a year.

Mail pours into mutual fund offices by the ton. Each piece must be opened, coded with an account number, and put in the right "in" basket. Checks are credited to the right client accounts at the day's closing price. Then they're shipped off to the bank.

Checks and confirmations from the previous day's transactions are mailed out to clients, making good on the claim that mutual funds are among the most liquid investments.

A typical mutual fund mailroom handles about 15,000 pieces of mail in one day—that's 3,750,000 pieces a year.*

* Based on 1994 statistics.

OTHER WAYS TO BUY FUNDS

One big question investors face when buying mutual funds is whether to buy directly from the fund—the process that's described here—or through a broker, bank, or other financial agent. They may wonder, for example, whether professionals can identify better performing funds than they can pick on their own.

The bottom line, statistically at least, is that direct purchase funds do at least as well and cost less than those bought through an agent. Among the reasons: Brokers and other agents sometimes push funds sponsored by the companies they work for, and sometimes buy the same no-loads people could buy themselves, tacking an advertising fee on top.

By the time a typical fund manager leaves the office any given day, $150 million in securities have been traded.*

Fund managers and analysts are always in the market for new securities that meet their investment objectives. Their research staff provides up-to-the-minute price information and analysis.

Trading managers authorize the buy and sell orders. Traders, looking for the best price, keep their eyes on the computer screen and their hands on the telephone. Other employees keep a running count of the fund's balance sheet.

Details of the fund's current value and the change from the day before are calculated by the staff and sent to the National Association of Securities Dealers, which disseminates the prices to news organizations.

Investors open accounts, send checks, or have money transferred into their accounts throughout the day. As the orders are processed, the money is invested in shares of the fund. Written confirmations follow all the telephone and electronic transactions. As a result of this follow-up documentation, the industry has extremely high quality control.

Telephone reps keep busy answering client questions and acting on orders. Conversations are recorded to back up the actions the reps take. There are very few transactions that can't be done by phone—as long as the client signs up for the services when the account is opened. Fund transfers, though, have to go to accounts registered in the same name.

At most funds, customers can talk to a service rep after the markets close, placing orders that will be filled on the next day. After the people go home, automated phone systems provide details about earnings, balances and recent trades, as well as other account and performance information. Funds also provide such information online.

Mutual Funds Quotations

As the popularity of mutual funds has grown, so has the information about them.

As investors have put more money into mutual funds, there's been a revolution in the way that fund performance is reported. Many daily newspapers track the return on individual funds, changes in share price and the cost of buying particular funds. Some newspapers print more comprehensive fund information on different days during the week.

The funds themselves supply the basic information daily to the National Association of Securities Dealers (NASD), which in turn, distributes it to the public and to analytical services.

Funds vary greatly in size, although each must have a minimum number of shareholders, as well as a minimum asset value, to be listed.

MUTUAL FUNDS

NAV	Net Chg	Fund Name	Inv Obj	YTD %ret	4Wk %ret	Total Return			Max Init Chrg	Exp Ratio
						1Yr	3Yr-R	5Yr-R		
		Columbia Funds:								
20.78	+0.05	Balance	MP	+5.3	+0.4	+11.0 C	+10.0 B	NS ..	0.00	0.69
20.59	+0.05	ComStk	GI	+11.3	+1.8	+18.3 B	+15.1 B	NS ..	0.00	0.80
12.79	+0.03	Fixed	AB	−1.0	−0.9	+3.7 B	+4.0 B	+7.7 C	0.00	0.65
8.16	+0.01	Govt	SG	+1.2	−0.4	+4.2 C	+3.8 C	+5.6 D	0.00	0.79
32.68	+0.24	Grth	GR	+9.5	+1.9	+12.7 C	+14.6 B	+15.2 B	0.00	0.75
9.05	...	HiYld r	HC	+3.5	+0.5	+8.7 E	NS ..	NS ..	0.00	1.00
14.25	+0.06	IntlStk	IL	+9.0	+0.6	+13.4 A	+8.5 B	NS ..	0.00	1.54
12.03	+0.03	Muni	SS	+0.7	−0.9	+3.6 D	+3.5 C	+6.2 E	0.00	0.57
14.09	+0.05	ReEEq	SF	+14.0	+3.9	+23.2 A	NS ..	NS ..	0.00	1.18
23.33	+0.18	Specl	MC	+8.8	+3.2	+9.3 D	+14.9 C	+17.4 A	0.00	0.98
		Commerce Funds:								
27.45	+0.16	AggrGr	MC	+6.7	+1.7	+7.6 D	NS ..	NS ..	3.50	1.32
23.05	+0.14	Balanced	MP	+4.9	+0.3	+9.4 C	NS ..	NS ..	3.50	1.13
18.61	+0.06	Bond	IB	−1.8	−0.9	+3.0 D	NS ..	NS ..	3.50	0.88
27.39	+0.20	Growth	GR	+10.9	+1.6	+17.4 B	NS ..	NS ..	3.50	1.11
20.60	+0.01	IntlEq	IL	+7.1	−0.2	+9.9 B	NS ..	NS ..	3.50	1.81
18.21	+0.02	STGovt	SG	+1.0	−0.3	+4.1 C	NS ..	NS ..	3.50	0.68
		Common Sense:								
18.26	+0.16	EmGrIIA p	MC	+14.5	+3.5	NA ..	NS ..	NS ..	5.50	2.75
18.04	+0.15	EmGrIIB t	MC	+13.8	+3.4	NA ..	NS ..	NS ..	0.00	3.49
10.15	+0.03	Govt	LG	−1.8	−0.9	+2.4 C	+3.0 B	+6.2 D	6.75	0.83
17.60	+0.10	GrInc	GI	+8.3	+2.2	+15.5 C	+13.1 D	+13.3 C	8.50	0.96
17.60	+0.10	GrIncIIA p	GI	NA	NA	NA ..	NA ..	NA ..	5.50	2.44
17.5	+0.10	Gr..B t	GI			NA ..	NA ..	NA ..	0.00	3.15

NAV is the fund's **net asset value**. A fund's NAV is the dollar value of one share of stock in the fund, the price a fund pays you per share when you sell. It's figured by totaling the value of all the fund's holdings, minus expenses, and dividing by the number of shares. For example, the NAV of the Columbia Growth Fund is $32.68.

Net change is the difference between today's NAV and the NAV on the previous trading day. A (+) with the number means the fund's value is up, and a (−) means it's down.

Generally, the change is small—less than 1%.

The **mutual fund company's name** appears first. Then its different funds are listed in alphabetical order.

r after the fund name means the fund charges a fee to redeem shares for cash.

p after the fund name means the fund charges a fee for marketing and distribution costs, also known as **12b-1 fees**.

t after the fund name means both r and p apply: you pay redemption and 12b-1 fees.

Every Friday in The Wall Street Journal, each fund is ranked by return performance, based on several time periods. In this example, the third ranking covers performance over the last five years. The code assigns an **A** to funds, like Columbia Special Fund, that rank among the top 20%, on down to an **E** for those that rank in the bottom 20%. When no ranking appears, it's usually because the fund didn't exist at the beginning of the time period.

Many mutual funds charge a commission, or **load**, to buyers. The **maximum initial charge** column tells you the commission as a percentage of your total investment. If this number is 0.00, that means you pay no sales commission when you buy. While some funds charge a commission when you sell, others are no-load funds, which means there is no commission when you buy or sell.

Expense ratio is the total of all charges and fees, including distribution fees, expressed as a percentage.

Total return is the percentage of gain (+) or loss (−) on an investment, assuming all distributions have been reinvested.

Many newspapers report total return for every mutual fund on a year-to-date (YTD) basis. In addition, they often show annual and multi-year returns on a weekly basis.

Here, Diversified's Balance Fund is up 6.3% since the beginning of the current calendar year, 0.5% in the last 4 weeks and 10.9% in the last full year. It's too new to have a longer performance history.

QUOTATIONS

Net Chg	Fund Name	Inv Obj	YTD %ret	4Wk %ret	Total Return			Max Init Chrg	Exp Ratio	NAV
					1Yr	3Yr-R	5Yr-R			
	Diversified Funds:									17.66
0.09	AggrEq p	MC	NS	+3.9	NS	NS ..	NS ..	0.00	NA	19.69
0.05	Balance p	MP	+6.3	+0.5	+10.9 C	NS ..	NS ..	0.00	0.87i	21.93
0.20	EqGrow p	GR	+10.3	+1.2	+6.6 E	NS ..	NS ..	0.00	1.01i	10.07
0.05	EqInc p	EI	+8.2	+1.9	+17.0 C	NS ..	NS ..	0.00	0.90i	10.00
0.05	EqVal p	GI	NS	+2.6	NS	NS ..	NS ..	0.00	NA	10.51
0.03	GovCorp p	IB	−1.5	−0.9	+4.1 A	NS ..	NS ..	0.00	0.85i	9.80
0.09	Gro&Inc p	GI	+12.0	+1.3	+21.9 A	NS ..	NS ..	0.00	1.03i	10.26
0.01	HiQual p	SB		−0.1	+5.2 B	NS ..	NS ..	0.00	1.00i	10.42
0.02	IntGvt p	SG			NS	NS ..	NS ..	0.00	NA	10.09
0.01	IntlEq p	IL				NS ..	NS ..	0.00	NA	9.42
0.05	SAFAgg	GI								10.06
0.01	SAFCon	M								
0.03	SAFMod	M								
0.13	SpecEq p	SC								
	Dodge & Cox:									
0.18	Balan	M								
0.03	Inco	A								
0.25	Stock	G								
0.13	Dom Social	G								
0.11	DomInsgtGr	C								
	Dreyfus:									
0.04	A Bond									
0.42	AggGr									
0.11	Aprec									

MUTUAL FUND OBJECTIVES

Categories compiled by The Wall Street Journal, based on classifications by Lipper Analytical Services Inc.

STOCK FUNDS

Capital Appreciation (CP): Seeks rapid capital growth, often through high portfolio turnover.

Growth (GR): Invests in companies expecting higher than average revenue and earnings growth.

Growth & Income (GI): Pursues both price and dividend growth. Category includes S&P 500 Index funds.

Equity Income (EI): Tends to favor stock with the highest dividends.

Small Company Growth (SC): Shares of lesser-known, small companies.

MidCap (MC): Shares of middle-sized companies.

Sector (SE): Health/Biotechnology; Natural Resources; Environmental; Science & Technology; Specialty & Miscellaneous; Utility; Financial Services; Real Estate; Gold Oriented funds.

Global Stock (GL): Includes small company global. Can invest in U.S.

International Stock (IL) (non-U.S.): International; European region; Pacific region; Pacific Ex-Japan; Japanese; Latin American; Canadian; Emerging Markets; inter-national small company.

TAXABLE BOND FUNDS

Short-Term (SB): Ultrashort obligation and short, short-intermediate investment grade corporate debt.

Short-Term U.S. (SG): Short-term U.S. Treasury; Short, short-intermediate U.S. government funds.

Intermediate (IB): Investment grade corporate debt of up to 10-year maturity.

Intermediate U.S. (IG): U.S. Treasury and government agency debt.

Long-Term (AB): Corporate A-rated.

Long-Term U.S. (LG): U.S. Treasury; Corporate BBB-rated.

General U.S. Taxable (GT): U.S. government; zero coupon.

High Yield Taxable (HC): Can invest in different types of bonds.

Mortgage (MG): Ginnie Mae and general high yield high-risk bonds.

World (WB): Short world multi-market; Adjustable-Rate Mortgage. Income foreign bonds; Emerging-Markets debt. short world single-market and general world

INVESTMENT OBJECTIVE

The two-letter abbreviation following the fund name describes its investment objective. A chart explaining the objectives is printed every day in the Mutual Funds Quotations.

Each category includes from one to eight closely related but differently named objectives. **Sector funds**, for example, are abbreviated as SE and include all the stock funds that invest in narrowly defined segments of the economy, like utilities or financial services. SG stands for short-term government bonds, including Treasury bonds and U.S. government funds.

Tracking Fund Performance

There are several formulas for measuring mutual fund performance. The bottom line is whether the fund is making money now—and how it has done in the past.

Whether a mutual fund aims for current income, long-term growth, or a combination of the two, there are three ways to track its performance and judge whether it is profitable. Investors can evaluate a fund by:

- Following changes in share price, or **net asset value (NAV)**
- Figuring **yield**
- Calculating **total return**

They can compare a fund's performance to similar funds offered by different companies, or they can evaluate the fund in relation to other ways the money could have been invested—stocks or bonds, for example.

Because performance can be figured differently for each type of investment, there isn't a simple formula for comparing funds to individual securities.

NAV CHANGE

$$\frac{\text{value of fund} - \text{expenses}}{\text{number of shares}} = \text{NAV}$$

for example

$$\frac{\$52,500,000}{3,500,000} = \$15$$

A fund's **share price**, or **net asset value (NAV)**, is the dollar value of one share of the fund's stock after expenses. NAV is figured by dividing the current value of the fund by the number of shares. The NAV increases when the value of the holdings increases. For example, if a share of a stock fund costs $15 today and $9 a year ago, there's been a **capital gain** (or profit) of $6 a share (or about 66%) before expenses.

YIELD

$$\frac{\text{distribution per share}}{\text{price per share}} = \text{Yield (\%)}$$

for example

$$\frac{\$ \ .58}{\$10.00} = 5.8\%$$

Yield measures the amount of income a fund provides as a percentage of its current price, or NAV. A long-term bond fund with a NAV of $10 paying a 58¢ dividend per share provides a 5.8% yield. Investors can compare the yield on a mutual fund with the current yield on comparable investments to decide which is performing better. Bond fund performance, for example, is often tracked in relation to individual bonds (see pages 82-83).

TOTAL RETURN

$$\frac{\text{current value}}{\text{cost of initial investment}} = \text{Return (\%)}$$

for example

$$\frac{\$15,000}{\$ \ 5,000} = 300\%$$

Total return tells investors how much—as a percentage—they've made or lost on an investment over time. It's figured by dividing the current value of an investment, plus income and capital gain distributions, by the cost of the initial investment. (The current value is the number of shares times the NAV.) If the distributions have all been reinvested, they are already included in the current value and don't have to be added as a separate item. For example, an investment worth $15,000 that cost $5,000 has a return of 300%.

MUTUAL FUNDS

USING BENCHMARKS...

Lipper Analytical Services provides daily total return indexes for nine categories of mutual funds. The gain (+) or loss (–) a particular fund has shown over the last week and since the end of last year can be compared to the performance of all the funds in that group.

In this example, **Capital Appreciation Funds** have had a total return of 1.06% since last week and 3.88% since December 31. **Growth Funds** are doing better for the year, up 5.28%.

Another measure of a fund's performance is how it stacks up against the movement of a major market index that reports on the same kind of investments the fund makes. For example, a gain or loss in a general stock fund could be compared to the direction of the Standard & Poor's 500 Stock Index, while a bond fund could be compared to a Government/Corporate Bond Index. However, some index figures don't include reinvested dividends or interest, or the costs of buying and selling, so they can't be compared directly to total return figures.

LIPPER INDEXES

Friday, June 25

Indexes	Prelim. Close	Percentage chg. since Prev.	Wk ago	Dec. 31
Capital Appreciation	389.43	+ 0.85	+ 1.06	+ 3.88
Growth Fund	706.55	+ 0.56	+ 0.83	+ 5.28
Small Co. Growth	389.40	+ 1.02	+ 0.90	+ 2.76
Growth & Income Fd	1074.31	+ 0.17	+ 0.67	+ 6.28
Equity Income Fd	695.31	+ 0.16		
Science & Tech Fd				

Mutual Fund Scorecard/Balanced

INVESTMENT OBJECTIVE: Investment balance through holding both stocks and bonds; must have 25% minimum in stocks and bonds

(Ranked by 12-month return)	NET ASSET VALUE[1] SEP. 23	TOTAL RETURN[2] IN PERIOD ENDING SEP. 23				ASSETS JUNE 30 (In millions)
		4 WEEKS	SINCE 12/31	12 MONTHS	5 YEARS	
TOP 15 PERFORMERS						
Cgm Tr:Mutual Fund[3]	$30.84	1.12%	20.17%	30.98%	127.76%	$710.5
Parnassus:Balanced[3]	18.38	0.77	16.72	26.31	**	7.0
Evergreen Foundation[3]	13.45	0.45	15.11	23.48	**	133.0
Eclipse:Balanced[3]	19.75	0.25	15.58	21.80	**	18.4
BOTTOM 10 PERFORMERS						
Pax World Fund[3]	$13.67	– 0.94%	– 2.48%	– 1.33%	65.83%	$503.3
Green Century Balanced[3]	10.20	– 0.20	– 2.20	0.03	**	2.8
Principal Pres:Balanced[4]	10.29	– 0.77	– 0.15	2.53	**	16.6
Pasadena Inv:Balanced	21.69	0.00	– 0.32	3.45	94.11	8?.?
?v Cox Balanced	?.??	18.99	18.48	93.36	371.1	
Evergreen American Ret[3]	12.04	0.42	13.59	18.33	74.26	28.6
AVG. FOR CATEGORY		0.05%	8.63%	13.31%	79.97%	
NUMBER OF FUNDS		110	98	83	46	

...AND MAKING COMPARISONS

A mutual fund's performance is also measured in relation to other funds. For example, comparing one fund's results with others that have the same objective shows how successful that fund has been. Every day many newspapers highlight a particular type of fund, giving performance details for the top and bottom funds in the category.

In this example, the funds invest in a balance of stocks and bonds. The top-ranking fund has performed significantly better than the average for the category over the last five years—with a total return of 127.76% compared with 79.97%. It's done more than twice as well during the last year—30.98% compared to 13.31%—and is also stronger than average for the last four weeks.

In contrast, several funds in the bottom 10 had five-year returns that came close to or exceeded the norm, but have fallen off dramatically in the last year. (The ** means the funds weren't operating five years ago.)

The Prospectus

The prospectus provides a detailed roadmap of a fund—covering everything from its objective and fees to its portfolio holdings and manager.

Mutual funds are tightly regulated by the Securities and Exchange Commission (SEC). One of the cardinal rules has been that all potential investors have access to a **prospectus** before they buy into a fund. The prospectus must be explicit about objectives, management, fees, performance and all the details of the fund's operation.

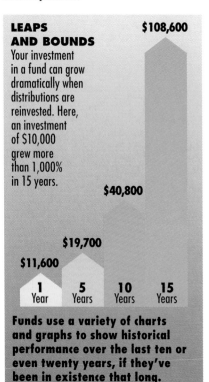

LEAPS AND BOUNDS
Your investment in a fund can grow dramatically when distributions are reinvested. Here, an investment of $10,000 grew more than 1,000% in 15 years.

$108,600

$40,800

$19,700

$11,600

| 1 Year | 5 Years | 10 Years | 15 Years |

Funds use a variety of charts and graphs to show historical performance over the last ten or even twenty years, if they've been in existence that long.

THE FUND'S OPERATION

The prospectus explains the programs and policies the fund's management uses to achieve its investment goals.

Investors have the right to vote on changes a fund proposes in its underlying financial policies. Since mutual fund investors are actually shareholders of the fund, they vote just as corporate shareholders do. Like corporate shareholders, too, their votes affect only major issues. In most cases they don't vote on day-to-day matters like the fee structure.

FEES

A summary of fees and expenses appears near the beginning of the prospectus. The fees can range up to 3%, with no-load bond fees at the bottom and international equity load funds at the top.

- **Management fees** are annual charges to administer the fund. All funds charge this fee, though the amount varies from a fraction of one percent to over two percent.
- **Distribution fees** (called 12b-1 fees) cover marketing and advertising expenses. About half of all funds charge them.
- **Redemption fees** are assessed when shares are sold to discourage frequent in-and-out trading. In contrast, a **deferred sales load**, a kind of exit fee, often applies only during a specific period—say the first five years—and then disappears.
- **Exchange fees** can apply when money is shifted from one fund to another within the same mutual fund company.

PORTFOLIO TURNOVER RATE

All open-end mutual funds trade securities regularly—some more regularly than others. A fund's **portfolio turnover rate** reveals how much buying and selling is going on. The range is enormous, sometimes reaching as high as 200% to 400% annually. In general, high turnovers mean higher stockbroker expenses. That means the fund needs higher returns to offset the cost. There's no rule that says which approach works better, since both styles can produce high performance results.

The financial information that the fund reports to the NASD, the National Association of Securities Dealers, is used by independent analysts to determine how the fund is doing.

THE NUTS AND BOLTS...

The prospectus also tells investors how to buy and sell shares in the fund, as well as how to use all the fund's services.

Minimum investments exist for most funds. A higher amount is required for opening an account than for adding to it. Sometimes the minimum initial investment is as low as $500, sometimes as high as $100,000.

Investment options let people buy over the phone, by mail, through a broker, or with automatic direct deposit.

Reinvestment options let shareholders decide what to do with the money they earn. They can plow their distributions back into the fund, take the money in cash, or some combination of the two.

Exchange services let people transfer money from one fund to another.

Redemption options provide lots of ways for shareholders to get their money out of the fund. They include checks, wire transfers, electronic transfers and automatic withdrawal plans.

Check writing privileges let shareholders use checks to redeem their holdings or pay their bills. However, redeeming stock and bond funds by check has tax consequences since there's always a profit or loss on the investment. Money market funds are the only ones that really work like checking accounts.

...AND THE GADGETS

Most funds have automated telephone services that provide 24-hour information on many details of an account. By using a series of codes, shareholders can find out their account balance, as well as the fund's current yield, price and dividends. The same information is available through many online computer services. And as the digital revolution expands, the information options will undoubtedly follow suit.

Prospectus

International Equity Funds

- **Statement of Objective**
- **Investor Programs**
- **Fund Fees and Expenses**
- **Fund Performance**
- **Result of $1,000 Investment**
- **How To Purchase Shares**
- **Shareholder Services**
- **How To Redeem Shares**

While a prospectus provides all the details of a fund's operation, it also tries to portray the fund in the best possible terms. Smart investors carefully sift through all the information.

International Funds

If someone needed to invent a reason for the existence of mutual funds, investing abroad might be the best one.

Mutual funds that invest in overseas markets have become extremely popular in recent years. And for good reason. In addition to diversity, professional management and ease of investing, overseas funds give even small investors access to markets they couldn't enter on their own. Overseas stock, bond and money market funds appeal to a variety of interests. While they're often referred to generically as **international funds**, there are actually four specific categories of funds: international, global, regional and country.

INTERNATIONAL FUNDS, also known as **Overseas Funds**, invest in foreign stock or bond markets. By spreading investments throughout the world, these funds balance risk by owning securities not only in mature, slow-growing economies, but also in the booming economies of many small nations.

GLOBAL FUNDS, also called **World Funds**, include U.S. stocks or bonds in their portfolios as well as those from other countries. The manager moves the assets around, depending on which markets are doing best at the time or have the brightest prospects. That might mean that the percentage invested in U.S. stocks could vary widely, depending on their performance in comparison with others around the world.

> Despite what the name suggests, global funds sometimes invest up to 75% of their assets in U.S. companies.

REGIONAL FUNDS concentrate on particular geographic areas like the Pacific Rim, Latin America or Europe. Many mutual fund companies that began by offering international or global funds have added regional funds to capitalize on the growing interest in overseas investing and on the strength of particular parts of the world economy.

Like the more comprehensive funds, regional funds invest in several different countries so that even if one market is in the doldrums, the others may be booming.

> Regional funds work well when the countries they include are small— like the Netherlands— and may not market enough securities to justify a single country fund.

EUROPE

THE RISK OVERSEAS

Investors who put money into overseas funds don't have to deal directly with currency fluctuations or calculating foreign taxes—they're handled by the fund. But the value of any fund that invests in other countries is directly affected not only by market conditions but by exchange rates.

Overseas bond funds are less dependable than U.S. funds as income producers because changes in the dollar's value directly affect the fund's earnings. For example, if a bond fund is earning high interest, but the country's currency is weak against the dollar, the yield is less. If a fund earns £100 when £1 equals $2,

the yield is $200. But if the pound drops in value, and £1 equals $1.50, the yield is only $150, and the fund's return plummets.

So if international markets are paying high dividends, a U.S. investor can make money, especially when the dollar is weak. However, if the dollar strengthens by 10% during a year that an overseas stock fund gains 10%, there would be no profit. And if the dollar strengthens by 20%—which happens as part of the regular ebb and flow of international currency exchange—there would actually be a loss of 10%.

COUNTRY FUNDS allow investors to concentrate their investments in a single overseas country, even countries whose markets are closed to individual investors who aren't citizens. When a fund does well, other funds are set up for the same country, so that there are currently several Germany funds and several Mexico funds. Most single country funds are closed-end funds that are traded through a broker once they have been established.

By buying stocks and bonds in a single country, investors can profit from the rapid economic growth as small countries start to industrialize or expand their export markets. This has been the case in Asia and Latin America in recent years, which is one reason those funds have been so popular. The risk of investing in emerging country funds, however, is that their value can be eroded in the event of market turbulance or political turmoil.

GERMANY

Closed-end funds that buy big blocks of shares in a country's industries can influence share prices and sometimes corporate policy, just as institutional investors do when they buy U.S. stocks.

INTERNATIONAL INDEX FUNDS, like other index funds, provide a way to invest with low expenses in world markets without taking a chance on the performance of an individual sector or industry. As the interest in international investing continues to grow, the number of index fund choices has increased, as it has in the domestic market.

MUTUAL FUNDS AROUND THE WORLD

Investors around the world can put their money into pooled investments that are similar to mutual funds. And while a majority of these funds invest in domestic stocks and bonds, most of them also offer international and regional funds that follow many of the same markets as U.S. funds.

Futures and Options

For some, futures and options are high-risk investments. For others, they're protection against dramatic price changes.

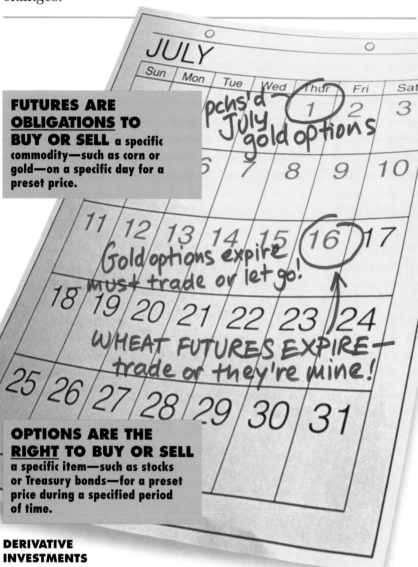

FUTURES ARE OBLIGATIONS TO BUY OR SELL a specific commodity—such as corn or gold—on a specific day for a preset price.

OPTIONS ARE THE RIGHT TO BUY OR SELL a specific item—such as stocks or Treasury bonds—for a preset price during a specified period of time.

DERIVATIVE INVESTMENTS

One reason futures and options are complex is that they're **derivative**, or hybrid, investments. Instead of representing shares of ownership—like stocks—or the promise of loan repayment—like bonds—each futures contract and option is once or twice removed from a real product. A crude oil futures contract, for instance, is a bet on which way oil prices will move. What happens to the oil itself is of little interest to the investor. Even more esoteric are products like an S&P 500 futures contract. It doesn't represent ownership in anything. It's merely a bet on how the stocks in that index will perform over a given time.

REDUCING THE RISK

For some people, futures and options are a way to reduce risk. Farmers who commit themselves to sell grain at a good price are protected if prices drop. Investors who sell options on stock they own can offset some of their losses if the market collapses.

But most investors trade futures and options to take risk, because the possibility of a big loss is balanced by the opportunity for a huge gain. Individual investors are usually small players in the futures and options markets because the stakes are high and the returns are unpredictable.

LEVERAGE ENHANCES RISK

Leverage, in financial terms, means using a small amount of money to make an investment of much greater value. That means you can buy a **futures contract** worth thousands of dollars with an initial investment of about 10% of the total value. For example, if you buy a gold contract worth $35,000 (when gold is $350 an ounce) your cost would be about $3,500 and your leverage would be $31,500.

Every time the price of the contract gains 10¢, the value of your investment increases by $10, as shown below.

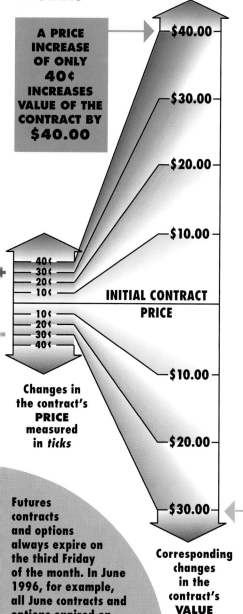

BUYS A $35,000 CONTRACT

A $3,500 INVESTMENT

100oz. GOLD

**|← LEVERAGE →|
OF
$31,500**

When Leverage Works

A PRICE INCREASE OF ONLY **40¢** INCREASES VALUE OF THE CONTRACT BY **$40.00**

$40.00

$30.00

$20.00

$10.00

40¢
30¢
20¢
10¢

INITIAL CONTRACT PRICE

10¢
20¢
30¢
40¢

Changes in the contract's PRICE measured in *ticks*

$10.00

$20.00

$30.00

When Leverage Hurts

A PRICE DECREASE OF ONLY **30¢** DECREASES VALUE OF THE CONTRACT BY **$30.00**

Corresponding changes in the contract's VALUE

Futures contracts and options always expire on the third Friday of the month. In June 1996, for example, all June contracts and options expired on the 21st.

In a commodity as volatile as gold, price swings of $100 within the lifespan of the contract are entirely possible. So, if the price went up $100, to $450 an ounce, the value of your investment would jump $10,000—almost a 300% gain.

But of course, the opposite can happen. If the price falls and the value of your investment drops 300%, it could cost you more than $10,000—sometimes a lot more—to make good on the loss. So while leverage makes the initial commitment easy, you can dig a very big financial hole to crawl out of by investing this way.

CREATED TO EXPIRE

While futures and options are deals for the future, the future they're talking about isn't very far away. Futures contracts on grains and other food sources generally expire within a year, though it is possible to find contracts on certain financial futures— like Eurodollars—that last five years.

Options normally expire in five months or less, although they may last as long as seven months. LEAPS, longer-term options (up to 30 months), were introduced for the first time in 1990.

The Futures Exchanges

Futures are traded on exchanges which offer markets in everything from pork bellies to stock indexes.

Most futures contracts are traded on one of the 10 futures exchanges in the U.S., or on exchanges in London, Winnipeg and others around the world. Exchange contracts trade only on the exchange that issues them. For example, if an investor buys a contract on the Chicago Board of Trade, all the transactions are handled there during the exchange's hours and at the exchange's prices.

Orders sent to the exchange are filled by **open outcry**. That means every order to buy or sell must be called out publicly, in a type of auction process called **price discovery**. It also means that those who scream the loudest often make the most deals. It's probably a major factor in creating the wild image that the exchanges enjoy in the public mind—along with the occasional broken arm suffered as a result of pushing and shoving.

THE COST OF TRADING

Traders charge their clients hefty commissions to execute their orders. Unlike the commissions on stock transactions, one for buying and another for selling, futures brokers charge only once, called a **round-turn commission**, to open and close a position. Commissions are higher though, often 18% or more of the cost of the transaction.

For the first time, futures exchanges are facing competition from brokerage firms who are creating their own derivatives for their clients. The appeal is that futures can be custom designed and timed to fit specific needs—and the clients aren't at the mercy of the pit traders.

MARKET REGULATION

The Commodities Futures Trading Commission (CFTC) is the federal watchdog agency responsible for monitoring the activity on the various exchanges. It does for futures trading what the **SEC** does for stock transactions. The exchanges themselves, stung by accusations of corrupt practices and indictments of some traders, also scrutinize trading activities and enforce regulations through the **National Futures Association (NFA)**.

Some legitimate trading rules, however, seem to permit conflicts of interest not allowed in stock trading. It's legal, for example, for a trader to be trading for himself and for clients at the same time—a practice called **dual trading** that has been singled out as less than fair. Clients' trades can be executed at less advantageous prices when the trader's self-interest takes precedence.

On the plus side, exchanges provide standardized rules, an accurate record of prices, and trading limits to prevent excessive price fluctuations.

Where The Exchanges Are

The 10 U.S. futures exchanges whose trading is reported in The Wall Street Journal are located in five different cities. Each one specializes in particular commodities.

CHICAGO

CBOT Chicago Board of Trade: grains, Treasury bonds and notes, precious metals, financial indexes

CMER Chicago Mercantile Exchange: meat and livestock, currency, stock market indexes

MACE Mid America Commodity Exchange: financial futures, currency, livestock, grain, precious metals

PHILADELPHIA

PBOT Philadelphia Board of Trade: foreign currency

MINNEAPOLIS

MGRX Minneapolis Grain Exchange

NEW YORK

CCTN, FINEX New York Cotton Exchange and its Financial Instrument Exchange

NCSE Coffee, Sugar and Cocoa Exchange

NMER New York Mercantile Exchange: petroleum, natural gas, precious metals

NYFE New York Futures Exchange: financial futures

KANSAS CITY

KBOT Kansas City Board of Trade: grains, livestock and meats, food and fiber, stock indexes

How They Work

Exchange floors are divided into pits where the actual trading occurs. To impose some order, each commodity is usually traded in one specific area on the floor, although pits for soybeans, gold and even stock index futures may stand side by side. **Options** on the futures contracts (see page 131) always trade in an area next to the corresponding futures trading area.

A **trading pit** is usually tiered into three or four levels. During heavy activity, traders jockey for position to see over the heads of the traders in front of them. Some pits are divided into sections so several different commodities can be traded at the same time. At COMEX a small trading area is called a **ring**.

Every trading area has **pit recorders**, whose job is to pick up the trading cards thrown to them, time-stamp them and key the information into a computer. Trades are recorded on **trading cards**, the only written record of the details of a transaction. Some exchanges have begun the move to hand-held computers to create an instant electronic record. Using these records, the exchange has the responsibility to guarantee that an agreement between a buyer and a seller is fulfilled.

Brokerage firm traders and some individual members, called **locals**, can work on the trading floor. While all market players have indirect access to the trading floor through a broker, only members of the exchange can actually trade on the floor.

Large **electronic display boards** circle the trading floor. They're constantly updated with new trade data, which is simultaneously sent out to the rest of the world through electronic vendors.

Trading Futures Contracts

You don't need to invest much to enter a futures contract, but you need nerve—and luck—to ride this financial rollercoaster.

To trade futures, an investor gives an order to buy or sell a commodity on a particular date in the future—like October wheat, or December pork bellies, or June '97 Eurodollars. The price is determined in trading on the floor of the exchange where there's a market in that commodity.

The cost of the contract is what the commodity will be worth if it is delivered. But the price of buying the contract is only a fraction (2% to 10%, depending on who the client is) of that total. It's paid as a good faith deposit, called the **initial margin**. For example, a contract for 5,000 bushels of wheat is $17,500 if wheat is $3.50 a bushel. The margin required would be about $1,750.

AFTER THE ORDER

When an order is filled, the contract goes into a pool at the exchange with all the other filled orders, with buyers and sellers anonymously paired. Since contracts are traded aggressively, the pairing process is always in motion.

Since the price of a contract changes daily—usually many times over—the value of an investor's account changes, too. At the end of each trading day, the exchange moves money either in or out of all the accounts on record depending on the shifting worth of the contracts. The process is called **marking to the market**. The financial effect on a portfolio is often dramatic, as shown below.

Winning and Losing with a Futures Contract

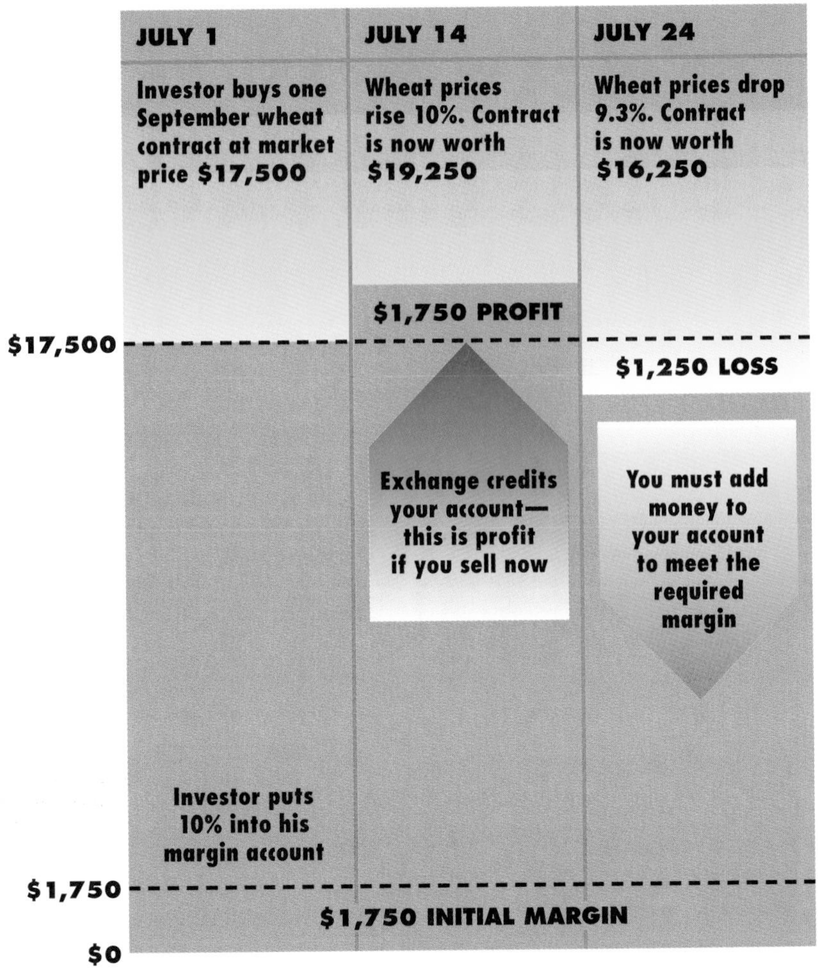

JULY 1	JULY 14	JULY 24
Investor buys one September wheat contract at market price $17,500	Wheat prices rise 10%. Contract is now worth $19,250	Wheat prices drop 9.3%. Contract is now worth $16,250

$1,750 PROFIT

$17,500

$1,250 LOSS

Exchange credits your account—this is profit if you sell now

You must add money to your account to meet the required margin

Investor puts 10% into his margin account

$1,750

$1,750 INITIAL MARGIN

$0

THE LANGUAGE OF FUTURES

Futures trading involves contracts that cancel, or offset, each other: for every buy there's a sell and vice versa. The language of futures trading reflects this phenomenon.

To Enter the Market	Which Means	To Leave the Market	Which Means
GO LONG	**ENTER A FUTURES CONTRACT TO BUY**	**GO SHORT**	**ENTER A FUTURES CONTRACT TO SELL**
GO SHORT	**ENTER A FUTURES CONTRACT TO SELL**	**GO LONG**	**ENTER A FUTURES CONTRACT TO BUY**

MEETING THE MARGIN

An investor's margin level must be kept constant, in part to reassure the exchange that the terms of the contract will be met. If an account is down at the end of the day, it has to be brought up to the required margin level. For example, if wheat slipped from $3.50 to $3.25 a bushel—a little more than a 9% drop—the margin account would be down $1,250 (a loss of 25¢ a bushel x 5,000). When that happens, the investor must add money to the account to bring it up to the required minimum.

Similarly, if the price of wheat dropped again the next day—perhaps on news of a bumper crop in Russia—the same thing would happen again. The original margin required could grow quickly to many thousands of dollars while the underlying value of the commodity continued to fall.

LOCK-LIMIT PROTECTION

The exchanges do have a mechanism, called the **lock-limit**, to protect investors in a fast-moving market. If a contract price moves up or down to the pre-established price limit, the market locks up or locks down, and doesn't open for trading again until the price gets to an acceptable level.

In reality, the lock-limit system often means that investors sustain huge losses or benefit from comparable gains because they are unable to sell a contract until the price has stabilized at the underlying commodity's new real price. A suddenly devalued currency, for example, could send futures contracts on that currency into a tailspin. And when the dust cleared, the value of the contract would probably be significantly less than it was when trading began.

> The average individual investor keeps an account open about 11 months before packing it in and taking what's left somewhere else to invest.

LEAVING THE MARKET

Fewer than 2% of all futures contracts actually result in the transfer of goods. The remaining contracts have been **offset**, or neutralized, with a contract that carries the opposite obligation.

For example, if you buy a September wheat contract at $3.50 per bushel with a $1,750 margin payment, you expect the price to go up.

If the price of the contract climbs to $3.80 after a storm-plagued July week devastates the wheat crop, your account is credited with $1,500, so you're ahead of the game.

You then sell a September wheat contract, which cancels your obligation to buy, take your profit and your margin amount (minus commissions and other expenses), and invest in a different futures contract.

But it can work the other way, too. If prices drop and you're losing money, you may sell an offsetting contract at the best price you can get to cancel your obligation and get out of the market before your losses are any greater. Statistics suggest that somewhere between 75% and 90% of all futures traders lose money every year.

REDUCING THE RISKS OF TRADING

The strategy called **spread trading** is one of the techniques used by futures traders to reduce the risk of losing large sums of money from a sudden shudder in the market, though it also limits rewards.

Basically, it means buying one contract and selling another for the same commodity at the same time. One contract will always make money and the other one will always lose. The key to ending up with a profit is getting the **spread**, or the difference between the two contracts' prices, to work in your favor. For example, if you lose money on a sell contract but make money on a buy contract, the difference between those prices is the spread. If it's 5¢ in your favor, you'd make $250 on a wheat contract. If it's 5¢ against you, the $250 would be your loss.

Financial Futures

Stocks, bonds and currencies are the commodities of the investment business.

Just as dramatic changes in the price of wheat affect farmers, bakers and ultimately the consumer, so changes in interest rates, the future value of currencies and the direction of the stock market send ripples—and sometimes waves—though the financial community.

With the creation of a market in financial futures, traders like pension and mutual fund investment managers, and securities firms that rely on financial commodities, can protect themselves against the unexpected. They're the **hedgers** of the financial futures market.

Financial Futures in Action

THE HEDGERS

Like other hedgers, financial investors sell futures contracts. It's also known as taking a sell position. Investors who plan to buy the products, buy contracts, or take a buy position.

Mutual Fund that owns S+P 500 stocks	**Hedges by taking a sell position** to protect against losses	**If stock stays strong,** gets out of market by buying offsetting contract **If stock prices drop,** offsets losses by selling contract at profit
Mutual Fund that plans future purchase of U.S. Treasury bonds	**Hedges by taking a buy position** to protect price	**If rates stay high,** sells offsetting contract to neutralize position **If rates drop,** and prices increase, fund's price is protected by being locked in

THE SPECULATORS

Speculators gamble on price changes	**Buy when they think prices are lowest**	**Sell when they think prices are highest**

SPECULATION RUNS RAMPANT

As in other futures markets, **speculators** keep the markets active by constant trading. Speculators buy or sell futures contracts depending on which way they think the market is going. World politics, trading patterns and the economy are the unpredictable factors in these markets. Rumor, too, plays a major role.

Financial speculators are no more interested in taking delivery of 125,000 francs than grain speculators are in 5,000 bushels of wheat. What they're interested in is making money on their gamble. So the offsetting technique works here as well, with speculators trying to get out of a contract at what they think is its highest point.

For example, the September contract on the **British pound**, which closed here at $1.5056, was as low as $1.3980 per pound and as high as $1.5800. If a speculator bought low and sold high, the gain (before commissions and other charges) would have been 18¢ per pound or $11,250 on a contract worth £62,500.

CURRENCY

	Open	High	Low	Settle	Change	Lifetime High	Low	Open Interest
BRITISH POUND (CME) – 62,500 pds.; $ per pound								
Sept	1.4880	1.5070	1.4826	1.5056	+ .0190	1.5800	1.3980	32,026
Dec	1.4830	1.4980	1.4770	1.4968	+ .0188	1.5670	1.3930	444
Est vol 16,304; vol Mon 14,125; open int 32,507, –2,398.								
SWISS FRANC (CME) – 125,000 francs; $ per franc								
Sept	.6625	.6670	.6603	.6654	+ .0042	.7100	.6380	3?
Dec	.6630	.6645	.6585	.6636	+ .0041	.7050	.640?	

WHAT'S BEING TRADED

The large variety of financial futures contracts in the marketplace is always in flux. Like other commodities, they trade on specific exchanges, in some cases as the most actively traded commodity. The Chicago Board of Trade's U.S. Treasury Bonds futures, the nation's most actively traded contract, accounts for two-thirds of the exchange's business. Similarly, trade in Eurodollar futures at the Chicago Mercantile Exchange dwarfs the volume of other trades there.

The contracts divide, roughly, into three general categories:

- **Currencies**
- **Stock and bond indexes**
- **Interest rates**

Currency trading has the longest history in the futures market, dating back to the 1970s. Stock index futures trading was added in 1982, and interest rate futures were broken out as a separate category by The Wall Street Journal in 1988.

Reflecting the international scope of financial futures trading, many of the contracts tracked in The Wall Street Journal are traded on the London International Financial Futures Exchange (LIFFE).

ARBITRAGE: MANEUVERING THE MARKETS

Indexes, and futures contracts on those indexes, don't move in lock step. When they are out of sync, the index futures contract price moves either higher or lower than the index itself. Traders can make a lot of money by simultaneously buying the one that's less expensive and selling the more expensive. The technique is known as **arbitrage**, and the chief tool is a very sophisticated computer program that follows the shifts in price.

Often, the price difference is only a fraction of a dollar. But arbitragers trade huge numbers of contracts at the same time, so the results are significant—if the timing is right. And since many arbitragers are making the same decisions at the same time, their buying and selling can produce changes in the markets they are trying to manipulate.

LOST INTEREST
The London International Financial Futures Exchange stopped trading futures contracts in U.S. Treasury bonds in the spring of 1993 because there wasn't enough trading to keep the markets active.

INDEX

S&P 500 INDEX (CME) $500 times index

	Open	High	Low	Settle	Chg	High	Low	Open Interest
Sept	452.30	452.30	450.20	451.45	− 1.20	458.55	391.00	179,853
Dec	453.30	453.30	451.10	452.35	− 1.30	459.30	429.70	4,198
Mr94	453.90	454.20	452.80	453.65	− 1.25	458.80	434.00	362

Est vol 38,621; vol Mon 36,995; open int 184,484, +1,618.
Indx prelim High 45
S&P MIDCAP 400 (
Sept 168.40 168.70 16
Est vol 267

INTEREST RATE

TREASURY BONDS (CBT) – $100,000; pts. 32nds of 100%

	Open	High	Low	Settle	Chg	Yield Settle	Chg	Open Interest
Sept	114-00	114-05	113-24	114-00	....	6.717	....	311,125
Dec	112-27	112-31	112-18	112-25	− 1	6.820	+ .03	19,486
Mr94	111-23	111-23	111-16	111-21	− 1	6.915	+ .02	9,022
June	110-19	110-21	110-16	110-19	− 2	7.007	+ .05	1,984
Sept	109-17	109-23	109-16	109-20	− 3	7.092	+ .08	2,103
Dec	....	....	....	108-25				
Mr95				108.00				

READING THE FINANCIAL FUTURES CHARTS

The details of financial futures trading are recorded daily.

The value of an index contract is calculated differently from other futures contracts. That's because an index is two steps removed from the commodity. Instead of dollars per yen or tons of soybeans per dollar, U.S. indexes settle at $500 times the index. Rather than taking delivery of the contract—which is only numbers in a computer—you would take delivery of the cash value of the contract.

For example, if this September contract had reached its expiration date, it would be worth $225,725, or the settle price of 451.45 x $500.

Interest rate futures contracts also differ somewhat from other contracts. Their value is figured as percentage points of 100%, or in the case of U.S. and U.K. bonds, in 32nds of 100%, to correspond to the way changes in value are measured in the bonds themselves (see page 90). For U.S. Treasury notes and bonds, and for Eurodollars, the tables report current yield rather than lifetime highs and lows.

A World of Options

Options are opportunities to make buy and sell decisions down the road—if the market takes the right turns.

Holding an option gives you the right to buy or sell a specific investment at a set price within a preset time period. The particular item that an option deals with—stock, index, Treasury bond, currency or futures contract—is called the **underlying investment**. If the stock or futures markets move in the direction an investor thinks they will, exercising the option can mean a healthy profit.

Options are traded on stock or commodity exchanges at a specific **strike (or exercise) price**, which is the dollar amount you'll pay or receive if the trade takes place. The strike price is set by the exchange. The market price rises or falls depending on the performance of the underlying investment on which the option is based.

BUYING OPTIONS

Buying options is a way to capitalize on changes in the market price. People who buy **call** options are betting that the price of the underlying investment is going up. Conversely, people who buy **put** options think the price is going down.

With either type of buy option, the potential loss is limited to the **premium**, or dollar amount, paid to buy the option. That's known in the securities industry as a limited, predetermined risk.

SELLING OPTIONS

The biggest difference between buying options and selling them is the nature of the commitment. Buyers have no obligation to do anything. They can simply let the option expire. Sellers, on the other hand, are required to go through with a trade if the party they sold the option to (by **writing a put** or **writing a call**) wants to exercise the option.

WRITING COVERED CALLS

The most basic form of option trading is **writing covered stock calls**, and it's the first type of option trading most people do. It means selling the right to some other party to buy stocks from you which you already own for a specific price. The key is that you own them—that's what makes the call **covered**.

NAKED— BEARING IT ALL

The greatest risk in options trading is **writing naked calls**. That means selling an option that allows someone to buy something from you that you don't already own. In a typical worst-case example, you'd write a naked stock call. The price of the underlying stock would pass the strike price, the option would be exercised, and you'd have to buy the shares at the market price in order to sell them at the agreed on price. Your cost—and loss—is potentially unlimited.

THREE WAYS TO BUY OPTIONS

Investor buys ten **CALL OPTIONS** (1,000 shares) on Stock X	
Price: $55/Share	① **HOLD TO MATURITY AND TRADE AT THE STRIKE PRICE**
Strike Price: $60/Share	② **TRADE FOR PROFIT OR LOSS BEFORE OPTION EXPIRES**
Premium: $750	③ **LET THE OPTION EXPIRE**

TWO WAYS TO SELL OPTIONS

Investor owns 1,000 shares of Stock X	① **WRITE TEN COVERED CALLS** Strike Price: $60 Collect premium: $750
Price: $55/Share	
Investor owns no Shares of Stock X	② **WRITE TEN NAKED CALLS** Strike Price: $60 Collect Premium: $750

THE LANGUAGE OF OPTIONS

In the specialized language of options, all transactions are either puts or calls. A put is the right to sell and a call is the right to buy.

	CALL	PUT
BUY	The right to buy the underlying item at the strike price until the expiration date.	The right to sell the underlying item at the strike price until the expiration date.
SELL	Selling the right to buy the underlying item from you at the strike price until the expiration date. Known as **writing a call**.	Selling the right to sell the underlying item to you until the expiration date. Known as **writing a put**.

TRADE OR EXERCISE

Like futures contracts, options can be closed out for a profit before the expiration date or neutralized with an offsetting order. Unlike most futures contracts, though, options are frequently exercised when the underlying item passes the strike price. That's because part of the appeal of options, and stock options in particular, is that they can be converted into real investments even though the options themselves are intangible.

THE OPTIONS KEEP CHANGING

The underlying investments on which options are available keep growing. At the time of publication, five types of exchange-listed options are generally traded:

- Individual stocks
- Stock and bond market indexes
- Currencies
- Treasury bills and bonds
- Futures contracts

IF STOCK PRICE RISES TO 65
Trade option at strike price of 60

$5,000	from trade
– $750	premium

$4,250 PROFIT

IF STOCK PRICE RISES TO 60
Trade option at strike price of 60

less your
premium only

$750 LOSS

IF STOCK RISES TO 62
Trade option before expiration at strike price of 60

$2,000	from trade
– $750	premium

$1,250 PROFIT

IF STOCK PRICE RISES TO 60½
Trade option before expiration at strike price of 60

$500	from trade
– $750	premium

$250 LOSS

IF STOCK PRICE DROPS TO 45
There are no takers for an option with a 60 strike price

less your
premium only

$750 LOSS

IF STOCK PRICE RISES TO 57
No takers—options expire

keep the
premium

$750 PROFIT

IF STOCK PRICE RISES TO 60¾
Buy 10 calls to cancel obligation and prevent losing stocks

$750	premium collected
– $750	premium on offsetting calls

BREAK EVEN

IF STOCK PRICE RISES TO 57
No takers—options expire

keep the
premium

$750 PROFIT

IF STOCK PRICE RISES TO 65
Option is exercised: You must buy 1,000 shares to sell to meet call

$750	premium
+ $60,000	proceeds from sale
– $65,000	to buy stock

$4,250 LOSS

Reading Options Tables

Successful stock option trading requires lots of attention to detail—including information on what's happening in the marketplace.

The price and trading volume of stock options are closely tied to the way the underlying stocks themselves are doing. The most actively traded options have **strike prices** that are usually quite close to actual stock prices except when there's been a dramatic gain or drop in price. That's because the exchanges establish the strike prices with the benefit of lots of analysis. Those options where the differences between prices is large don't trade often enough to get reported in the tables.

In fact, the relationship between actual price and strike price is so important to the way options trade that there is a special vocabulary to describe it. **In the money** options are those where the actual price is above the strike price for calls and below it for puts. **At the money** options mean the stock price equals the strike price. **Out of the money** options mean the actual price is below the strike price for calls, but above it for puts. Out of the money options have a price spread large enough to make them potentially very lucrative. While you have a lot more potential buying out of the money options, the probability of actually making money is much lower than other option investments.

LISTED OPTIONS

—Call— Vol.	Last	—Put— Vol.	Last	Option/Strike		Exp.	—Call— Vol.	Last	—Put— Vol.	Last	Option/Strike		Exp.
53	2⅞	20	1⅛	Exbvte	7½	Nov	...	...	95	⁵/₁₆	JeffPl	50	Jan
500	⅜	...	...	Exxon	60	Oct	30	5⅞	25	⅛	57⅜	55	Apr
115	⅞	25	1³/₁₆	65⅝	65	Sep	343	¾	...	...	JohnJn	35	Oct
480	⁵/₁₆	...	....	65⅝	65	Oct	556	1⅝	22	⅞	38¾	35	Jan
		36	1¹¹/₁₆	65⅝	65	Jan	10	2⁷/₁₆	30	2¼	38¾	40	Sep
70	¼	...	....	65⅝	65	Apr	73	3	...	...	38¾	40	Oct
47	1	...	...	65⅝	70	Oct	10	⅛	151	4¾	38¾	45	Jan
35	1⅞	9	2¹/₁₆	65⅝	70	Jan	328	¹¹/₁₆	...	...	K mart	20	Sep
26	¹/₁₆	...	...	FNM	75	Sep	10	3¾	100	⅛	22¾	22½	Sep
...	...	40	³/₁₆	78½	75	Oct	45	4½	131	⅞	22¾	22½	Dec
30	3⅝	...	...	78½	75	Dec	20	5⅞	3	2	22¾	22½	Mar
225	1	...	...	78½	75	Mar	20	7⅛	...	...	22¾	25	Sep
50	¹³/₁₆	...	...	78½	80	Sep	168	⅜	1	1¾	22¾	25	Oct
183	2¼	...	...	78½	80	Oct	1581	¹¹/₁₆	1	3⅛	KLA In	17½	Dec
30	⅝	...	...	78½	80	Dec	31	3	30	4⅜	22	20	Mar
30	2⅞	...	...	78½	85	Mar	45	2⁹/₁₆	...	...	KLM	20	Mar
5	3	28	½	78½	90	Dec	75	½	...	...	Kellog	50	Sep
30	4⅜	...	...	F P L	40	Dec	31	1⅛	...	...	54⅜	50	Oct
300	⅞	...	...	FFB	45	Sep	20	4	...	...	54⅜	55	Sep
5881	1⅜	...	...	48⅞	50	Sep	25	¼	...	...	54⅜	55	Mar
30	1⁵/₁₆	...	...	48⅞	50	Dec	35	2¼	125	2⅞	54⅜	60	Mar
50	13½	...	...	48⅞	55	Mar	50	1⅜	...	...	KelyOil	12½	Sep
95	10⅛	12	¹/₁₆	FHLB	50	Sep	20	2	370	¼	13¼	12½	Oct
73	10½	...	...	51⅜	55	Oct	20	7/₁₆	...	...	13¼	12½	Nov
41	11⅝	3	½	Ford	45	Sep	12	8¾	45	¹/₁₆	13¼	15	Sep
47	9⅞	2	1¼	53⅝	50	Sep	410	3¾	337	⅞	13¼	15	Nov
		47	¼	53⅝	50	Oct	40	4½	35	½	13¼	17½	Oct
				53⅝	50	Dec					13¼	17½	...

The **number** in the first column—often the same number several times, for each option—is the current price of the underlying stock. The relationship between the current price and the strike price is one factor affecting how actively the option is traded. In this example, for instance, Exxon sold for 65⅝ a share at the end of the previous trading day, and two of the three most actively traded options had a strike price of 65.

The **name** of the stock being optioned is often abbreviated, and in alphabetical order. Some big names, like Exxon and Ford, are easily recognized. Others, like FHLB, need deciphering. (It's Federal Home Loan Bank.) The abbreviations are often, but not always, the same ones that are used in the stock tables.

Information about the most actively traded options and LEAPS, or long-term options, is given separately, at the beginning and the end of the regular listed options columns.

OPTIONS PRICES

Option prices are quoted in whole numbers and fractions that represent a dollar amount. To convert a whole number and a fraction to an option price, multiply the whole number by 100 and the fraction by 10 and add the results.

for example	
2⅝ =	(2 x 100) + (⅝ x 10)
=	(200) + (6.25 x 10)
=	200 + 62.50
2⅝ =	$262.50

This chart gives the decimal equivalent of the fractions:

1/16	=	0.625
1/8	=	1.25
3/16	=	1.875
1/4	=	2.50
5/16	=	3.125
3/8	=	3.75
7/16	=	4.375
1/2	=	5
9/16	=	5.625
5/8	=	6.25
11/16	=	6.875
3/4	=	7.50
13/16	=	8.125
7/8	=	8.75
15/16	=	9.375

stops trading on the third Friday of that month. The strike price is the dollar amount a trade would cost if the option were exercised. For example, an LSI Sep 17½ means that anytime up to the third Friday in September, an option holder could buy 100 shares of LSI stock for $17.50 a share.

Often the same month appears several times with different strike prices, with the groupings by price rather than date.

For example, if Pfizer has options at 55, 60, 65, 70, 75 and 85, all the 60s are together, and so on.

The **expiration date** and **strike price** are listed beginning with the closest month and lowest price. The date is given as a month, and the option

QUOTATIONS

	—Put—	Option/Strike	Exp.	—Call—		—Put—		Option/Strike		Exp.	—Call—	
st	Vol.Last			Vol.	Last	Vol.	Last				Vol.	La
⅜	... ...	Komag	20 Sep	...	...	25	2¹/₁₆	Pet	15	Sep	10¼	15/
½	... ...	Kroger	20 Oct	50	1⅞	...	...	15⅞	15	Oct	21½	17/
	2020 ¼	21½	22½ Jan	650	1⅜	...	...	15⅞	17½	Sep	59	
...	98 1¹/₁₆	L S I	17½ Sep	23	½	...	...	15⅞	17½	Oct	256	
¼	8 1¼	17⅞	17½ Oct	24	1⁷/₁₆	...	...	15⅞	17½	Dec	72	
/₁₆	... ...	LAC	7½ Jan	40	1³/₁₆	...	...	Petrie	25	Sep	50	
¾	... ...	LAGear	10 Sep	30	⅛	...	...	PfdHlth	20	Oct	5	2³/
•⁵/₈	1 ¹/₁₆	9⅜	10 Oct	156	⁷/₁₆	53	1⅛	Pfizer	55	Sep		
/₁₆	29 ⁵/₁₆	LDDS	40 Sep	83	3¾	...	...	61⅜	55	Dec	18	8
/₁₆	7 1	LILCO	30 Oct	...	...	50	1³/₁₆	61⅜	60	Sep	148	
¾	22 1⅝	28½	30 Mar	32	½	...	...	61⅜	60	Oct	519	3
/₁₆	5 2⅞	LamRs	45 Sep	30	6¼	...	...	61⅜	60	Dec	...	
⅛	... ...	LawInt	12½ Dec	30	1¾	...	...	61⅜	60	Mar	...	
⁷/₈	... ...	Legent	17½ Sep	60	2	...	...	61⅜	65	Sep	407	
³/₄	... ...	19½	20 Sep	32	¼	...	...	61⅜	65	Oct	564	
	25 1¾	19½	20 Oct	25	⅞	5	2	61⅜	65	Dec	155	2
¼	... ...	19½	30 Oct	40	¹/₁₆	...	...	61⅜	70	Sep	100	¹/
¼	... ...	Lilly	45 Oct	20	3⅝	16	⅜	61⅜	70	Oct	150	⁵/
/₁₆	15 1¼	48¼	50 Sep	56	⅛	12	1⅞	61⅜	75	Dec	23	
•³/₈	... ...	48¼	50 Oct	30	¾	48	2⁷/₁₆	61⅜	85	Dec	1701	
⅝	13 6¾	48¼	50 Jan	35	1⅞	1	3⅞	Ph Mor	45	Sep	66	3
¼	20 ¹/₁₆	Limitd	20 Nov	...	...	28	¹/	47⅞	45	Oct	56	3
•⅛	... ...	21¾	22½ Sep	41	³/₁₆	54	¾	47⅞	45	Dec	210	4
¼	... ...	21¾										

Call options—or options to buy—are reported separately from **put options**—or options to sell. Sometimes calls and puts are traded on the same option, and sometimes only one or the other is being traded. When that happens dashes appear in the non-trading column, as they do for Kellogg's September and October 50 contracts. When volume and price are similar for both calls and

puts, as they are for KLM's March 20 option, they are often offsetting trades.

Volume reports the number of trades during the previous trading day. The number is unofficial, but gives a sense of the activity in each option. Generally, trading increases as the expiration date gets closer if the strike price is in the money. For example, there's much more action in Kellogg's September 55 option than

in the March option at the same price.

Last is the closing price for the option on the previous trading day. In this case, the Lilly January 50 put closed at 3⅞, or $387.50 for an option on 100 shares at $48.25. Generally the higher the price, the greater the profit the trader expects to make—like the people buying Ford's September 45 call option for $875 or Pfizer's December 55 call for $850.

Using Options

Options can produce a lot of income quickly, if the price moves the right way and the options are exercised or traded before they expire.

Options are appealing to many traders because they don't cost very much to buy—though the commissions are a significant factor in their cost. By paying only a fraction of the cost of actually buying stocks, Treasury notes, or whatever the underlying investment is, a trader has **leveraged** the purchase, or used a little money with the potential to make a lot within a relatively short time—usually five to seven months or less. If the option is traded or exercised profitably, the yield can be hundreds or even thousands of times the original investment amount.

THE COST OF AN OPTION

The **premium**, or nonrefundable price, of an option depends on several factors. Officially, the factors are the type of investment the option is on, the investment's underlying price, how volatile the price has been over the last year, the current interest rate and the time remaining until expiration.

The premium fluctuates so you can get back more or less than you paid to buy the option when you decide to sell.

Sellers take their money up front when they write options. It's called a **price premium**, and it's also nonrefundable. In fact, collecting the premium is often the primary reason for writing options.

USING OPTIONS AS INSURANCE

In addition to the highs that speculating can provide, stock options have practical uses for traders who follow the markets closely and have specific goals, such as providing some insurance for stock market investments.

One method of reducing risk with options is to buy a **married put**. This means buying a stock and a put (sell) option on the same stock at the same time. If the price of the stock falters or goes down, the put option goes up in value, and part of the loss on the stock can be offset

The Following Rules of Thumb

The greater the difference between the exercise price and the actual current price of the item, the cheaper the premium, because there is less chance the option will be exercised.

The closer the expiration date of an "out of the money" option (where the market price is higher than the strike price), the cheaper the price.

Option/Strike			Vol	Exch	Last	Net Chg	a-Close	Open Int
Pfizer	Sep	75	829	AM	1 3/16	...	69¼	6,573
Pfizer	Dec	75	77	AM	2½	+ ⅜	69¼	1,521
Pfizer	Dec	85	225	AM	⅝	+ 1/16	69¼	3,317
Ph Mor	Jul	45						
Ph Mor	Sep	45						
Ph Mor	Jul	50						
Ph Mor	Jul	50						
Ph Mor	Aug	50						
Ph Mor	Sep	50						
Ph Mor	Sep	50						
Ph Mor	Dec	50						
Ph Mor								

Option/Strike				Vol	Exch	Last	Net Chg	a-Close	Open Int
CaesrW	Aug	45		100	AM	2¾	− ¾	44⅝	426
CasMag	Jul	22½	p	123	CB	1½	+ ⅜	23½	82
CasMag	Aug	22½	p	93	CB	2¾	+ 9/16	23½	105
CasMag	Nov	22½	p	68	CB	4¾	+ ⅝	23½	139
CasMag	Aug	25		148	CB	2¼	...	23½	19
CasMag	Aug	30		62	AM	1	− ¼	23½	57
CasMag	Nov	30		437	CB	2 7/16	− 9/16	23½	622
Caterp	Jul	75	p	75	AM	2 9/16	+ 7/16	74½	913
				[illegible]	CB	[illegible]	[illegible]	[illegible]	84

When Pfizer is trading in July at 69¼, a **December 75** option costs $250 but a **December 85** is only $62.50.

When CasMag is trading at 23½ in July, an **August 30** option is $100 but a **November 30** option is $243.75.

by selling the put. A similar technique, called a **strangle**, involves writing a call (buy option) with a strike price above the current market price and a put (sell option) with a strike price below it. That means that you've collected your premium and neutralized your position at the same time.

Straddle, or **spread**, trading means buying and writing options on the same stock at different strike prices. Then if you are forced to buy or sell because someone exercises the option you've sold them, you can cover the deal by exercising your own option to buy or sell. A **covered straddle** involves buying the stock and writing (selling) equal numbers of calls

and puts at the same time. Whatever happens, you've collected your premium and have stocks to boot. The premiums can either increase the return you get on your shares or reduce the cost of buying additional shares if the price drops.

LEAPS

Long-term stock options, actually **Long-term Equity Anticipation Securities**, lasting up to three years were introduced to the options marketplace in 1990. Because they last longer than other options, they are considered less risky. That's true in part because the price of the stock or stock index has much longer to perform as expected. It's also true that the money saved in buying an option instead of the stock itself can be invested elsewhere. (You could buy a January 1997 30-call option for 100 shares in Apple Computer for $250 in July 1996, when 100 shares cost $2,900 in the open market.) On the other hand, options don't pay dividends.

The drawback of LEAPS, like all options, is that the stock must still perform as expected, and the decision to trade, exercise, or let the option expire must be made within the option's lifespan.

Plus, only a limited number of LEAPS are available—about 250 in the summer of 1996—while more than 1,600 stocks have regular options available.

Usually Apply to Options

The more time there is until expiration, the larger the premium, because the chance of reaching the strike price is greater and the carrying costs are more.

Call and put options move in opposition. Call options rise in value as the underlying market prices go up. Put options rise in value as market prices go down.

Option/Strike		Vol	Exch	Last	Net Chg	a-Close	Open Int
Exxon	Jan 65	56	CB	3	− ¼	65½	225
Exxon	Jul 65	140	CB	1⅛	− ½	65½	7,376
Exxon	Jan 70	66	CB	1⅛	− ⅛	65½	1,392
Exxon	Oct 70	87	CB	9/..	− 3/..	65½	4,343
F N M	Jul 80						
F N M	Jul 85						
F N M	Jul 85						
F N M	Aug 85						
F N M	Sep 90						
FFB	Sep 50						
FHLB	Jul 50						
FHLB	Jan 55						
FHLB	Jan 55 p						
F lntste	Jul 65	88					
FM Cop	Sep 25						
FM Cop	Dec						

Option/Strike			Vol	Exch	Last	Net Chg	a-Close	Op
G M	Jul 40		671	CB	4¼	− ¼	44	4,
G M	Aug 40		68	CB	4⅞	+ ¼	44	2
G M	Aug 40	p	69	CB	7/16	...	44	2
G M	Sep 40		73	CB	5⅛	− ¼	44	8,
G M	Sep 40	p	146	CB	¾	...	44	
G M	Dec 40		56	CB	6¼			

In early July when the price of Exxon stock is 65½, one **January 65** option on Exxon stock costs $300 but a **July 65** is $112.50.

The **August 40 call** on GM stock that's trading at 44—obviously higher than was expected—costs $487.50, but the **August 40 put** (shown with a **p** in the margin after the information about date and price) is selling for $43.75.

Other Options

Options are a growth industry: New ways to speculate on what the future holds crop up regularly.

Options on currencies, Treasury bills, notes and bonds, stock and bond indexes and futures contracts are currently traded. Because they are **derivatives**, a step or sometimes two removed from an actual investment, they can be difficult for individuals to understand and use profitably.

These types of options, like stock options, appeal to traders who want to:

- Protect investments against major swings in market prices, or
- Speculate on market movements

OPTIONS ON STOCK INDEXES

Buying **put options** on stock indexes is a way for investors to hedge their portfolios against sharp drops in the market. It gives them the right to sell their options at a profit if the market falls. The money realized on the sale will—hopefully—cover the losses in their portfolios resulting from the falling market.

For this technique to work, though, the options have to be on the index that most closely tracks the kind of stocks they own. And there have to be enough options to offset the total value of the portfolio. Since options cost money and expire quickly, using this kind of insurance regularly can take a big bite out of any profits the portfolio itself produces.

Speculators use index options to gamble on shifts in market direction. Like other methods of high-risk investing, this one offers the chance of making a big killing if you get it right. Otherwise there wouldn't be any takers. But the risks of getting the price and the timing right are magnified by the short lifespan of index options.

A complicating factor is that indexes don't always move in the same direction as the markets they track. When indexes are out of kilter, there are big profits to be made, too—by the arbitrage traders with computer programs fine-tuned enough to take advantage of the movements.

The value of an index option is usually calculated by multiplying the index level by $100.

OPTIONS ON CURRENCY

People with large overseas investments sometimes hedge their portfolios by buying options on the currencies of countries where their money is invested. Since the investment's value depends on the relationship between the dollar and the other currency, using options can equalize sudden shifts in value.

For example, if the value of the British pound lost ground against the dollar, U.S. investments in British companies would be worth less than they were when the pound was strong. But an option to buy pounds at the lower price could be sold at a profit, making up for some of the loss in investment value.

Speculators also buy currency options, sometimes making hefty profits. But it's generally accepted that currency speculation, like interest rate speculation, is not the right market for individual investors.

TO MARKET, TO MARKET, TO BUY...

The hogs that end up as pork in the supermarkets also supply the futures and options markets—at 40,000 pounds per contract. The hogs get sold, the futures contracts are traded and the options on those contracts are exercised—or expire. The farmer makes money if the hogs are sold for more than it cost to raise them. Futures contract traders make money if the cash price for the hogs means they can trade their contracts at a profit. But option buyers make money only if they guess right on what price a futures contract will be on a specific date. That's what a derivative market is all about.

OPTIONS ON INTEREST RATES

Options on interest rates are actually options on bonds issued by the U.S. Treasury, municipalities, or foreign countries. As always with bonds, a change in interest rates produces a change in price.

Bondholders can hedge their investments by using interest rate options, just as stockholders can hedge by using index options. Interest rate options are intended to offset any loss in value between the purchase date of the option and the date the bond matures. If the money from the maturing bond has to be reinvested at a lower rate, the profit from trading the option can make up for some of the loss—if the cost of the option doesn't eat it up.

A put option on bonds, with the right to sell at a certain price, is worth more as the strike price gets higher and the exercise date is further away. Call options, with the right to buy, are more valuable the lower the strike price. Since interest usually increases over time—and bond prices go lower—calls increase in value as the exercise date gets further away.

TRADING OPTIONS

Options are traded through option trading firms on futures exchanges (see page 119), on the Chicago Board Options Exchange, and on four stock exchanges: the American, Philadelphia, Pacific and New York. Like futures contracts, options contracts are traded exclusively on the exchange which makes, or originates, them.

Trades are handled through the exchanges where they take place. Buy and sell orders are matched anonymously, and can be canceled by using an offsetting contract.

Individual stock options can also be traded on more than one exchange. The SEC has initiated a controversial program with stock options to have them multiple-listed—or available for sale at all of the exchanges—the way that stocks themselves are. Currently, the Chicago and American exchanges, which trade contracts in many blue chip stocks, control more than 75% of the business, with the Philadelphia and Pacific exchanges at about 22%.

One change that multiple listing means is a shift to the increased use of telephone and computer-generated trading, introducing opportunities for comparison shopping and for arbitrage.

OPTIONS ON FUTURES CONTRACTS

Options on futures contracts are the right to buy or sell an obligation to buy or sell. These seem to be—whether or not they actually are—the furthest removed from reality and the most difficult to use. An option on a futures contract on feeder cattle, for example, is a long way from the corral. And since the hedgers in the futures business buy contracts, not options on contracts, these vehicles belong almost exclusively to the speculators.

There is money to be made in the futures markets, so options on futures are traded regularly, though generally in smaller numbers than options in Treasury bonds, indexes and the most active individual stocks.

Tracking Other Options

The most active options trading is reported regularly in several different tables, each keyed to the underlying product.

As the variety of options available in the marketplace has increased, so have the number of tables providing information about current trades. All option tables provide the same basic information, including the strike price, the expiration date and the current price of the option.

But there are some differences. The sales unit for each option is based on the item being optioned—100 shares of stock, 44,000 pounds of feeder cattle, $50,000 Australian dollars. So are the expiration dates, which in some cases follow a regular pattern and in other cases are random.

INDEX OPTION TRADING

Like stock options, index options are closely tied to the underlying item—in this case various stock indexes. In fact, the ranges of the underlying indexes are printed in The Wall Street Journal accompanying the details of the trading.

Index options generally have a short time frame and a broad range of prices. That's because they're so volatile. Trying to predict with any precision where an index will be is even more difficult than with most other options. The further in the future, the more difficult it becomes.

INDEX OPTIONS TRADING

Strike	Vol.	Close	Net Chg.	Open Int.	Strike	Vol.	Close	Net Chg.	Open Int.	Strik
CHICAGO					Jul	400 c	151	18½	– 1	5,244	Call
					Jul	400 p	1,867	½	+ 1/16	29,591	Put
S & P 100 INDEX(OEX)					Aug	400 p	725	1 15/16	+ 3/16	12,645	
					Sep	400 p	436	3½	+ ¼	9,155	
Jul	370 p	233	1/16	...	4,156	Oct	400 p	38	4⅞	– ⅛	1,338	Se
Aug	370 p	210	⅜	...	955	Jul	405 c	582	13¾	– ⅞	6,931	Ji
Sep	370 p	68	¾ + 1/16	1,449	Jul	405 p	2,669	¾	+ 1/16	34,185	A
Jul	375 p	165	1/16	...	3,951	Aug	405 p	327	2¾	+ 3/16	3,575	J
Aug	375 p	155	7/16	1/16	1,317	Sep	405 p	128	4⅝	+ ⅛	1,031	A
Sep	375 p	15	15/16	...	675	Jul	410 c	4,024	9⅜	– ¾	29,674	
Jul	380 p	192	⅛ – 1/16	6,681	Jul	410 p	8,508	1⅜	+ ⅛	42,427	
Aug	380 p	344	⅝ + 1/16	7,651	Aug	410 c	1,181	11¾	– ⅞	5,995	
Sep	380 p	207	13/16	3/16	2,174	Aug	410 p	1,596	3⅞	+ ¼	13,305	
					Sep	410 c	20	13½	– ⅞	728	
					Sep	410 p	240	6⅛	+ ⅜	1,0	

The **Index** on which the options are offered is listed. Traders can buy options on a wide variety of indexes, from the S&P 100 to the much broader Russell 2000. There are some indexes that track specific industries or stock markets in other countries.

The **Exchange** on which the index options are traded is shown first.

The **Strike** column shows the expiration date, strike price and whether the option is a put (p) or a call (c). In this example of S&P 100 index option trading, the puts predominate at the lower end (375) of the price scale, suggesting that those traders think the market is headed down. At the upper end (410), calls increase, suggesting some traders think the market is going up.

Volume reports the number of trades during the previous trading day. In index option trading, the heaviest volume is usually in options closest to expiration—in this case July.

Close is the closing price of the option at the end of the previous day's trading. As with stock options, prices are given in whole numbers and in fractions. (To get the actual price you multiply the number by 100, since each option is for 100 shares.) For example, the July 400 call is trading at 18½, or $1850.

Net Change is the difference between the price reported here and the closing price two trading days ago. When the two are alike, all the outstanding options have been neutralized by opposing trades.

FUTURES OPTIONS PRICES

Futures options trading includes agricultural products, other raw materials and financial commodities like international currencies and interest rates.

The **futures contract** on which the option is based, the exchange on which it is traded, the number of units in the contract and the price units by which the price of the commodity is figured are shown. In this example, the futures contract is on soybeans traded on the Chicago Board of Trade. Each contract is for 5,000 bushels and the price is quoted in cents per bushel, so that 575 means $5.75 a bushel.

Industry group is a grouping of similar commodities traded on various exchanges. They include options on futures contracts in agricultural products, oil, livestock currency, interest rates and stock and bond indexes.

Puts gives the dates of the put options available in each commodity. Prices for puts and calls move in the opposite direction, because they reflect the price movement of the underlying commodity. When calls are selling for more, puts are selling for less, as they are for feeder cattle here.

FUTURES OPTIONS PRICES

Tuesday, June 22,

AGRICULTURAL

SOYBEANS (CBT)
5,000 bu.; cents per bu.

Strike Price	Calls—Settle			Puts—Settle		
	Aug	Sep	Nov	Aug	Sep	Nov
575	45½	51¾	57½	2¾	6¾	10½
600	28½	36	43	10½	16⅝	21⅝
625	18	27½	33¼	25	32	37
650	12⅜	22½	26½	44	51½	54
675	8⅛	17½	21¼	....	...	74
700	6	14⅝	18¼	....	...	96½

Est vol 15,000   Mon 14,310 calls 5,-945 puts
Op int Mon   109,516 calls 41,064 puts

SOYBEAN MEAL (CBT)
100 tons; $ per ton

Strike Price	Calls—Settle			Puts—Settle		
	Aug	Sep	Oct	Aug	Sep	Oct
185	10.50	12.45	13.25	1.25	3.25	3.70
190	7.50	9.75	10.50	3.25	5.25	5.95
195	5.50	8.00	9.00	6.00	...	9.50
200	4.00	6.60	7.50	....	...	12.90
210	2.20	4.75	5.50	....	19.75	20.80
220	1.40	3.60	4.50	....	...	....

Est vol 1,300   Mon 1,585 calls 951 puts
Op int Mon   16,262 calls 8,144 puts

SOYBEAN OIL (CBT)
60,000 lbs.; cents per lb.

Strike Price	Calls—Settle			Puts—Settle		
	Aug	Sep	Oct	Aug	Sep	Oct
2100	1.430	1.700	....	.250	.400	.460
2150	1.080	1.430	....	.400	.640	....
2200	.800	1.220	1.400	.650	.930	
2250	.650	1.050	....			
2300	.500	.920	1.08.			
2350						

CATTLE-FEEDER (CME)
44,000 lbs.; cents per lb.

Strike Price	Calls—Settle			Puts—Settle		
	Aug	Sep	Oct	Aug	Sep	Oct
82	4.85	4.10	3.92	0.32	0.60	0.75
84	3.00	2.50	2.47	0.47	1.00	1.30
86	1.60	1.25	1.37	1.05	1.75	2.20
88	0.70	0.55	0.65	2.10	....	....
90	0.22	0.20	....	3.57	....	....
92	0.17					

Est vol 278   Mon 40 calls 167 puts
Op int Mon   1,853 calls 7,340 puts

CATTLE-LIVE (CME)
40,000 lbs.; cents per lb.

Strike Price	Calls—Settle			Puts—Settle		
	Jly	Aug	Oct	Jly	Aug	Oct
70	....	3.57	....	....	0.17	0.47
72	....	1.97	2.70	0.07	0.55	0.95
74	....	0.75	1.52	0.75	1.32	1.75
76	0.05	0.20	0.72	....	2.75	2.92
78	....	0.05	0.32	....	....	4.50
80	....	....	0.12	....	....	....

Est vol 1,787   Mon 179 calls 5.
Op int Mon   12.90.

HOGS—LIVE (C
40,000 lbs.;

Strike Price
44
46
48
50
52
54

contracts and the options on those contracts may not trade at the same pace, the exchange will adjust an option's price to coincide with its futures price at the end of the day.

So the settle price for the August 575 option is 45½ (45½¢) a bushel, or $2,275. The futures contract itself is worth $28,750.

Estimated volume reports the number of trades on the previous trading day, separated into puts and calls.

Open interest shows the number of outstanding options contracts, broken out by puts and calls, that have not been offset by an opposite transaction.

Strike price is the price at which the option owner may buy or sell the corresponding futures contract by exercising the option. Each commodity has options covering a range of prices which increase in a regular sequence (200/210/220).

Calls gives the dates of the call options currently available on this commodity. In this example, options on soybean futures contracts are available for August, September and November.

Settle shows that the exchange has adjusted the price to reflect market values at the end of trading. Because futures

Qualified Retirement Plans

If you cultivate tax-deferred investments, you'll have a cash crop to live on when you retire.

To produce a healthy supply of cash—and to be sure it's there when you need it—you have to invest for retirement while you're working. You can participate in employer-sponsored retirement plans, invest in retirement savings plans of your own, or both. As long as you're using a plan that meets the government's legal requirements, it counts as a qualified retirement plan.

GREENBACK QUALIFIED RETIREMENT PLAN

GROWS FAST TAX-RESISTANT

- SOW EARLY AND OFTEN
- CULTIVATE WELL
- DO NOT HARVEST UNTIL MATURE

PRIZE-WINNING PLANS

Many types of plans are qualified, and, in general, they work like this: In return for postponing taxes until you start receiving your retirement income, you give up access to the money that's invested.

If you're contributing to a plan that you set up yourself, as you might do if you're self-employed, you have to be sure your plan complies with the regulations. But if your plan is employer-sponsored, the plan administrator is responsible for following the rules:

ELIGIBILITY
A plan must apply eligibility rules consistently.

ANNUAL CONTRIBUTION
There are specific limits on the amount you can contribute each year to qualified retirement plans.

PAYOUT REGULATIONS
A number of restrictions apply to withdrawals from qualified plans before retirement. For example, you will be penalized in most cases if you start to withdraw from a retirement plan before you are 59½ years old. There is also a limit on the amount you can receive from all your qualified pension plans in any year before you owe additional tax.

TYPES OF QUALIFIED PLANS

Both employer-funded plans and employee contribution plans can be qualified. The major difference is the source of the money that's invested—whether your employer puts it in, over and above your salary, or it's taken out of your salary. You may participate in several different plans, either at the same time or at different points in your working life.

Pension plans are funded by your employer, with money that's separate from your salary. Your employer gets to deduct the contribution from corporate income tax.

Savings plans are funded with a portion of your earnings. The amount of your contribution is subtracted from the amount reported as income to the IRS, decreasing your current taxes.

Many employers also match your contributions to your retirement savings plan, often as a percentage of your contribution, up to a fixed cap.

A Qualified Advantage

With a qualified retirement plan, you postpone or defer paying taxes on contributions and investment earnings, until you begin withdrawing money. The difference in growth between a tax-deferred and a taxable investment is shown dramatically in the chart below. For example, it can mean that $100,000 invested at 8% annual interest grows to $466,096 before taxes after 20 years—instead of $292,884. That's an unqualified advantage.

WITH A QUALIFIED PLAN

PAY NO TAX ON CONTRIBUTIONS AND ANNUAL EARNINGS UNTIL YOU WITHDRAW

PAY TAX* AS YOU WITHDRAW

 INVESTMENT **+** **ANNUAL EARNINGS** **=** **TOTAL RETURN**

*You will owe taxes at your regular rate as you withdraw from your tax-deferred plan.

WITH A REGULAR INVESTMENT**

PAY TAX ON ALL EARNINGS ANNUALLY

INVESTMENT **+** **ANNUAL EARNINGS** **−** **ANNUAL TAX** **=** **TOTAL RETURN**

** Taxes must also be paid on initial investment.

OTHER TAX-ADVANTAGED PLANS

Like qualified retirement plans, certain other arrangements let you defer taxes on pay and investment earnings. But with these other plans you or your employer may have to pay taxes on the money before you invest it, which means you have less to invest. But if you aren't eligible for a qualified plan, or if you've invested all the money you can in a given year, you can use another tax-advantaged plan to save for retirement.

For example, you can invest in variable annuities or certain types of insurance that accumulate tax-deferred. Or maybe you can persuade your employer to provide retirement benefits through a non-qualified plan designed for you. You won't have to deal with qualified plan restrictions, including how much can be invested.

Pensions

You can collect a pension after you retire—if you work for an employer that provides a pension plan.

Under traditional pension plans, called **defined benefit plans**, employers put money into funds that pay retired workers, and sometimes their survivors, a regular income for the rest of their lives. The amount is usually based on what they were earning and how long they worked.

In recent years, many employers have modified their approach to pension plans. Using **defined contribution plans**, employers put money into individual pension fund accounts for each employee. In a defined contribution plan, the employer doesn't guarantee the retirement benefits employees will receive.

The amount you get from a pension can vary enormously, from a small check at the time you retire to a generous percentage of your final salary every year. The payout depends on the kind and level of plan your employer provides, how well it's managed and how long you participate.

WHO'S COVERED... AND WHO'S NOT

Any business that has employees and anyone who is self-employed can set up a pension plan. Most large companies with more than 250 employees—and virtually all government agencies—provide pension plans for their employees. Most small companies don't.

In the early '90s, for example, only 14% of all businesses with fewer than ten employees offered plans, leaving millions of people without pensions. Part-time workers are rarely covered by a pension plan, even when they're long-time employees. The same applies to seasonal workers, and to people who work in low-paying retail and service jobs.

> **Employer contributions to 401(k) plans average 3%–3½% of your salary.**

Though there are tax incentives for workers without pension plans to establish Individual Retirement Accounts, many don't, either because it doesn't seem important or because they have a hard time putting aside the money they are entitled to invest.

PENSION FINE PRINT

An **integrated plan** is a variation of a pension plan, which can leave you with less retirement money than you expected. In an integrated plan, your employer counts their contribution to Social Security in determining contributions or

THE HISTORY OF PENSIONS

The first pensions we know about were paid to aged and disabled Roman soldiers who could no longer fight for the Empire. Military pensions in the U.S. date back to before the American Revolution. In 1636, the Plymouth Colony provided: "If a person shalbee sent forth as a soldier and shall return maimed hee shalbee mayntained competently by the Collonie during his life."

By the early 1800s, government workers in several European countries were supported after they retired. In 1859, a plan was created for the New York City Police. The U.S. government introduced pensions in the 1920s. Generous pensions have since become a hallmark of public-sector jobs, compensating civil servants for lower salaries than they could earn in the private sector.

The history of most corporate pensions in the U.S. began in the 1930s, and is linked closely to the aftermath of the depression, the introduction of Social Security, and to World War II wage and price controls.

EVERY WORKER DESERVES A PENSION

Two Kinds of Plans

THE COMPANY PUTS MONEY INTO A PENSION FUND IN YOUR NAME

DEFINED BENEFIT PLAN

" Company A guarantees you a yearly pension equal to 30% of your salary if you've worked for them for at least 25 years before you retire. "

DEFINED CONTRIBUTION PLAN

" Company B agrees to invest an amount equal to 5% of your salary in your retirement account each year, and may offer you a variety of investment options. "

the benefits they pay to you, and then reduces the amount of your pension accordingly. It's perfectly legal, and it must be explained in the material you're given when you enroll in the retirement plan. But many people miss that detail until it's too late.

PENSIONS AND THE LAW

The federal government does not require companies to provide pension plans, but it does offer them substantial tax incentives to do so. To help insure that plans live up to their promises to pay, and to protect tax revenues, the government carefully regulates and monitors them. As a result, many small companies have shied away from participating, and in recent years a number of companies that had traditionally offered plans have ended them.

Some companies have used their pension funds to buy policies with insurers who take over the responsibility of paying retired workers. Others offer bonuses and salary increases instead of retirement

account contributions, or give employees a check for the amount accumulated in their pension account.

What these changes mean for the future is that workers will have a much greater long-term responsibility for funding their retirement themselves.

PENSION PLAN LIMITS

The government limits the size of the annual contribution an employer can make to any defined contribution plan. The cap runs from 15% to 25% of salary, depending on the plan. There's also a dollar limit for each type. For example, in 1996, the defined contribution plan maximum is $30,000.

Defined benefit plans don't have a contribution limit, but there is a cap on the total amount that an employee can receive from the plan in any single year. For 1996, the IRS has set that amount at $120,000, or 100% of a recipient's average salary, whichever is less.

Defined Benefit Plans

Defined benefit pensions are a lot better to look forward to than death and taxes—but they aren't always as certain.

Traditional employer-funded pension plans, known as **defined benefit plans**, are designed to pay a fixed, pre-established benefit when you retire. If there's a defined benefit plan where you work, you'll probably be included in it if you work full-time. And chances are you won't have many options about how the plan works or how the money is invested. That's one of the trade-offs for the advantages the defined benefit plan provides.

Defined benefit plans generally pay you a regular monthly benefit for your lifetime, sometimes with a final payment to your survivors. In other cases, though, you may be able to choose a lump sum payment when you retire, which you can reinvest (see page 156). With a generous plan, you might expect an annual income equal to between 30% and 50% of your final salary. But there's no law about how much a pension has to promise to pay, and some workers end up getting very little.

CALCULATING YOUR PENSION

The way your employer figures the amount you get is spelled out in the plan itself. In some plans, for example, there is a standard pension for everyone who meets minimum years-in-service requirements. In others, the annual amount you get reflects what you were earning, with better-paid employees getting higher pensions.

The rules are clear, though, so you can calculate ahead of time what your pension will be. Usually, the major factors in determining the amount you'll receive include:

- **Your salary**
- **The time you've been on the job**
- **Your age**

GETTING ADVICE

Since defined benefit pension plans vary, you need to understand the fine print of any one you're depending on.

Your employer's benefits officer should know the answers to questions like these:

- Is your pension based on your average compensation, your final year's salary, or some other amount?
- Do different length-of-service requirements apply to employees who were hired at different times?
- What's the normal retirement age? What happens to your pension amount if you retire sooner?
- Is there any advantage to working past age 65?
- Is there a Cost Of Living Adjustment (COLA) after you retire?

LONGER IS BETTER

One common formula for setting your pension amount is to multiply the years you've been on the job times a certain percentage, such as 1.5%, and then multiply the result times your final salary

$$\text{Years on job} \times .015 \quad \times \quad \text{Final salary} \quad = \quad \text{Pension}$$

for example

	30	Years
x	**.015**	
=	**.45**	
x $	**72,000**	Final salary
= $	**32,400**	Annual pension

YEARS ON THE JOB

10 YEARS

20 YEARS

30 YEARS

STAYING PUT

Even if you can also count on pensions from a couple of earlier jobs, you'll probably wind up with less money than if you'd been with the same employer for your entire career. That's one reason some workers prefer the more portable defined contribution plans.

EMPLOYER RETIREMENT PLANS

BEING VESTED

Being **vested** means you have the right to collect a pension benefit at a specific age, even if you've left the job before then. Without vesting rights, you forfeit any benefit when you leave, and the money becomes part of the general fund.

Today, the law requires that you be vested under one of two minimum schedules. You are either:

- **100% vested after five years, or**
- **20% vested after three years and fully vested after seven years.**

With some employers, you are vested more quickly, and in certain cases immediately. A few plans—including some for government employees and for many unionized workers—still require you to be on the job for ten years or longer before you're vested.

501 HOURS

If you leave your job before you're vested, you usually lose the credits you've built up toward retirement. But there are ways to keep up your ties and your benefits. One is part-time work. In most cases, working 501 hours a year, the equivalent of 12½ weeks, is enough to keep you on the pension books. However, if you end your career working part-time, your pension could be reduced—since your final salary may determine the amount you get.

You won't lose pension credits, either, if you take up to 501 hours of family leave to care for a new baby or a sick family member.

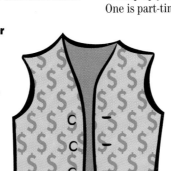

SALARY	PENSION	
$55,000	**$8,250**	
$72,000	**$10,800**	**THE MORE YEARS YOU SPEND ON THE JOB, THE LARGER YOUR PENSION**
$55,000	**$16,500**	
$72,000	**$21,600**	
$55,000	**$24,750**	**TIME ON THE JOB CAN HAVE A BIGGER IMPACT THAN FINAL SALARY**
$72,000	**$32,400**	

WHAT'S IN A COLA

Once you retire and your pension is calculated, the amount is usually fixed. Fewer than 5% of private U.S. pensions come with COLAs, or cost-of-living adjustments, that increase the amount of your pension to keep pace with inflation. Some employers voluntarily increase pensions for retired workers from time to time. Government pensions, on the other hand, are generally adjusted annually to make up for increased living costs.

PENSION

Defined Contribution Plans

The potential risks of defined contribution plans are offset by their potential rewards.

The way retirement plans are funded and run is still changing. Since the mid-1970s, the trend has been away from defined benefit pensions, with their guaranteed payments, to **defined contribution pension plans**. In a defined contribution plan, your employer contributes to an account in your name, but has no obligation to provide a fixed amount when you retire. The amount of your pension is determined by how much is invested and the way it grows. If the economy is healthy and your pension account does well, you'll be in good shape. But if your account's performance lagged, you could end up

with less. While account statements offer an indication of your likely return, there's no way to predict what you'll get until the day you actually retire.

One major advantage of these plans is that they offer employees strong growth potential and a greater sense of control, plus the ability to transfer them to a new employer.

WHO OFFERS THEM?

More and more employers, both private and public, are offering defined contribution plans. In 1980, 70% of all pension plans fit into this category. By 1996, more

Types of Defined Contribution Plans

Type	Funding	Contribution
MONEY PURCHASE PLANS	Employer	Employer contributes to plan based on a formula that covers all participating employees
PROFIT-SHARING PLANS	Employer	Employer contributes percentage of profits; some plans are based on total profits, while others use a sliding scale
EMPLOYEE STOCK OWNERSHIP PLANS (ESOPS)	Employer	Employer contributes stock or subsidizes employee purchase of stock
401(k) PLANS	Employee and Employer	Employee contributes pre-tax salary to the plan; employer may, and often does, contribute an amount based on an announced formula. Plan may also allow employee to make after-tax contributions
403(b) PLANS	Employee and Employer	Employee contributes pre-tax salary to the plan; employer may, and often does, contribute an additional amount
SECTION 457 PLANS	Employee	Employee contributes pre-tax salary to the plan

PACKING YOUR PLAN

Portability is a major attraction of defined contribution plans, along with quicker, or even instant, vesting rights. When you switch jobs, you can often move your accumulated assets to your new employer's plan. That way, you're not starting at pension zero each time you move. If you can't move it, you can often leave your account with your former employer so that it goes on growing until you're ready to retire.

than four of every five employers who supplied pensions offered a defined contribution plan. Some employers offer them as supplemental savings plans in addition to defined benefit plans. Others have replaced their conventional plans entirely. Most employers setting up plans for the first time choose to make a defined contribution rather than provide a defined benefit.

It's easy to see why. Defined contribution plans are easier to administer and less subject to government regulation. And they can provide employees with investment choices.

Eligibility	Loan Privileges
All eligible company employees	NO
All eligible company employees	YES
Employees of stock-issuing businesses	NO
All eligible employees of companies that sponsor plans (not available to state and municipal workers)	YES
Restricted to employees of certain tax-exempt employers and certain public school teachers	YES
Restricted to state and municipal workers and some employees of tax-exempt organizations	YES

VARIETY SPICES UP THE PENSION STEW

Some employers offer only one type of defined contribution plan, like a profit-sharing or money purchase plan. In most cases, these plans are funded by the employer, with the year's contribution tied to how well the company did.

Other employers let you choose among a variety of plans or participate in more than one. Usually, when you have a choice, you have to contribute before your employer's contribution kicks in.

IT'S YOUR CHOICE

Many defined contribution plans are optional. You get to choose whether you want to participate. What you agree to if you do participate is that you'll contribute some of your current salary to fund your pension. On the plus side, you don't owe tax on the amount you put away until you begin to receive benefits. But you will have less take-home pay.

With voluntary plans, employees who decide not to participate—because they think retirement is too far off or because they're reluctant to cut back on their take-home pay—may end up without enough in retirement.

Salary Reduction Plans

If you want to control your retirement fund investments, 401(k)s, 403(b)s and 457 plans may be the right vehicles.

More than $1 trillion is currently in **salary reduction plans**—about a sixth of all pension fund money in the U.S. And that share is growing, as more people recognize the advantages of making tax-deferred investments when they have the chance.

The 401(k)s, 403(b)s and 457s—their catchy names are the sections of the tax code that describe them—are also increasingly popular because they are sometimes the only game in town—or at least the only way many employees can participate in a pension plan.

A Double Plus

The double advantage of tax-deferred plans is saving on your tax bill and investing for retirement

The more money you put in a 401(k) plan...

the lower your taxable income...

WITH A 401(k) PLAN you save on taxes while you invest for retirement*

$	75,000	Gross pay
−	6,000	401(k) investment
= $	69,000	Taxable income

WITHOUT A 401(k) PLAN you pay more in tax and you must set aside savings from income after tax

$	75,000	Gross pay
−	0	401(k) investment
= $	75,000	Taxable income

*Based on 1996 rates. Tax figures include the personal exemption and the standard deduction, which everyone is entitled to receive.

THE NEW SAVINGS SUPERSTAR

There are about 40 million workers currently covered under salary reduction plans, and the number keeps growing. Between 1988 and 1993, the number of workers with an employer that sponsors a salary reduction plan jumped by over 40%.

HOW SALARY REDUCTION WORKS

You invest in a salary reduction plan by having a percentage of your salary deposited in your pension account. The amount you deposit is tax-deferred—it does not count as part of your taxable income for that year.

Employers who offer salary reduction (or salary deferral) plans usually arrange for you to invest your money in different fixed-income, equity, or money market accounts. You choose among the options, and pay the costs of investing, such as

administrative fees. But you do not have to pay any tax on these funds or their earnings until you withdraw from the account.

A ROSE BY ANY OTHER NAME...

If you work for a nonprofit organization, you may not recognize the name 403(b), even if you're participating in one. Salary reduction plans are frequently known by other names, including TSAs, tax shelters and savings plans, especially when they're offered as supplements to defined benefit plans.

at the same time. For example, if you're single, make $75,000 and put 8% of your salary in a 401(k), 403(b) or 457 plan, you'll pay $1,860 less in federal income taxes, and you'll have $6,000 growing tax-deferred.

the less tax you pay...

$14,495** — Taxes on $69,000 income

$16,355** — Taxes on $75,000 income

and the faster your investment grows.

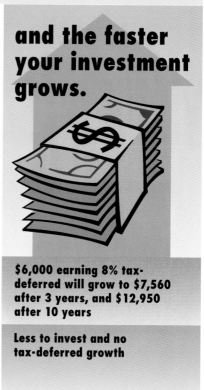

$6,000 earning 8% tax-deferred will grow to $7,560 after 3 years, and $12,950 after 10 years

Less to invest and no tax-deferred growth

**In most places you will also save on state income taxes.

THE 400 FAMILY

While 401(k)s are the best known of the salary reduction plans, they're just one of a group of defined contribution pension plans available to people who work for different types of organizations. Each of these plans is restricted to a specific group of workers, and each has an annual contribution maximum.

The plans also have different rules on employer contributions, who can partici-

pate, and the way the plan is administered, although they operate under similar government regulations. They may also play different pension roles. In some cases, a 401(k) plan may be the only way for employees to participate in a pension plan. In contrast, federal, state and non-profit salary reduction plans like 403(b)s and 457 plans and 401(k) plans of larger employers are often set up to supplement defined benefit pensions.

Matching and Switching

Getting the most from your retirement investment requires some fancy footwork.

Many corporate employers who offer salary reduction plans match, or add to, your contribution, up to a limit. A typical formula is to match 50% of what you put in, up to 6% of your salary. There's also usually a cap on the amount an employer will contribute in each pay period. That means you'll end up with more if you spread out your contributions to qualify for matching instead of having your share taken out in big installments early in the year.

How Matching Funds Work

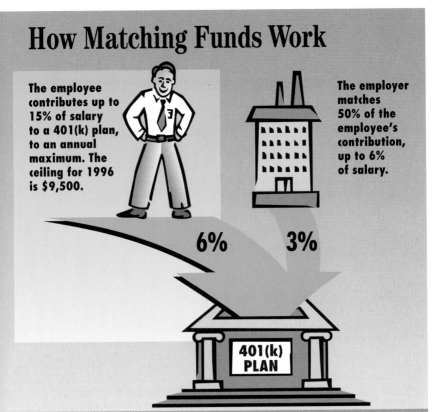

The employee contributes up to 15% of salary to a 401(k) plan, to an annual maximum. The ceiling for 1996 is $9,500.

The employer matches 50% of the employee's contribution, up to 6% of salary.

6% 3%

401(k) PLAN

The Employee The Employer

	Contribution	Contribution	
4% of $90,000 income	**$3,600**	**$1,800**	**50%** of employee contribution
6% of $90,000 income	**$5,400**	**$2,700**	**50%** of employee contribution
10% of $90,000 income	**$9,000**	**$2,700**	**50%** of **6%** of employee income ($5,400)

MOVING THINGS AROUND

Generally, a salary reduction plan lets you put money in as many of the available options as you choose and move your investment from one option to another. Some plans permit only annual transfers, but others allow them quarterly or even daily. In some cases, though, there are large surrender fees when you switch between different types of investments, or from one fund to another.

The reason for using different options is to keep your investment diversified. Moving assets around works best when you have a strategy for investing your retirement funds, like balancing growth and income. It makes less sense to move between funds if you're constantly trying to guess how the markets will move (called timing the market), or you're reacting in panic to a downturn in the stock or bond markets.

THE 403(b) ADVANTAGE

If you work for a college or university, a school system, or certain other nonprofit groups, you may be able to participate in a 403(b), the most flexible salary reduction plan. Generally, you have more investment choices than 401(k) or 457 plans provide, and you may be able to contribute a larger percentage of your salary, up to an annual cap of $9,500 and sometimes more.

You may also have the right to make a tax-free transfer from any option your employer offers to another 403(b) mutual fund or annuity of your own choosing. In some cases, you can only transfer money you have contributed yourself, but not the matching funds contributed by your employer.

The advantage is that you can move money into high-performance, low-fee funds. And while the transfers may be tax-free, they may not be fee-free. Some 403(b)s impose surrender charges, which can total 7% or more of the assets you're moving, especially when the transfer occurs during the first few years after you have contributed money.

403(b) CATCH UP

If you didn't begin contributing to a 403(b) as soon as you were eligible, or you didn't contribute the maximum, you have a chance to catch up—an uncommon phenomenon in the world of retirement savings. The usual pattern is to increase the percentage of salary you

MAKING THE GRADE

There are limits on how much you can contribute to a 401(k), 403(b) or 457 plan. In 1996, the IRS set these ceilings at $9,500 for 401(k) and 403(b) plans and $7,500 for 457 plans. There are even more rules that tie these ceilings together—so if you're lucky enough to be eligible for both types of plans, what you contribute to a 457 plan will reduce the amount you can contribute to a 401(k) plan, and vice versa.

In addition to the limits on contributions, there are rules that govern what percentage of salary employees can contribute to a defined contribution plan like a 401(k). Basically, the rules tie the contributions of owners and higher paid employees to the contributions of employees who make less. For example, the higher paid employees can in many cases contribute only 2% more of their salaries than the average percentage contributed by the rest of the employees. That means that sometimes higher paid employees won't be able to contribute up to the $9,500 ceiling.

defer and exceed the normal dollar limit of $9,500 each year for five years. It's an easy way to play catch-up that also saves on your current tax bill.

IS THE SWITCH WORTH IT?

Often, the answer is yes, even if you pay fees. If the fund or annuity you're switching to has a better track record, or provides greater diversity, than your current investment, the long-term returns may be worth the cost of the transfer. But you do have to compare fees carefully, as they can vary significantly.

New participants in 403(b) plans now have many more options than were available before, so they may be less likely to get caught in the surrender fee crunch.

Paying for the Plans

Bigger is cheaper, as this chart shows. 401(k) investors typically pay their account administrators higher fees than corporations and other large employers pay to have their pension funds managed. But even the higher fees for smaller plans are more than offset by the tax advantages.

TYPE	ASSETS	AVERAGE FEE
BIG PLANS	**$150 MILLION** (12,000 employees)	**0.5%**
401(k) PLANS	**$1.5 MILLION** (115 employees)	**1.4%**

Self-directed Pension Plans

Contributing to your pension plan is only the beginning of the story. Along the way, you may be responsible for managing it, too.

MUTUAL FUND

One major difference between defined benefit and defined contribution plans is who takes responsibility for how well your pension fund performs. In defined benefit plans, you have no say at all over investment decisions. In fact, you probably have no idea where the money is invested. But if you contribute to a defined contribution plan, like a 401(k) or a 403(b), making decisions about pension fund investments is usually your responsibility. The choices you make determine the return you'll get when it's time to collect.

GROWING NUMBER OF CHOICES

Often, you can choose where to put your money. Many plans provide between four and seven options, including mutual funds, annuities, stock purchases and savings bonds. Usually, there's at least one stock fund, a balanced fund, a bond fund or fixed-income account, and maybe a money market account. And sometimes you can choose from as many as two dozen or more different funds.

PUT MORE STOCK IN STOCK

Although stocks, and stock funds, historically provide better returns than other investments, only 25% of the people participating in defined contribution plans own stock or stock funds, and only 3.7% have half or more of their investment in stock or stock funds.

Stock ownership in defined contribution plans

75% HAVE NO STOCKS

ONLY **3.7% HAVE MORE THAN 50% IN STOCKS** →

25% HAVE STOCKS

FINDING SOLUTIONS

Your freedom to choose the best investments is limited, of course, by the options your employer's plan offers. And your investing decisions have to take into account your age, other sources of income, and your tolerance for risk. But there are questions you can ask to help you decide which option you'll choose:

- **What are my investment choices?**
- **What are the objectives of each option, and what are their risks?**
- **How well have the various options been doing over various time periods?**
- **How do the annual expenses compare?**
- **Who pays the investment fees and administrative charges?**
- **Are there commissions or surrender charges?**

GETTING INVESTMENT ADVICE

Some employers provide very little, if any, investment advice about which options to choose or how to allocate your money for the best return. They may fear being

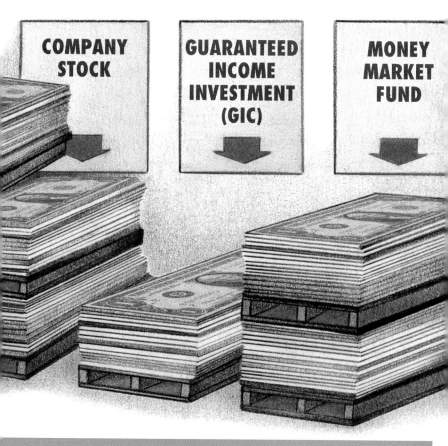

SOME DISAPPOINTING RESULTS

Despite the vast sums that employees have contributed to self-directed pension plans—some current estimates make it close to $1 trillion—financial experts caution that these investments may not produce as much as they should. Three reasons are frequently mentioned:

FEAR OF RISK Employees are not making the best choices among the options offered—usually because they don't realize that in choosing what seems safest, they are limiting their return. In 1993, one study showed that close to 50% of 401(k) money was invested in Guaranteed Investment Contracts (GICs), which are designed to provide guaranteed payments, and thus are likely to pay less than the stock market.

SHORT-TERM THINKING Investing for retirement requires a long range view. Some participants invest as if they need to keep their nest egg available to spend tomorrow. When they do, they get lower returns and risk losing the fight with inflation. Wise long-term investors, on the other hand, have a better chance of staying ahead of inflation.

NOT ENOUGH DIVERSITY Too many employees put all their eggs in one basket. In this case, the old wives' tale is correct. By diversifying investments—putting some in stocks, some in bonds and a little in the shorter term investments—pension savings get a buffer from periodic ups and downs of any one investment option.

held liable if their advice doesn't produce good returns, so they shy away from providing advice at all. In addition, self-directed pension funds are generally administered by human resources directors, who are typically not financial managers with expertise in providing investment advice. Whatever the explanation, if you need advice, you may have to get it from other sources.

Supplemental Retirement Plans

A company's basic retirement plan may be only the starting point for some employees.

Since the promise of a secure retirement is a way to recruit and keep valuable employees, companies use non-qualified plans, sometimes called **SERPs** or **Supplemental Executive Retirement Plans**, to help feather certain nests. The tighter the restrictions get on regular retirement plans, the more widespread supplemental plans become—despite their limitations for both employers and employees.

HOW SERPS WORK

If you're covered by a supplemental plan, it pays to know how they work for you— and sometimes against you. On the plus side, because SERPs are non-qualified plans provided by your employer, there are no limits on the amount that can be contributed. And since you have limited access to the money—you usually can't get it before you leave or retire—your tax liability is deferred until the money is paid out.

SERPS HAVE DRAWBACKS

First, you might never collect. Supplemental retirements are paid out of a company's general operating budget, not a special pension fund. Your share is an entry in the company's books, but there's no ownership protection, no insurance, and no government watchdog. So if the company goes bankrupt, or if it's sold, there's no guarantee you'll ever get the money you were promised. Some

Supplementing Your Retirement Plans

WHAT COMPANIES CAN CONTRIBUTE

Supplemental Plans	Standard Plans	Your Position
The company may provide SERPs, but is most likely to offer them to employees earning the higher salaries in this range	The company contributes to qualified pension plans on the same basis for all workers, usually a set percentage of the employee's contributions	Senior Management (above $150,000) 
		Middle Management ($66,000–$150,000) 
		Rank & File Workers (under $66,000) 

SERP
NON-QUALIFIED

QUALIFIED PENSION PLAN

companies, however, buy insurance or set up trusts to provide some protection for SERP money.

A second potential problem is how your employer values the growth of your investment. If the money is not actually invested anywhere, it isn't providing a real return. If your employer assumes a money market return of around 4%, instead of a well-performing stock fund return, which might be closer to 12%, your account will be worth much less than it could have been.

When you do get the SERP money you were promised, you'll owe tax on the amount. That's because you can't roll the payout over into an IRA or a retirement plan at your new job since SERPS aren't qualified plans.

NEW RULES/NEW WRINKLES

Until recently, SERPs—sometimes referred to as **top hat plans**—were pretty much limited to highly paid executives. Over the last 15 years, the limits on contributions and benefits under qualified plans have been tightened by the government. Most recently, in 1994, the top salary on

which contributions to qualified pension plans could be figured was lowered from $235,840 to $150,000. As a result, more employers are looking for ways to put more retirement money away for employees who fall into that range and might not have needed special treatment before.

MIRROR PLANS

Employers have great flexibility when they design SERPs. Some are specially created for individual employees. Others cover a broader range of management employees.

There are a number of reasons why the government imposes fewer rules on SERPs. The most important is that SERPs don't get all the same tax advantages that apply to qualified plans. Another reason: SERPs are only available to management employees.

One common type of SERP is a **mirror plan**. A mirror plan "wraps around" a qualified plan, providing the benefits that an executive was not able to get because of the limits the government puts on qualified plans. For example, if your salary is $150,000, a 15% contribution to a 401(k) plan would come to $22,500. But the law limits your 401(k) plan contribution in 1996 to $9,500. A mirror 401(k) plan would allow you to save the additional $13,000.

Like qualified 401(k)s, the $13,000 investment grows tax-deferred. But there are some catches:

- **Your contribution is not part of the 401(k) plan. It is kept separate and remains subject to your employer's creditors.**

- **When it's time to start distributions, you won't be allowed to roll over the mirror plan balance to an IRA.**

- **Your ability to choose distribution options may be limited.**

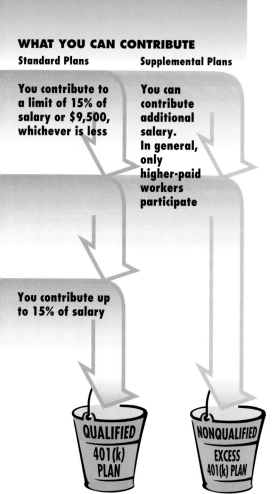

WHAT YOU CAN CONTRIBUTE

Standard Plans

You contribute to a limit of 15% of salary or $9,500, whichever is less

You contribute up to 15% of salary

Supplemental Plans

You can contribute additional salary. In general, only higher-paid workers participate

QUALIFIED 401(k) PLAN

NONQUALIFIED EXCESS 401(k) PLAN

Pension Distributions

When you're mapping out the best route to collecting your pension, there'll be several forks in the road.

Once you've decided to retire, you may have to make a decision about how to collect your pension. The choice is usually between a **lump sum** payment and a lifetime **annuity**, or series of equal payments. The most unnerving element in the process is that once you've committed yourself, you can't change your mind.

If you choose the lump sum, you'll also have to decide what to do with the money. One common option is to put it into an IRA rollover, but you might decide to take a cash payment instead.

THE CRITICAL FACTORS

While you don't have to decide until you're actually ready to stop working, making the best choice is critical. The factors you have to consider are your age and health, what you want to provide for your family, and what other sources of income you'll have. In some cases, too, you have to consider your employer's economic health.

For example, if you're in poor health and concerned about providing for your spouse, you might choose a joint and survivor annuity that will continue to pay while either of you is alive. On the other hand, if your spouse is seriously ill, you might choose a single life annuity that will provide a larger amount for you each month than a joint annuity would. Usually this requires your spouse's consent.

HOW TO COLLECT

Individual plans set their own rules for collecting a pension, just as they do for qualifying. You might have to be a certain age, have worked a certain number of years, or a combination of the two.

For example, sometimes you're not eligible to collect a pension until you reach 65, although other plans allow you to begin sooner. The minimum is usually 55—provided you've participated in the plan for at least ten years. If you're younger, you have to wait to collect.

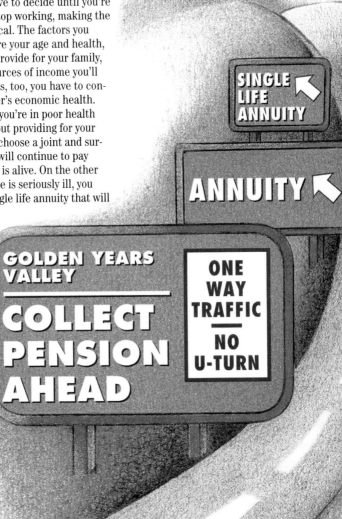

In most cases, though, your pension is paid when you actually retire. You usually can't postpone the payout, although it may be possible to defer part of it.

DEFINED BENEFIT PENSIONS

Most employers who provide defined benefit pensions provide experts to give you advice on the differences between the payout options. Even though the final decision is yours, the advisor should give you a detailed comparison showing how each option would work and the money you can expect to receive. When you choose, you have to consider not only how much you'll collect, but for how long, and what the tax consequences will be.

While 65 is no longer the hard and fast retirement age it once was, many defined

A CORPORATE FIRST

American Express is generally thought to have established the first corporate plan in 1875. In 1913, AT&T established its own comprehensive corporate pension plan. It paid retirement benefits to workers aged 60 and above who'd been with the company 20 years or more. It also provided accident and disability insurance to long-time employees.

benefit retirement plans are still set up as though 65 were still the norm. If you retire earlier, your employer may recalculate the pension you were promised to take into account the added years you'll be collecting instead of working.

If you go on working after 65, federal rules require that your pension keeps on growing until you actually retire and collect on it. That should provide a boost to your income, and perhaps act as an incentive to delay retirement.

DEFINED CONTRIBUTION PENSIONS

If you have a defined contribution pension plan, you probably have to make fewer choices at retirement. While sometimes you can choose an annuity or periodic payments, frequently the assets are sold and you get a lump sum distribution, which you are responsible for investing to provide income during your retirement. If you've participated in a stock purchase plan, you can hold onto the shares and continue to collect dividends, or sell your shares and reinvest the money. Again, it's up to you.

PAYOUT LIMITS

There's a limit—$155,000 for 1996—on the amount of money you get from all your qualified pension plans in any single year before owing a penalty. If you get more than the limit, you'll owe the IRS up to 15% of the excess amount. If you have only one employer-sponsored pension, you're not

apt to go over the limit, as the plan's administrator keeps tabs on its payouts. But if you're collecting from several different qualified retirement plans—perhaps including a Keogh, a SEP, or several IRAs—complying with the limits is your responsibility.

The one exception is for lump sum payments. In 1996, you take your money all at once so that you can get a $775,000 payout without penalty.

Pension Choices

Understanding the small print helps you balance the pros and cons of payout options.

There's no universal right answer about how to take your pension payout, but when you have to make a decision, it helps to know the advantages—and the disadvantages—of your options.

WHAT THE ISSUES ARE

How comfortable you are with investing money is a major consideration in deciding between a lump sum payout and an annuity. If you've been investing successfully for years, the prospect of building your portfolio and your profits with a lump sum pension payout can be appealing—and realistic. The challenge, of course, is producing enough income during retirement.

But if you don't want to worry about outliving your assets, you may opt for the relative security of an annuity. Knowing that the same amount is coming in regularly makes budgeting—and occasionally splurging—a lot easier.

Taxes are also a major consideration. If you'll still be in a high tax bracket after you retire and you're eligible for **forward averaging** (see page 157), you may make out better paying the taxes you owe up front. On the other hand, if your tax rate will drop after you retire because your pension is providing the bulk of your income, you may owe less by taking an annuity or rolling your payout over into an IRA.

TAKING YOUR TIME

The good thing about making pension payout choices is that usually you have plenty of time, as retirement doesn't usually take you by surprise. Defined benefit pensions have been in place long enough so that their managers understand the consequences, good and bad, of the various options. Or, you can get additional advice from your union representative, tax consultant, or lawyer.

A Close Look At Some

Type	What it is
 ANNUITY	An annuity is a regular, monthly payment, usually for your lifetime
 PERIODIC PAYMENTS	Periodic payments are installment payments of roughly equal amounts paid over a specific period, often 5–15 years
 LUMP SUM	A lump sum is a cash payment of the money in your pension fund
 IRA ROLLOVER	An IRA rollover is a lump sum (or qualifying periodic) payment deposited into a special IRA account. You can either deposit it yourself or ask your employer to do it directly

PENSION MAX
Pension maximization

is salesperson's lingo for a single life annuity repackaged to make it seem more attractive to people trying to get the most out of their pension. With **pension max**, you use part of the higher payment under a single life plan to buy a life insurance policy to cover the needs of the surviving spouse. It should come as no surprise that the person selling the policy is usually the one who suggests maximizing. The consensus among those who don't stand to profit from selling the insurance plans is that almost everyone is better off choosing a joint and survivor annuity, especially surviving spouses.

LOCATING THE MISSING

Sometimes pensions get lost in the shuffle—because people forget about them or forget to tell their survivors. Or sometimes a defined benefit plan folds, leaving incomplete records. The Pension Benefit Guaranty Corporation tries to locate the approximately 1,000 people a year who are entitled to pensions but aren't collecting. If you, or someone you know, was part of a plan but has lost touch with the employer, you can contact the Pension Benefit Guaranty Corporation at 1200 K Street NW, Washington, DC 20005. Write to the Administrative Review and Technical Assistance Division.

Important Retirement Choices

Advantages	Drawbacks
• Security of knowing that payments will come in on a regular basis • Option of spreading the payments out over your spouse's lifetime as well as your own • Peace of mind in knowing you can't outlive your resources	• Most annuities not indexed for inflation, which means that your fixed annuity will buy less and less as time goes by. Variable annuities are designed to help address this issue • Tax due on the amount you get each year • May lose ability to claim certain tax advantages
• Assurance of a regular payment at regular intervals • Relatively large payments because of limited time frame • May have option of rolling some or all payments into an IRA	• Commitment to payment schedule limits ability to get at lump sum, if needed • No assurance of lifetime income • Might leave yourself or spouse without funds after payments end • Taxes may be due at higher rate • Inflation can erode purchasing power of payments
• Control over investing and gifting your assets • May be eligible for forward averaging, which reduces taxes, and in some cases for other tax breaks	• Tax due immediately • Possibility of spending too much too quickly • Vulnerable to making poor investment decisions • No assurance of lifetime income—might leave yourself or spouse without funds if assets are exhausted
• Money continues to grow tax-deferred • Allows you to invest as you want and take money as you need it • Protection from early withdrawal penalties if you're not yet 59½	• May lose ability to claim certain tax advantages • Withdrawal schedule required after you reach age 70½

Pension Annuities

A pension annuity's distinguishing feature, and its greatest charm, is regularity.

A pension annuity pays you a regular retirement income. It can last your lifetime, or your lifetime plus the life of a survivor. But once you choose, it's set.

GAMBLING ON SURVIVAL

If you choose an annuity, you also have to decide whether you want a **single life** (sometimes called **straight life**) or a **joint and survivor option**. In a single life annuity, you get a regular payment every month for your lifetime. Basically, the payment is figured by dividing the

amount that has built up in your pension account and what you can expect it to earn over your remaining lifetime, by your life expectancy (figured using standard actuarial tables).

If you live longer than statistics predict, you still get your annuity. For example, a woman who retires at 65 can expect to live until she's 85. If she's still collecting her pension when she's 95, the system has worked in her favor. On the other hand, if she dies at 68, the balance in her account reverts—in most cases— to the general pension fund. (There are some exceptions. Certain pension funds make a lump sum payment of the balance of your retirement account to your estate. It's something you should check.)

In a **joint and survivor annuity**, your pension covers your lifetime and the lifetime of your designated survivor—often, but not necessarily, your spouse. The amount of your monthly check is usually less than it would be for a single life annuity. But after you die, your survivor gets a percentage of your pension each month for life. The advantages of the joint and survivor option are clear, especially in cases when your designated survivor is apt to live a long time and doesn't have a separate pension or other income. In fact, the financial benefits that joint and survivor policies provide (for elderly widows in particular) is such good social policy that the law requires companies to provide this

THREE KINDS OF ANNUITY PAYOUTS

The chart below compares an example of a single life payout with the amounts you'd get with a 50% joint and survivor annuity and with a 100% one. The type of annuity you choose determines the size of your monthly payout. As this example shows, a single life annuity pays the most, but a 100% joint and survivor annuity protects your survivor better.

Type of payout	Retiree's monthly payout UNTIL DEATH	Death of retiree	Spouse's monthly payout STARTING AFTER RETIREE'S DEATH
Single life	$4,167		Nothing
50% joint and survivor	$3,705		$1,853
100% joint and survivor	$3,335		$3,335

option automatically to married employees.

The drawbacks of joint and annuity pensions—the smaller payment and the possibility that your survivor might die before you do—are things you have to weigh before choosing this option. But both you and your spouse must agree—in writing—to waive the joint and survivor option if you select a single life annuity or a lump sum payment.

Period certain annuities provide survivor benefits for a set amount of time after the death of the pension holder. Because the payout period is limited—usually to five or ten years—the amount of the basic payment is higher than a joint and survivor annuity. The best reason for making this choice is to provide short-term support for a younger survivor, a minor child for example. The limited-term payments can be used to pay college tuition or make the down payment on a house, among other things.

Not all 401(k) and profit-sharing plans offer an annuity option. Instead, they will sometimes make periodic payments, over five, ten, or fifteen years. You can roll over periodic payments into an IRA if they're paid out in fewer than ten years and they are not part of the mandatory distributions discussed below. And you can choose to roll over some of the payments and take the others. That gives you much greater flexibility than you get with defined benefit pensions.

PENSION PAYOUTS

The law requires that qualified plans make mandatory distributions when you reach age 70½. Because pension plans are administered by the company—even if you decide how the money is invested—the company may, and often does, determine the way your annuity is calculated.

If a lifetime annuity is chosen, there are two ways to figure the minimum payment each year: the period-certain method and the recalculation method.

401(k) PIONEERS

Defined benefit pensions are well-mapped territory, but if you're counting on your 401(k) investments, you're traveling in uncharted lands. Most of the people who've invested in 401(k)s haven't retired yet, so depending on the investments you choose, there may be some new ground to cover in figuring the amount of your benefit, the schedule on which it should be paid and whether it will last as long as you do.

COMPANY PENSION FUND

COMPANY PENSION FUND

PAY TO THE ORDER OF JOHN J. PENSIONER

THREE THOUSAND TWO HUNDRE

Monthly pension FOR payment No. 00037

The Compan

Period certain means you get the same amount every year based on your life expectancy when you retire. **Recalculation** means the amount is refigured every year based on your new life expectancy. The employer plan may specify which method is used, or may give you the option. If the plan does not provide any rule, you get the recalculation method by default. Generally, the recalculation method provides a slower payout of the benefits.

Lump Sum Distributions

Sometimes you can take your pension in a lump sum and invest it yourself.

Lump sum suggests the comforting image of a mass of money—a bulwark against financial perils. If you invest it right, you can shore up the future by beating inflation, which causes annuities to lose their value. But you do need to be concerned about decreasing assets.

HOW LUMP SUM PAYMENTS WORK

When you take a lump sum distribution from a defined benefit plan, your employer figures out how much you would get if the plan paid you an annuity over your projected lifespan, and then calculates how much the pension fund could have earned in interest on that amount during the years of your payout. Your lump sum share is what you would have been entitled to, reduced by a factor of the projected interest earnings known as the discount rate.

If interest rates are high—as they were through much of the 1980s—your lump sum will be less than in a period of low interest. Once you have the lump sum, the responsibility for investing your pension to make it last through your retirement is yours.

MAKING IT LAST

You can use the discount rate the company uses to calculate your lump sum as a guide to how well you're doing with your investments. If you're earning the discount rate, you ought to do about as well, but if your money is earning less than that, you may come up short.

IT'S YOURS, NOW

You can take a lump sum distribution in cash—or perhaps more precisely by check. Or you can roll over the money into a special Individual Retirement Account (IRA). The only catch is that all the money you roll over must be pretax contributions and their earnings. You can't roll money into an IRA if you've already paid tax on it (as you would have on after-tax contributions to company thrift plans).

MAKING THE CHOICE

If you roll over your pension distribution to an IRA, you'll save taxes. Often, you'll also be better off over the long haul compared to taking a lump sum distribution, even with the tax advantages of forward

CASH DISTRIBUTION

ADVANTAGES

- Can use money immediately
- May be able to reduce taxes owed
- No minimum or maximum limits on withdrawal amounts

DRAWBACKS

- Easy to spend too fast
- Taxes due immediately
- Must make initial investment decisions quickly
- Owe additional taxes on investment gains

averaging, especially if you don't have to start drawing money right away.

WITH IRA ROLLOVER

$350,000	IRA rollover
x **8%**	Earnings (tax deferred)
$755,623	IRA balance after 10 years
− **278,802**	Tax if withdrawn (1996 rates)
$476,821	Balance after 10 years (after tax)

VS. LUMP SUM DISTRIBUTION (WITH AVERAGING)

$350,000	IRA rollover
− **84,180**	Tax (with averaging—1996 rates)
$265,820	After tax balance
x **8%**	Earnings (taxable annually)
$465,373	Balance after 10 years (after tax)

The longer you delay withdrawals (especially if you make withdrawals a little at a time), the better the IRA rollover option. But if you need the money right away, a lump sum distribution (with forward averaging) may be the way to go. If you don't qualify for forward averaging, the rollover is always the best way to reduce your taxes.

LUMP SUM

IRA ROLLOVER

ADVANTAGES

- Defer taxes on distribution until you withdraw funds
- Investment continues to grow tax-deferred
- May retain ability to claim forward averaging later

DRAWBACKS

- Might pay more taxes in the long run
- May lose access to large cash sum because of limits on annual withdrawal amounts
- Must begin periodic withdrawals by age 70½

A ONE-SHOT DEAL

To qualify for forward averaging, which you can do only once in your life, you have to:

- **Be at least 59½ and in the plan at least 5 years.**
- **Stop working for the employer who is paying you the lump sum.**
- **Take the entire pension amount as a lump sum directly from your employer.**

In addition, you can't forward average in a year when you're planning to roll over any money from another source into an IRA. If you do, you may lose the tax deferral and have to pay tax on that amount, too.

If you were born before 1936, you may be eligible for ten-year forward averaging, or the right to pay tax on your earnings as if they were capital gains taxed at a 20% rate. Either method would reduce your taxes. One thing you can't do is forward average money that's been rolled over into an IRA, unless you roll it back to a qualified employer-sponsored plan.

WHAT IF YOU'RE NOT 59½?

If you get your pension as a lump sum before you reach 59½—because you take the option of retiring, change jobs, are disabled, or are let go—you could face the double hit of taxes and penalties.

If you stop working after age 55, the penalty is automatically waived. The same is true if you can't work. But if you're healthy, younger than 55, and get the money as a lump sum, you'll have to roll over the whole amount into a special IRA or set up a special payment plan to avoid extra tax and penalties.

You must set up a **segregated**, or special, IRA for your pension payout, otherwise known as your preretirement distribution. You can't add anything to this IRA. But you may be able to roll the amount into a retirement plan at a new job or start withdrawing from it when you retire.

FORWARD AVERAGING

When you take a lump sum distribution, you have to pay the tax that's due on the entire amount. Any way you figure it, the tax will take a big bite out of what you have coming. But if you're at least 59½, you may qualify for **forward averaging**. That means you will owe less, even though you'll still owe it all at once.

When you forward average, you figure the tax as if the lump sum had been paid in equal payments over five years and were your only income in those years. For example, if your lump sum payment were $350,000, forward averaging would let you calculate as if you had received $70,000 in each of five years. You can't take any deductions or exemptions, and you pay at the single taxpayer rate.

WITH FORWARD AVERAGING

1 Divide your lump sum payout by five to find your taxable annual income.

2 Using the tax tables provided by the IRS, find the tax due. Multiply the annual tax by five to find your total tax bill.

3 Compare that amount with the tax that would have been due on the entire amount.

$ 350,000 Lump sum	**$ 16,836** Tax on 70K*	**$ 118,176** Tax on $350,000*
÷ 5	**x 5**	**− 84,180** Averaged tax
$ 70,000 Per year	**$ 84,180** Total due	**$ 33,996** TAX SAVINGS

*These examples use 1996 tax rates.

Changing Jobs, Changing Pensions

Retirement savings are portable…if you know what you have to move and where to store it.

If you change jobs—about 12% of the population does every year—protecting your retirement pension and investments may require some tough choices. Of course, what you can do depends on the type of plan, or plans, you've participated in. Sometimes your employers make all the decisions. But in many cases you'll be responsible for choosing a new home for the money. Even if you're short of cash, the biggest mistake you can make is spending it. You'll need it more after you retire.

CHOOSING WISELY

As a rule, if you're part of a 401(k), a profit-sharing plan, or a stock purchase plan, you'll get a distribution of the money that's been invested in your name, plus whatever the investment has earned. Then you'll have to decide what to do with the money, before taxes gobble up a big share of it. The chart below summarizes the details of the most frequent options.

Your options and their consequences

OPTION	TAX CONSEQUENCES	PLUSES AND MINUSES
Transfer money directly to IRA	None	Rollover money must go into separate IRA. Retain right to roll money into future employer's plan, preserving forward averaging option (see page 157)
Roll distribution into IRA yourself	20% withheld. Total amount must be deposited within 60 days, including the 20%, or subject to tax and 10% penalty if younger than 59½	Gives you short-term access to money, with potential penalties (see page 168)
Begin periodic withdrawals	Tax on distributions, but no early withdrawal penalty	Distributions must continue for five years or until 59½, whichever is longer. Depletes money earmarked for retirement
Leave money in former employer's plan (not always available)	None	In defined contribution plan, investment continues to grow undisturbed. Later, can be rolled into an IRA or moved to new employer's plan
Take cash as lump sum	Taxed as current income, plus 10% penalty if younger than 59½. 20% withheld immediately to help cover taxes due	May be eligible for forward averaging. Flexibility to use some cash and roll rest into an IRA. Lose ability to roll money into new employer's plan. Risk depleting retirement savings

change careers, the amount in your plan continues to grow tax-deferred.

Some civil service pensions offer reciprocity: pension contributions you make as a state employee and time spent on the job count if you move to a federal job, or vice versa. A state police officer who joins the Secret Service, for example, begins the new job with a pension credit already on the books. The same is true for some union plans.

RESTRICTED RIGHTS

If you're part of a defined benefit plan, your employer often won't offer a lump sum when you leave, and won't start paying you a pension until you reach the minimum age for early retirement— sometimes 55, but often older. Then you get what accumulated up to the time you left, either in a lump sum or as an annuity.

Thanks to changes in vesting rules, you probably will be entitled to the money your employer has contributed to the plan. But if you change jobs at 40, and can't collect for 15 or 20 years, don't expect the pension to pay a lot. In some cases, your benefit will be based on your salary when you left the job. Over time, inflation will eat away the value of the benefit you eventually receive.

HANDLING THE DETAILS

If your pension has included a stock purchase plan, or if your employer has contributed stock to a profit-sharing plan, you can hold onto it since it's in your name, or sell if the price is right. If you hold onto the stock, you can continue to use your former employer as your agent, or you can transfer the stocks into an IRA rollover you open with a brokerage firm. The advantage of a broker can be easier access, and possibly smaller commissions when you do decide to sell.

AVOIDING THE HASSLE

Some pension funds, including many 403(b) annuities, aren't tied to a particular employer. If you move, your pension goes with you. And if you're vested, but

EARLY RETIREMENT PACKAGES

Sometimes employers offer incentives for retiring early, like adding three to five years to the years you've actually worked, increasing the percentage of salary your pension will replace or offering a pension supplement until you become eligible for Social Security. Together, the incentives could mean a significantly bigger pension.

Or your employer may offer you a bonus for leaving your job early. This lump sum **severance** payment is added on top of the pension you would receive if you retired early. A week's pay for each year you've been on the job is a common formula used to compute the lump sum.

If you have a choice between a bigger pension or severance, multiply the increase in monthly pension you've been offered times the length of time the increase is in effect (plus any investment income on the increase that you can expect to earn). Compare that figure to the amount of the severance offer plus what you can expect to earn on that amount.

For example, if at age 55 you're offered a $30,000 severance or $500 a month added to your pension for 10 years, you'd make out better with the pension:

	for example	
$	**500**	Added per month
x	**12**	Months
$	**6,000**	Added pension per year
x	**10**	Number of years
=	**$60,000**	Total expected payments
+	**28,159**	Earnings on expected payments over 10 years (approximate)
=	**$88,159**	Total value of pension increase
−	**59,970**	Severance offered, ($30,000 plus earnings over 10 years)
=	**$28,189**	Additional retirement income

Some Pension Problems

When defined benefit plans are short on cash, their performance doesn't stack up.

When pensions work the way they're supposed to, they help insure the financial security of millions of retired workers. But there can be major headaches for people who are counting on that income if a pension doesn't deliver what it promises.

That can happen if a defined benefit plan is **underfunded**. Typically, underfunding occurs when your former employer encounters financial difficulty. Though you can't prevent underfunding, recognizing that it can and does happen will help you make plans for replacing the income if your pension is delayed or reduced.

Underfunded means that a pension is short on the money it needs to meet its projected expenses

30% OF PUBLIC FUNDS ARE SHORT 75% OF WHAT THEY NEED

Fully funded means that a pension has the funding it needs to meet projected expenses

95% OF PRIVATE FUNDS HAVE OVER 75% OF WHAT THEY NEED

SHORT ON MONEY

Most defined benefit plans are adequately funded. But some private and public pension funds are currently underfunded, a few seriously. One reason is that bookkeeping rules have changed. Employers must forecast the future obligations differently than they have in the past, increasing the gap between what they've put away and what they'll owe.

In addition to the impact of the new rules, private plans come up short if:

- **The plan's investments don't do as well as expected.**
- **The employer doesn't contribute enough.**

Employers must meet minimum funding requirements if they set up a defined benefit plan. But those rules don't apply to public pension plans. Public plans are sometimes underfunded because state and local governments are reluctant, in the face of increasing opposition, to raise taxes enough to meet their projected obligations. Some states have also tried to use the contributions they should be making to the pension fund to meet short-term obligations.

THE OTHER SHOE

Underfunding also occurs because there are government limitations on what a company is allowed to contribute to a pension fund if it is fully funded. Just as you're limited to $2,000 in an IRA or $9,500 (for 1996) in a 401(k), a company can't make tax-deductible contributions that raise pension funds much above the full funding level defined by law. When the accounting rules changed, some funds went from fully funded to underfunded overnight.

People who look on the bright side of the underfunding issue see it primarily as the consequence of low interest and inflation rates, at least for private pensions. They predict that when the rates increase, underfunding will stop being a problem.

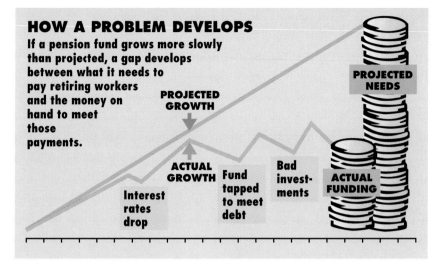

HOW A PROBLEM DEVELOPS

If a pension fund grows more slowly than projected, a gap develops between what it needs to pay retiring workers and the money on hand to meet those payments.

PROJECTED NEEDS

PROJECTED GROWTH

ACTUAL GROWTH

ACTUAL FUNDING

Interest rates drop

Fund tapped to meet debt

Bad investments

LOOKING FOR A WAY OUT

There are other solutions, too. As more and more people reach retirement age, some private employers are cutting back on pension promises to newer employees, renegotiating existing obligations, increasing the use of defined contribution plans (which can't be underfunded), or ending their defined benefit plans altogether.

ERISA, the Employee Retirement Income Security Act, does protect employees to some extent. If the plan where you work is ended, your employer must provide the money you're entitled to at that point, by buying you an annuity or making a lump sum payment. But neither of those is likely to provide the same level of long-term income a pension would provide.

MAKING NOBODY HAPPY

State and local governments, which have depended on the promise of generous pensions instead of high salaries to make themselves competitive with the private sector in attracting qualified workers, are also looking for ways to reduce their pension obligations.

One solution has been to make the biggest cuts in benefits to people working fewer than ten years, or to require them to work more years to qualify. Other approaches have been to increase the amount workers must contribute themselves to pension plans, to limit cost-of-living increases, and to reduce the use of overtime to boost final year salaries that are the basis for pension payouts. Elected officials, though, must weigh the political cost of public employee anger against the consequences of imposing higher taxes.

Public pension plans are not covered by ERISA, so they can make more radical changes than private plans can, including cutting or delaying benefits.

PENSION GUARANTEES

The Pension Benefit Guaranty Corporation, established in 1974, guarantees pension payments to approximately 40 million workers who are covered by 85,000 defined benefit plans. The PBGC doesn't promise you'll get the full amount you planned on, but it does guarantee that you will get something.

CHECKING UP

The Pension Rights Center, 918 16th Street NW, Suite 704, Washington D.C. 20006 is a resource for answers to your pension questions.
For information closer to home, you can ask your employer for a copy of Form 5500, which has to be filed every year with the government, reporting on the plan's investments and its financial health.

Pension Rights Center
918 16th St. NW, Suite 704
Washington D.C. 20006

IRAs: What They Are

IRAs are retirement plans for individuals—easy to set up, but not always easy to understand.

Individual Retirement Accounts (IRAs) are tax-deferred retirement plans that anyone who earns money can open.

$2,000 MAXIMUM ANNUAL CONTRIBUTION

The most you can contribute to an IRA each year is $2,000. Spouses can contribute up to $2,000 each into separate accounts.

SPOUSAL ACCOUNTS

Before August 1996, if your spouse didn't work, you could contribute an annual total of $2,250 divided between separate IRAs. As of August 1996, married couples can contribute up to $4,000 to their IRA accounts—whether or not both spouses earn income.

LIMITS ACCESS

What you give up with an IRA is access to your money. In most cases, you'll owe a 10% penalty for taking money out before age 59½, in addition to the taxes that are due.

DEFERS TAXES

You don't owe any tax on your earnings until you begin to withdraw from your account. That means your investment grows faster.

MAY REDUCE TAXABLE INCOME

If you're not part of another retirement plan, or if your income falls below certain levels, you can deduct your contribution from your tax-able income, reducing your current taxes.

INVESTOR-MANAGED PLANS

You can make all your IRA investment decisions yourself, including the choice of letting your broker decide how to invest your account.

OPEN AN
IRA
INDIVIDUAL RETIREMENT ACCOUNT

ASK INSIDE FOR INFORMATION

INVESTMENT OPTIONS

You can invest your IRA money almost any way you like, from sedate sav-ings accounts to volatile options on futures. And you can change your in-vestment when you please without paying tax on your gains.

1985	
$38 BILLION	
	1991
	$9 BILLION
Before change	After change

TOTAL IRA CONTRIBUTION

THE GOOD OLD DAYS

When IRAs were introduced in 1974, they were much less complex. Anyone who earned money during the year could open an IRA, contribute up to $2,000, and then take the amount of that contribution as a tax deduction. But when the deductibility rules changed, lots of people dropped out.

TO OPEN OR NOT TO OPEN AN IRA— THAT IS THE QUESTION

It's easy to open an IRA by filling out a relatively simple application provided by the financial institution you choose to be the **custodian**, or holder, of your account. Because IRAs are self-directed, meaning you decide how to invest the money, you're also the one responsible for following the rules.

WHO IS ELIGIBLE

You must have **earned income**—money you work for—to contribute to an IRA. Any amount you earn qualifies, and you can contribute as much of your earnings as you want, up to $2,000. But you can't contribute more than you earn. For example, if you earn $1,800, that is how much you can put in. And whether you earn $3,500 or $350,000, you can only contribute up to the $2,000 limit.

The one exception applies to a spouse who doesn't have a job. Since 1996, a single-income couple can contribute a total of $4,000 into two separate IRAs, one for each person.

WHAT IS DEDUCTIBLE

If you qualify, you may be able to deduct all or part of your IRA contribution from your taxable income. For example, you can deduct the entire amount if neither you nor your spouse is covered by another retirement plan. Otherwise, as your income gets higher, the amount you can deduct gets smaller, and is eventually phased out altogether.

Contributions are fully deductible for single people earning up to $25,000, and for married couples filing jointly earning up to $40,000. With additional income, you begin to lose some of your deduction—to ceilings of $35,000 and $50,000. Even if your contributions aren't deductible, you still get the benefit of deferring tax on your IRA's earnings.

DEDUCTIONS ARE GRADUALLY PHASED OUT

Single Deductibility
$2,000
$0
$25K · $30K · $35K
Income

Married Deductibility
$2,000
$0
$40K · $45K · $50K
Income

WHEN TO CONTRIBUTE

You have until April 15—the day taxes are due—to open an account and make the deposit for the previous tax year. Your account administrator will send you a statement by May 31 telling you how much you contributed for the previous tax year. But it's your job to keep track of your annual contribution. If you put in more than the $2,000 that's allowed, you'll owe a penalty.

You can contribute $2,000 to your IRA in a lump sum or spread the deposit out over the 15 months. You get the best return on your investment if you put in the whole amount the first day you can, January 2 of the tax year you're making the contribution for. But if you're like most people, you're more apt to make the deposit the last possible day.

January 2
Best day to deposit lump sum

April 15
Last day to deposit lump sum

Installment deposit over 15 months before taxes are due

F M A M J J A S O N D | F M A

Jan 1,1996   Jan 1,1997   Apr 15,1997

IRAs: Your Show

You call the shots on your IRA, so it helps if your goals are in focus.

You set up your IRA on your own with a bank, mutual fund or brokerage firm.

You can invest your IRA money in almost anything you can think of, from aggressive growth stocks to conservative savings accounts, or from high-interest junk bonds to government-insured certificates of deposit. The exceptions are life insurance and collectibles, including fine art, gems and some coins.

One strategy is to use your IRA for investments that return the highest income, since you are deferring the taxes and might as well rake in all you can. Another is to put IRA money into riskier high-growth investments, like stocks or certain mutual funds, early in your career, and gradually switch them to safer investments as you get older.

Among the investments you should avoid are municipal bonds or municipal bond funds, and investments that are designed to produce more capital gains than income. Here's why:

● The interest you earn on **municipal bonds** is tax-free, as long as they're outside an IRA. But once you include them in an IRA, their earnings are treated like all other IRA earnings and taxed when you make a withdrawal.

● The **capital gains tax rate** is lower than the rate for the top income tax brackets. If you're in a high tax bracket when you withdraw money from your IRA, you'll lose the benefit of the lower rate on these gains because all IRA earnings are taxed at your income tax rate.

Experts disagree about putting IRA money into variable annuities. The ayes stress the earning potential of annuities. The nays argue that since annuities are already tax-deferred, it's overkill.

SAVING ON FEES

Consolidating your accounts can save you money, because you generally pay an account fee of between $10 and $50 to maintain each IRA. The fee's the same whether you have $2,000 or $20,000 in the account. And some funds waive the fee entirely if your account is large enough.

You can let the bank or mutual fund deduct the fee from your account, or you can write a separate, tax-deductible check to cover it. That way, your entire investment can go on growing.

PRODUCER/DIRECTOR
Mr. Investor

HOLLYWOOD

CASTING CALL:
My Financial Future

STARRING ROLES
★ Mutual Fund IRA
★ Bank CD IRA
★ High-risk Stock IRA
Rated "A"

KEEPING TRACK OF YOUR IRAs

While you can set up a different IRA every year, keeping track of your accounts can be a nightmare long before you begin figuring your withdrawals (see page 172). That's an argument for using one broker, bank or mutual fund as the custodian. You can have several different types of investments, but your records will be on one statement that provides all the information you need.

Your recordkeeping is also simplified if all of your IRA contributions are deductible. You report the contribution (and the deduction) when you file your tax return. But you must report a non-deductible IRA contribution on Form 8606.

And you must keep those records for as long as you have your IRAs to avoid paying taxes twice on your nondeductible contributions. If the prospect of holding on to 50 years of tax forms is annoying, think how you'll feel if you can't prove that you've already paid taxes on several thousands of dollars of investment—and you have to pay again.

IRA PROTECTION

One reason people put their IRAs in bank CDs or savings accounts is that the money is insured by the Federal Deposit Insurance Corporation (FDIC). But the old level of protection has been revised—downward.

Accounts that were opened before December 19, 1993, are insured up to $100,000 apiece, no matter how many different ones you have in the same bank. But all accounts opened after that date are insured up to $100,000, *total*. If you have different types of accounts—an IRA, for example, and a Keogh (see page 176), or two separate IRAs—in the same bank, only your first $100,000 is protected. That's all you can collect on if the bank collapses.

But if the insurance is important to you, one solution is to use different banks, limiting your deposit to $100,000 in each one. Of course, the insurance applies only to bank deposits. If you're using a bank as your agent for buying mutual funds or other investments, that investment isn't insured by the FDIC.

NON-DEDUCTIBLE IRAs

Even if you can't deduct your contribution, you might still decide to open an IRA. What you earn on your investment is still tax-deferred until you begin to withdraw. But funding an IRA with money you have paid taxes on may not provide as big a payoff as some other investment options, especially ones with higher limits on annual investment amounts like 401(k)s, or no limits at all like variable annuities or municipal bonds.

INVENTING IRAs
IRAs were created on Labor Day 1974 when President Ford signed the Employee Retirement Income Security Act (ERISA). The story has it that the committee designing the plan to encourage personal savings struggled to find a name with a pronounceable acronym—and borrowed their solution from Ira Cohen, the IRS actuary who was working with them.

IRAs: Weighing the Merits

It's hard not to love an IRA, but look before you leap.

THE PLUSES

IRAs are great investments for many people. If you qualify to deduct the contribution, you'll certainly benefit from setting one up.

$31,000

START CONTRIBUTING AT AGE 18

STOP CONTRIBUTING AT AGE 28

For example, if you contributed $2,000 a year for ten years as soon as you started earning, and then stopped contributing, your $20,000 investment would go on growing, and you'd owe no tax until you were ready to withdraw.

If you earned 8% a year on the investment, you would have $31,291 in the account when you stopped putting money in at the end of ten years.

THE MINUSES

As terrific as IRAs are for some investors, they do have some drawbacks. For one thing, if you take the money out before you reach 59½, in most cases you'll owe a **10% penalty** on the amount you withdraw. For example, if you put $2,000 away earning 8% a year, your $2,000 investment would be worth $2,938 after 5 years. A 10% penalty would be $294, leaving you with earnings of $644, or a return of only about 6.5% a year. If you pull the amount out earlier, the tax bite can be even worse.

THE 10% HIT

$	2,938	Value of IRA before early withdrawal
–	2,000	Total contribution to IRA
–	294	10% penalty
= $	644	Earnings after penalty

You can't borrow from your IRA the way you can from some pension plans or insurance policies. But you may be able to get at the money in your IRA on a short-term basis—specifically 60 days—if you take money out of one account, use it for whatever you want, and open a new account with the full amount you withdrew before the 60 days are up. But if you miss the deadline, or you don't deposit the full amount, it counts as an early withdrawal and you'll owe the penalty.

Finally, IRAs are not necessarily the best choice for your retirement savings, especially if you can contribute to a pension plan where you work. That's because most voluntary plans, like 401(k)s and 403(b)s, or Keoghs and SEPs for the self-employed, allow you to contribute more, and many include employer matching contributions.

MIXING DIFFERENT IRAS: A RECIPE FOR TAX TROUBLE

While it's smart to put several years worth of IRA contributions into the same account, both to simplify your record-keeping and to increase your earnings, it's not smart to mix deductible and non-deductible contributions in the same account. That's because when it comes time to withdraw, figuring the tax you owe can be a problem.

For example, if, by the time you retire, you have put $40,000 in IRAs—$16,000 in deductible contributions and $24,000

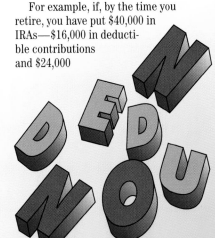

A $600,000 IRA provides at least $40,000 a year for 15 years

WAIT UNTIL AGE 70½

If you waited until you were 70½ to start withdrawals, your IRA would be worth around $600,000.

---

in non-deductible contributions—that has produced earnings of $56,000, how do you figure the tax that's due?

TAXES ON LUMP SUM WITHDRAWAL

$ 96,000	Total value of IRA
– 24,000	Non-deductible contributions
= $ 72,000	Taxable part of lump sum

If you were single and in the 28% tax bracket, the tax due on the entire $96,000 would be $25,290, based on 1993 tax tables. But you've already paid tax on $24,000. Subtract $24,000 from $96,000, leaving a taxable balance of $72,000 and a tax due of $17,850. That's not so hard.

BUT THERE'S A HITCH—OR TWO

Chances are you aren't going to withdraw your IRA money in a lump sum. That means you have to figure out what percentage of the money that has already been taxed is included in each withdrawal, and compute the tax you owe on the

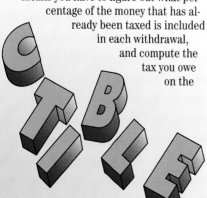

balance. Using the same example, you can figure out the taxable part of a $3,000 withdrawal in two steps, finding the taxable percentage and the taxable amount:

TAXES ON A $3,000 ANNUAL WITHDRAWAL

First:

$ 24,000	Non-deductible contributions
÷ 96,000	Total value of IRA
= 25%	Non-taxable percentage

Then:

$ 3,000	Total value of withdrawal
x .25	Non-deductible percentage
= $ 750	Is non-taxable, so you owe tax on $2,250

It won't work to say you're using up the non-deductible portion of your savings first. The IRS says you must treat withdrawals as if they came from all your IRAs proportionally, even if you have always kept the accounts separate and actually withdraw from just one.

That's one reason why so many people stopped putting money into IRAs when the deductibility rules changed. Chances are, if you have both types of accounts, you'll need the help of an accountant or tax professional to figure out the amount you owe.

167

IRA Rollovers

Rollovers are a hop, skip and a jump from conventional IRAs.

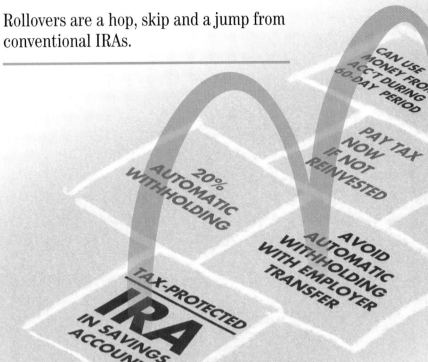

CAN USE MONEY FROM ACC'T DURING 60-DAY PERIOD

PAY TAX NOW IF NOT REINVESTED

20% AUTOMATIC WITHHOLDING

AVOID AUTOMATIC WITHHOLDING WITH EMPLOYER TRANSFER

TAX-PROTECTED

IRA IN SAVINGS ACCOUNT

Rollover IRAs are like other IRAs in many ways. You pay no tax on your earnings until you take the money out. And there can be penalties if you make withdrawals before age 59½.

The difference is where the money in the IRA comes from. Rollover IRAs are funded with money that's already been put away in a qualified retirement plan, like a 401(k), a Keogh, or another IRA. The rollover lets you move the money without owing any tax.

THERE ARE ROLLOVERS AND THEN THERE ARE ROLLOVERS

The word rollover does double duty when it comes to IRAs. If you close your IRA account, get the check for the amount you've accumulated, and deposit that amount into another IRA, you're rolling it over. As long as you put the money from the old IRA into the new one within 60 days, your IRA is intact.

You could accomplish the same thing by filling out the necessary forms and asking the institutions involved to transfer your IRA balance directly. You open a special IRA with a lump sum payment you get

from a qualified pension plan. That might happen when you retire, change jobs, or when a plan is disbanded and the money is paid out.

As always, there are rules

Like IRAs that you fund yourself, IRA rollovers from qualified plans are subject to certain regulations. Following the rules postpones taxes and protects you from fees and penalties.

DEPOSIT WITHIN 60 DAYS

First and foremost, the 60-day rule applies. If you put your pension payout into an IRA, you have to deposit the full amount within the official time period—and the clock starts ticking on the date the check is mailed to you.

A bigger problem is that 20% of the payout amount is automatically withheld as tax when you get the payment check. That means if you're going to deposit the full amount, you'll have to tap another source—like your savings—to come up with the 20% that's being withheld. You'll get the 20% back—after you pay

TAX-PROTECTED IRA IN BROKER ACCOUNT

60-DAY RULE ROLLOVER TIME LIMIT

WHY USE A ROLLOVER?

If you put your pension payout in an IRA, your investment can keep on growing and you can continue to postpone taxes until you make withdrawals. Then you owe tax at your regular rate.

Once the IRA rollover is set up, you can leave it or, in some cases, transfer it into a new employer's pension plan. You can invest the amount in an IRA rollover any way you wish, just as you can with any IRA.

IRA FEES

IRAs cost little or nothing to set up and aren't expensive to maintain. Banks rarely charge fees at all. Mutual funds and brokerages may charge between $5 and $50 to open your account and often a similar annual fee, although sometimes they'll waive the charges to attract or keep your business, especially if you have a sizeable sum.

Since some of the fees are fixed, and not based on the size of your IRA, they have a much smaller impact than the fees often imposed on other retirement savings plans. And you can subtract the annual fee as a miscellaneous deduction on your income tax return if you pay the fees by check rather than having them deducted from your account.

But the annual fees don't cover sales charges or commissions on the buying and selling you do within your IRA. Those costs can't be paid separately. They are based on the size of each transaction, and are not tax-deductible. As long as your return, including the cost of the trading fees, is more than the rate of inflation, your investment is growing.

FUTURE CONSIDERATIONS

You can extend the tax-deferred life of your IRA at least five years, and sometimes more, by leaving it to a living beneficiary rather than to your estate. That's because IRA withdrawals are based on life expectancy and an estate hasn't got one. So your account comes to a quick (and bad) end, with a tax bill to settle. It's an easy mistake to avoid.

---

your taxes for the year, possibly as long as 15 or 16 months later.

Worse yet, if you can't come up with enough to cover the full lump sum payment, the amount that was withheld counts as a withdrawal, even though you never had the money. If you're not 59½ yet, you owe the tax, plus a penalty for early withdrawal.

There is a way to avoid this problem: Have your employer transfer your pension payout to your IRA rollover directly, rather than sending you a check. (Legally, you must be offered this option.) That way, no tax is withheld. But if you want access to the cash during the 60 days, you're stuck.

2 KEEP IRAs SEPARATE

When you set up a special IRA, sometimes called a conduit IRA, you should keep it separate from any other IRAs you might have. It's especially important if there's a chance you might want to move the money into a new employer's pension plan. If you don't keep the money separate, you won't be able to move it.

3 DON'T MIX TAXED AND PRE-TAXED IRAs

The only contributions to a pension or retirement fund that can be moved into an IRA rollover are those which weren't taxed. If you've made any after-tax contributions, or if your employer has made supplemental contributions that aren't tax-deductible, that money has to be invested separately. The one advantage of the rule is that it will simplify figuring your tax when you begin to make withdrawals, since everything you take out will be taxable.

4 PUT AWAY PENSION PAYOUTS

You can put all or part of your lump sum pension payout into an IRA rollover. If the payout is made in a series of partial lump sums over a period of less than ten years, you can put some or all of those payments into an IRA rollover, too.

IRA Withdrawals

You have to be old enough to take money out of your IRA, but you don't have to retire first.

The first things you have to know about withdrawing from your self-directed retirement investments are the magic numbers. One is the otherwise unmagical 59½. That's the point at which you can begin to collect without paying a penalty.

Being eligible at 59½ doesn't mean you must start collecting then: You can wait until you actually retire—at 62 or 65 or 68—or until you're ready to add a source of income to your budget.

The only restriction is that you *must* begin withdrawing by the time you're 70½. At that time, you must set up a plan for getting all the money out of your accounts and into your pockets (and the taxes you owe into Uncle Sam's pockets).

WHAT YOU HAVE TO TAKE

If you want to take the minimum out of your IRA (a good move if you're trying to minimize taxes), you have to follow IRS rules. The rules are specific but not simple. Basically, your withdrawal schedule

59½ [60-70] 70½

Since insurance company actuarial tables consider you already 60 when you reach 59½, and still 70 until you're 70½, Congress used those ages to frame the withdrawal period from retirement accounts.

has to be set up so that if you followed it, you would get all the money out of all your retirement accounts within one of the following:

- **Your lifetime**
- **The joint lifetime of you and your spouse**
- **The joint lifetime of you and any beneficiary you choose**
- **Any period that's shorter than any of the others**

You get to set the length of the shorter period. Otherwise the length of time is dictated by the life expectancy tables the IRS provides in Publication 590, "Individual Retirement Arrangements."

THE TAX BITE

Because IRA investments are tax-deferred, you owe income tax on your withdrawals. For tax purposes, it's considered regular income. That means if your combined income for the year puts you into the 28% tax bracket, that's the rate at which your payouts are taxed.

Many people assume they'll be in a lower tax bracket when they retire, so they'll end up paying less tax. Even if that's not the case—and for many people it isn't—the real advantage of retirement savings plans is the rate at which the investments grow, not the rate at which they are taxed.

YOU <u>MUST</u> START IRA WITHDRAWALS

Since an IRA is a retirement account, with the tax-deferral advantage, the IRS doesn't want it to be a way to build the estate you're planning to leave your heirs. So when you reach age 70½, the law says you must start spending what you've saved— whether you need the money or not. One way to stretch the account (but not bend the rules) is to name a much younger person as your IRA beneficiary. When you die, that person may be able to spread payments from the account over a much longer time.

Happy 59½ᵀᴴ Birthday!

YOU **CAN** START IRA WITHDRAWALS

Once you reach age 59½ you can start taking money out of your IRA in any amount you want without penalty as long as your income from all your retirement plans isn't more than $155,000 a year. You'll owe tax on the amount you withdraw, but you can spend it any way you like.

THE PENALTY QUESTION

If you take money out of your IRAs before you're eligible—usually at 59½—you'll probably owe a 10% early withdrawal penalty on top of the taxes.

The IRS imposes the penalty to encourage you to leave your retirement money alone and to charge you for getting tax-deferred growth on investments you're making for other reasons.

The truth is that most people have no qualms about taking money out of their retirement savings if they need it. There are two views on enforcing the penalties:

One is to change the law so that people who use their retirement money for worthy causes— like education, buying a house, or health care—would be exempt from the penalty, no matter what their age. The other view is that a penalty is valid because it discourages people from spending the money they're going to need when they retire long before they get close to retirement.

There's a question, too, about whether people would participate in a stricter plan. Several polls suggest that the majority would not put money into an IRA if they knew there was no way to touch it until they hit 59½.

When It's Safe to Withdraw

10% PENALTY FOR EARLY WITHDRAWAL	NO PENALTY FOR WITHDRAWALS BETWEEN AGES 59½ AND 70½	50% PENALTY FOR LATE WITHDRAWAL
50	59½ 70½	80

EARLY WITHDRAWAL WITHOUT PENALTY

There is one way to get access to the money in your IRAs before you're 59½ and avoid the penalty. That's to **annuitize** your distribution. It means you establish a withdrawal plan that pays you, each year, a fixed amount of the money in your IRA, based on your life expectancy. The chief restriction is that the plan must cover at least five years or all the years left until you reach 59½, whichever is longer. Annuitization does have drawbacks, though. If what you really need is a large amount of money, you probably won't get it this way unless you're close to 59½. And you're using money that was intended for your retirement, so you're depleting, not adding, to your savings.

ANNUITIZED WITHDRAWAL FROM AGE 50	REGULAR WITHDRAWAL FROM AGE 59½
$23,000/YR	**$45,000/YR**

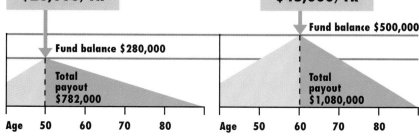

Fund balance $500,000

Fund balance $280,000

Total payout $782,000

Total payout $1,080,000

Age 50 60 70 80   Age 50 60 70 80

Taking Money Out

Investing in an IRA is the easy part. It's getting the mandatory withdrawals right that's tough.

When you're ready to start taking money out of your IRAs, you need a strategy to meet the legal requirements while getting the best return you can.

The more plans you have and the more money you have amassed, the more carefully you need to plan your withdrawals—not so much to avoid overspending, but to avoid the big penalties you'll have to pay for taking out too much or too little in any given year.

HAVING TOO MUCH

Though it seems a curious way to reward planning for the future, you get hit with a penalty if you've put too much away. In 1996, the most you're allowed to withdraw a year from your pension and retirement savings plans combined is $155,000. If you take more than that, you pay 15% of the amount over $155,000 on top of whatever tax is due.

Realistically, to get that large a payout, your retirement investments have to be substantial—probably several million dollars. But someone with a generous pension plus a SEP or Keogh, or someone who begins to put money away early in a successful career and invests it profitably might easily be in that position.

Since the one source of retirement income you can control is what you take out of your IRAs, one solution is to start your withdrawals earlier than 70½. By spreading out the number of years you collect, you can lower each annual amount. But for many people who continue earning through their 60s, and anticipate living well beyond that, withdrawing money they don't need now and might need later has serious drawbacks.

HOW LONG WILL YOU LIVE?

The funny thing about life expectancy is that it changes according to how old you are. A white American male born today can expect to live 73 years. (For white females, it's just under 80.) But if the man were 73 today, he could expect to live about 14 more years, to age 87. And if he were 87 today, he could expect to live another 6 years, to age 92.

1

ADD UP YOUR IRAs
Withdrawals are based on the total value of all your accounts.

SETTING THE AMOUNT

You can set the amount of your annual withdrawal for life when you are 70½ by choosing the term-certain method of withdrawal. **Term-certain** withdrawals are calculated, using your current life expectancy (based on your age alone). The amount is fixed, for as long as your withdrawals continue.

You can take the entire withdrawal from just one IRA account, even if you have several. One advantage is that you can avoid withdrawing from accounts that are growing at a faster rate. Another is simplified bookkeeping.

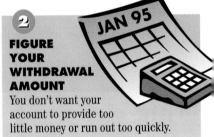

2

FIGURE YOUR WITHDRAWAL AMOUNT
You don't want your account to provide too little money or run out too quickly.

GETTING THE RIGHT NUMBERS

If you have $250,000 in your IRA, and you have a life expectancy of 18 years, you need to withdraw $13,888 a year. You can use the formula below for figuring out the size of the withdrawal you have to make:

$$\frac{\text{Account balance}}{\text{Life expectancy}} = \text{Minimum annual withdrawal}$$

for example

$$\frac{\$250,000}{18} = \$13,888$$

RECALCULATING THE AMOUNT

You can—within certain limits—change the amount you withdraw each year by recalculating your life expectancy annually. The advantage is that you can take smaller payments in the early years, letting your investments grow and reserving more for later years.

There are some drawbacks, though. Once you choose to recalculate, you commit yourself to doing it every year. And if your life expectancy calculation is based on two lives (yours and your spouse's, for example), and one of you dies, the surviving partner would have to increase the annual withdrawals

IRS PUB 590

You can get Publication 590 and other IRS information by calling:

1-800-TAX-FORM

The IRS Internet homepage is:

http://www.irs.ustreas.gov

enough to meet minimum requirements. That would mean more taxes, and the potential for spending down the money too rapidly.

For example, if you were 72 and your spouse was 70, you'd have a life expectancy of 19.8 years. But if your spouse died, yours would drop to 14.6. If your IRA balance was $100,000, you'd have to withdraw $1,799 more, and pay more tax too.

TABLE II (Joint Life and Last Survivor Expectancy)*

AGES	68	69	70	71	72	73
69	21.9	21.5	21.1	20.7	20.3	
70	21.5	21.1	20.6	20.2		
71	21.2	20.7	20.2	19.8		
72	20.8	20.3	19.8	19.4		
73	20.5	20.0	19.4	19.1		

TABLE I (Single Life Expectancy)*

AGE	DIVISOR	AGE	DIVI
70	16.0	108	
71	15.3	109	
72	14.6	110	

* Table I does not provide for IRA

JOINT AND LAST SURVIVOR

	$ 100,000	Value of IRA
÷	19.8	Life expectancy
= $	5,050	Annual withdrawal

SINGLE LIFE

	$ 100,000	Value of IRA
÷	14.6	Life expectancy
= $	6,849	Annual withdrawal

3

AVOID TAX PENALTIES

You'll owe extra tax for withdrawing too much or too little.

CAUTION

GETTING THE NUMBERS WRONG

If you miscalculate the amount you must withdraw, and take too little, you'll get socked with a 50% penalty on the additional amount you should have taken and didn't. That's true even if it was an honest mistake—unless you can prove to the IRS that you were completely befuddled.

If you take too much, of course, you pay more tax than you might have otherwise, and you deplete your account faster. But there aren't penalties for that unless you're over the $155,000 annual withdrawal limit.

4

DECIDE ON A SOURCE

Setting up mutual funds or money market accounts is one strategy.

IRA WITHDRAWAL
- ☑ Bonds
- ☑ Stocks
- ☑ CD
- ☑ Money Mkt.

FINDING THE CASH

Figuring out how much you must withdraw each year is only the first step. You also have to decide how to get at it. Since wise investment strategy suggests you diversify your retirement accounts into various moneymaking investments, you probably haven't got the right amount sitting around in a money market fund or savings account.

You could sell stocks, but what if the market is down? You might have to pay a penalty to take money out of a CD. A better option is to open a mutual fund or bank money market account to collect dividend and interest payments from various investments.

SEPs

Setting up a Simplified Employee Pension isn't exactly a piece of cake, but it can be a sweet addition to your retirement menu.

If you run a small business, a Simplified Employee Pension, or SEP, may offer the most effective way to put money away for retirement. That's because you can shelter a lot more than you can in an IRA and the rules, though they're involved, are a lot less stringent than for other qualified retirement plans, including Keoghs.

Because a SEP is a qualified plan, the amount you contribute each year can be deducted from your earnings, reducing your current taxes. The contribution limits are 15% of what you earn (the salary you pay yourself), with a cap of $22,500 for 1996.

You can change the amount of your contribution each year, skipping poor years and putting away the maximum in good ones. If you change jobs or end up being covered by another plan, you can roll over a SEP into an IRA without penalty and keep earning money on a tax-deferred basis.

WHAT YOU CAN'T DO WITH SEPs AND SAR-SEPs

There are a few limitations on SEPs that don't apply to other qualified retirement plans:

- **You can't forward average a lump sum distribution (see page 156)**
- **You can't roll over your SEP into a new employer's retirement plan**
- **You can't invest in insurance**

None of these by itself—or even the three together—are reason to ignore the advantages of a SEP. And, you don't have to file an annual report with the IRS the way you must with a Keogh.

EMPLOYEE PLANS

Since SEPs are actually specialized IRAs, sometimes referred to as SEP-IRAs, they're always set up and controlled by the person who benefits from them, even though they're funded exclusively by an employer.

That makes it easier for employers: They don't have to pay someone to run a

Comparing SEP-IRAs

Small-company employees may have the option of being included in two different types of SEPs to save for retirement. They are

SEP-IRA LIKE A PENSION, THE CONTRIBUTION COMES FROM YOUR EMPLOYER

Employer contributes up to 15% of your salary, to a cap of $22,500

You don't contribute

ALL ELIGIBLE EMPLOYEES MUST BE INCLUDED

pension plan. It's also better if you're an employee: All the money in your SEP account is yours from the minute it's deposited. You don't have to wait to be vested, as you do with some other qualified plans.

SAR-SEPs

SAR-SEPs, also known as salary reduction SEPs, are the equivalent of 401(k)s for small businesses with 25 or fewer employees. Employees can defer salary up to 15%, to a cap of $9,500 for 1996, and employers can provide matching amounts.

EQUALITY'S THE RULE

If you have employees, you have to give them the same kind of SEP benefits you give yourself. For example, if you contribute 10% of your earnings to your SEP, you have to contribute 10% of their earnings to accounts in their names.

and SAR-SEPs

funded differently and have different rules for participating.

SAR-SEP LIKE A 401(k), YOU MAKE THE BASIC CONTRIBUTION

You contribute up to 15% of your salary, to a cap of $9,500 in 1996

Employer may match part of your contribution to a total cap of 15% of salary

AT LEAST 50% OF ALL ELIGIBLE EMPLOYEES MUST AGREE TO PARTICIPATE

PUTTING MORE IN

You may be able to build up your pension by using a SAR-SEP to defer part of your earnings into the plan. However, the total annual contribution is limited to 15% of your salary, or $22,500. So if your employer plans to put the full 15% into a SEP-IRA, that amount would be reduced by what you put in yourself and you'd lose part of your employer's contribution.

But if your employer is putting in less than 15%, you might want to make up the difference. You may also make a deductible $2,000 contribution to an IRA

if your earnings are within the limit set by the laws (see page 163).

FIGURING YOUR CONTRIBUTION

Figuring the amount you can contribute to a SEP is a bit trickier than it seems if you're self-employed. That's because compensation, or earnings, as far as qualified retirement plans are concerned, aren't what you earn, but your earnings minus the amount you contribute to the retirement plan. The effect can be to reduce the maximum SEP contribution from 15% to about 13%. If you're self-employed, you also have to subtract half the money you paid in self-employment tax.

The IRS provides a workchart for you to use in figuring your contribution. Or you can get a sense of your potential maximum contribution using this formula:

$$\begin{array}{c} \text{Net earnings} \\ \text{minus 50\%} \\ \text{employment tax} \end{array} \text{x} \begin{array}{c} \text{Contribution} \\ \text{reduction} \\ \text{factor (.115)} \end{array} = \begin{array}{c} \text{Contribution} \\ \text{amount} \end{array}$$

for example	
$200,000	Net earnings
− 6,787	50% of employment tax
= 193,213	
x .115	Contribution reduction
= $ 22,219	Contribution amount

TIMING

Another appealing feature of SEPs, whether you're self-employed or the owner of a small corporation, is the timetable for setting up and contributing to the plan. Like an IRA, you can open a SEP and fund it when your tax return is due, including any extensions.

As with any savings that accumulate tax-deferred, you make more money if you contribute early in the tax year. But self-employed people in particular can't always be sure how much they'll make in any given tax year, or how much they'll be able to put away for the future. Since there are penalties for putting too much into a SEP, waiting until the end of your tax year can make it easier to get the right contribution amount.

SIMPLE

In 1997, a new retirement plan, Savings Incentive Match Plan for Employees (SIMPLE) will be available to companies with 100 or fewer employees. SIMPLEs allow salary deferrals up to $6,000.

Keogh Plans

A Keogh lets you invest for retirement while you're busy earning a living.

How to Qualify

If you're self-employed, earn money for work you do in addition to your regular job, or own a small business, you qualify to open a Keogh plan that lets you build up money for retirement by deferring taxes on the investments you make and the earnings they accumulate.

You can contribute a portion of your net earnings from one or more of these categories, but no income from other sources. There's no requirement that these earnings be your only source of income or the Keogh your only pension plan. In fact, you can be a fulltime employee covered by a defined benefits plan and still contribute to a Keogh if you earn money in a way that qualifies.

To set up a Keogh you must:

Own your own business and file a Schedule C with your tax return

Have a Subchapter S corporation

OPENING A KEOGH

To set up a Keogh, you need to file an IRS-approved plan. Banks and other financial institutions provide standardized plans, but you can have one specially designed by a lawyer or accountant who is a Keogh specialist. The advantage—some would say the necessity—of a specialized plan is the flexibility it provides for managing and investing your plan's assets.

KEOGHS FOR EMPLOYEES

If you have employees, and you have a Keogh plan for yourself, you must provide comparable benefits to the people who qualify to participate. For example, if you contribute 15% of your earnings to the plan, you must contribute 15% for each employee covered by the plan.

The law says you must have a plan administrator—you can take the job

KEOGH or SEP?

If you qualify to set up a Keogh plan, you also qualify for a SEP—though you can't open both for the same earnings. Each has some advantages and some limitations.

For most people, especially those without employees, the debate comes down to two issues—the option to shelter more money through a Keogh versus the simplicity of a SEP. For employers, the ability to set the standards for participation can also be an important factor.

Advantages	Limitations
SEP	
● Simpler and cheaper to set up	● Contribution amount limited to 15% of earnings
● Easier to administer, both internally and for the IRS	● Employers must cover everyone who works for them but can set eligibility at three years
● Doesn't commit you to annual contributions	
KEOGH	
● Offers several ways to structure plan	● Can commit you to contributions even in poor years
● Lets you shelter more money, sometimes much more	● Expensive to set up and administer
● Allows employers to establish criteria for employees to qualify for participation	● Complex tax-reporting requirements

THE MAN WITH THE PLAN
Keogh plans are named for Eugene Keogh, a U.S. Representative from Brooklyn, New York, who sponsored the legislation that established the plans. They went into effect in 1962.

Be self-
employed doing
something or
selling
something

Sit on
a corporate
board of
directors

Be a
partner in
a business
that files
a Schedule K

Work
as a
freelancer

yourself if you want—and dictates how to compute contributions based on your net profit. There's no law that requires you to hire a Keogh specialist to handle your plan—but you probably should.

HOW A KEOGH WORKS

A Keogh works like employer-sponsored pension plans in many ways. But like an IRA, it is often set up to benefit just one person—you. Like other qualified plans, a Keogh lets you deduct pension contributions on your tax return and imposes a penalty if you withdraw funds before you're 59½.

When you reach 70½, you must set up a specific withdrawal schedule. But unlike other plans, whether funded by your employer or yourself, a Keogh lets you go on making qualifying contributions even after you've started taking mandatory withdrawals.

Like a pension plan, a Keogh permits forward averaging for lump sum withdrawals (see page 157), and allows you to borrow against the funds accumulated in your plan, with some restrictions. Neither of those advantages is available with an IRA or a SEP-IRA.

HOLD THE APPLAUSE

Keoghs are a boon to self-employed people who would otherwise have no way to shelter money for the future, and to employees of small businesses that wouldn't otherwise offer a retirement plan. But being involved with a Keogh is complex.

To begin with, there are three different sets of Keogh regulations: one if you're self-employed, one if you own a business, and one if you're an employee of a company with a Keogh plan.

KEOGH CUSTOM TAILORING

**CUSTOMIZE—
IT MAY PAY**
Ask your lawyer or tax professional to recommend someone to set up your Keogh. Be prepared: A customized plan could cost several thousand dollars. But a plan that locks you into contributions you can't meet or options that limit what you can save costs more in the long run.

Once the account is set up—by December 31 of the first year you are going to take a tax deduction for your contribution—you can make annual or periodic additions to it as long as you don't put in more than the amount you're entitled to contribute in any given year. The deadline for depositing funds is the day your tax return is due, including any extensions you may get.

The same investment limitations that apply to IRAs apply to self-directed Keoghs, with an added prohibition on U.S. coins. But if your Keogh is a trust or custodial account, the money can be invested in anything at all—including wine.

Keoghs

Keoghs have several designs, plain and fancy, to appeal to a lot of different tastes.

While Keogh rules are notoriously complicated, the investment opportunities Keoghs provide have made them a staple of retirement planning. One major advantage is that you can choose the Keogh you want from among several types of defined contribution options or a defined benefit plan. The options mean that a wide range of people, with different sources of self-employment income, can participate.

Defined contribution plans, which are available in three different versions, are classic Keoghs. They work just like corporate defined contribution pension plans. You put money into the plan, and the amount you have at retirement depends chiefly on how well your investments do.

Defined benefit plans guarantee a specific payout but may require large contributions. They are not for everyone. But they can be ideal for people within 15 years or so of retirement who are making lots of money and don't mind the expense of sheltering it this way.

JUST DESSERTS

MAKE YOUR OWN

DIET SPECIAL

CHOOSE YOUR FLAVORS

DOUBLE SCOOPS

PROFIT-SHARING DEFINED CONTRIBUTION PLANS are the least complicated, and the most popular, Keoghs.

They let you decide each year whether to participate and how much to put away.

You can contribute up to 15% of your earnings, or $22,500, whichever is less.

MONEY PURCHASE DEFINED CONTRIBUTION PLANS are the most generous and the most rigid plans.

They let you put away up to 25% of your earnings, to a maximum of $30,000.

You must specify the percentage of earnings when you set up the plan, and you must contribute that percentage each year.

The minimum you can choose is 3%; if you don't put in enough, you'll owe a penalty of up to 100% of the amount you owed but didn't contribute.

PAIRED PLANS are the most flexible Keoghs, combining some of the best aspects of profit-sharing and money purchase. They do, however, lock you into an annual contribution even in years when you don't make much money.

You can set a money-purchase percentage low enough to meet comfortably each year—say 10%—and then contribute an additional amount—up to 25% total—through profit-sharing in good years.

WHAT YOU CAN CONTRIBUTE

The amount you can put into a Keogh each year is a fixed percentage of your earnings. Usually there's a cap, which is determined by the way your plan is set up. For 1996, the maximum contribution ranges from 15% to 100% of earnings, with most plans capped at $22,500.

Keogh earnings aren't what you earn, but what's left of your earnings after you subtract the amount you contribute to your Keogh plan. The effect is to reduce the contribution from 15% to about 13% in profit-sharing Keoghs and from 25% to 20% for money-purchase and paired-plan Keoghs. If you're self-employed you also have to subtract half the money you paid in self-employment tax from your earnings to find the amount your Keogh contribution is based on. IRS Publication 560 explains the details.

DEFINED BENEFIT PLANS guarantee a specific annual payout after you retire or reach age 65.

To fund the plan so that it produces the payout you choose (and incidentally to save yourself a lot of current tax), you may be able to contribute up to 100% of your annual earnings.

Figuring out what you must pay in each year is extremely complicated. The law requires that an actuary review your plan annually to determine what you have to put in to meet your projected payout; you must submit a copy of that report with your tax return.

KEOGH TRUSTS

If you want to diversify your Keogh investments without having to watch several different plans, you can set up a self-directed Keogh trust, make all your contributions to the trust, and invest the holdings as you choose. While setting up a trust can be costly and time-consuming, it does more than just save paperwork over time. With a trust, you can make more types of investments and shift your asset allocation among investments more easily. Perhaps most importantly, a trust simplifies the withdrawal process when the time comes to start taking your money out, since, unlike IRAs, you must withdraw the correct amount from each Keogh account separately.

KEEPING THE IRS UP-TO-DATE

Keoghs can be a recordkeeping nightmare. Every three years you have to file a Form 5500-C with the IRS. Other years you must file Form 5500EZ (if you're self-employed) or 5500-R (if you have employees). Even if you have to gather the records yourself, it's probably worth having an accountant or Keogh expert fill out the form for you.

IRS FORM 5500-C

IRS FORM 5500EZ

IRS FORM 5500-R

ELASTIC PLANS

If you have a Keogh, you can roll a pension payout from another job into it, instead of into an IRA. That lets you take a lump sum distribution and forward average the entire amount at some future date. That flexibility is an advantage when you start withdrawing from your retirement plans.

Or, if your self-employment income dries up and you can't keep up with a Keogh plan, you can call it quits and roll the money over into an IRA. You're out the money you spent to set your plan up, and might have to pay some penalties. But because a Keogh is a qualified retirement plan, you don't have to take a distribution and pay tax on it.